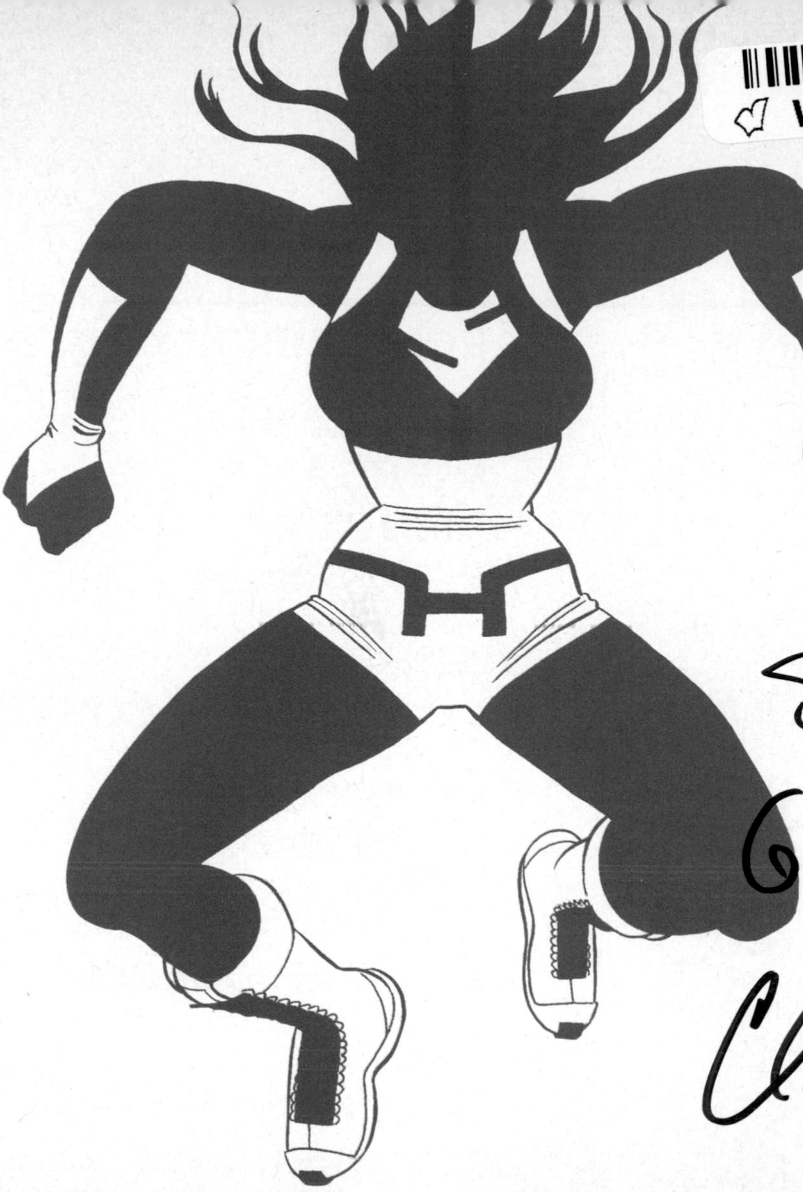

Stay Green!

SHE-HULK

LAW AND DISORDER

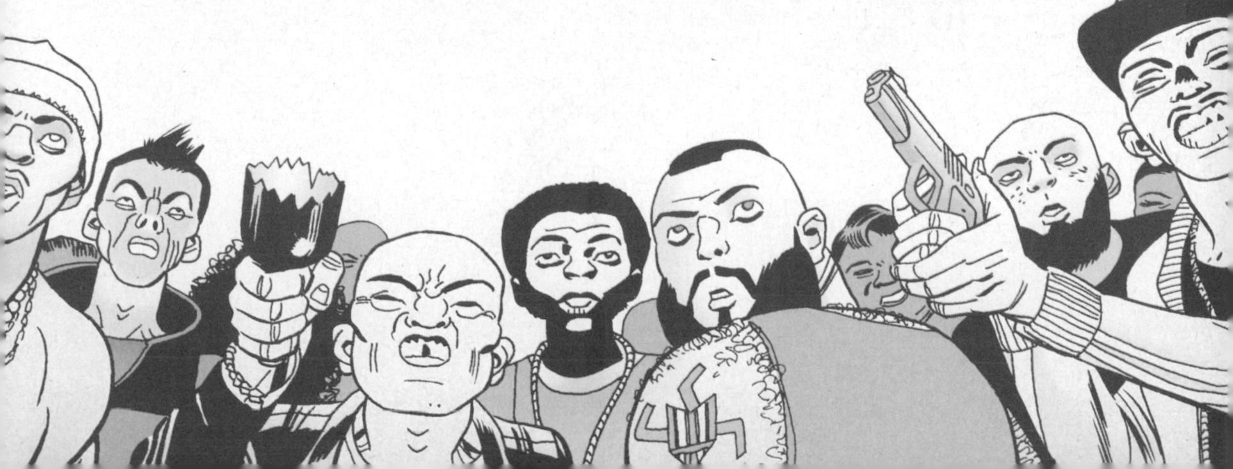

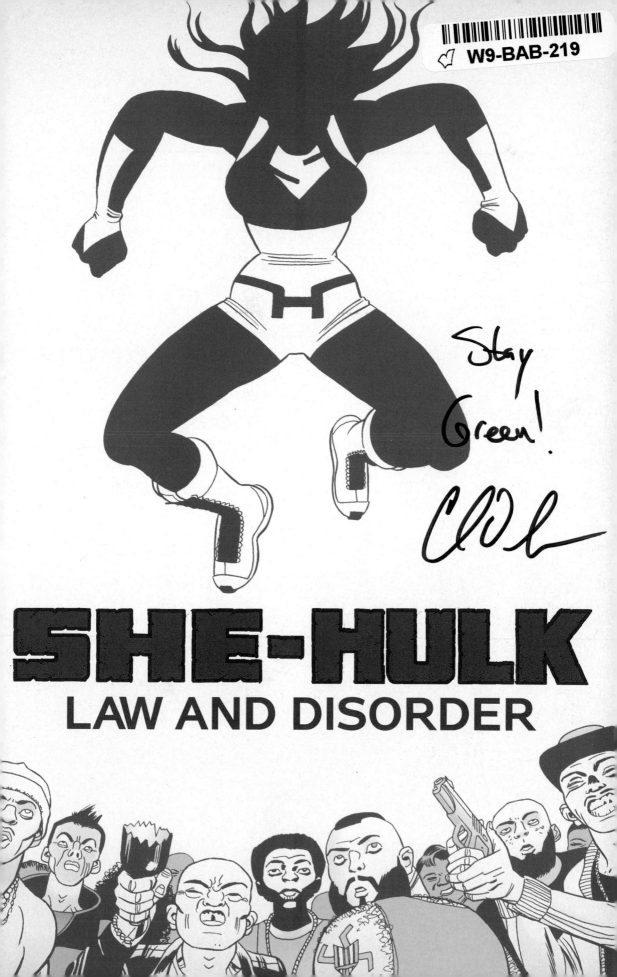

WRITER
CHARLES SOULE

STORYTELLERS
JAVIER PULIDO (#1-4) &
RON WIMBERLY (#5-6)

COLOR ARTISTS
MUNTSA VICENTE (#1-4)
RICO RENZI (#5) &
RON WIMBERLY (#6)

LETTERER
VC'S CLAYTON COWLES

COVER ART
KEVIN WADA

ASSISTANT EDITOR
FRANKIE JOHNSON

EDITORS
JEANINE SCHAEFER &
TOM BRENNAN

COLLECTION EDITOR: JENNIFER GRÜNWALD
ASSISTANT EDITOR: SARAH BRUNSTAD
ASSOCIATE MANAGING EDITOR: ALEX STARBUCK
EDITOR, SPECIAL PROJECTS: MARK D. BEAZLEY
SENIOR EDITOR, SPECIAL PROJECTS: JEFF YOUNGQUIST
SVP PRINT, SALES & MARKETING: DAVID GABRIEL
BOOK DESIGN: JEFF POWELL

EDITOR IN CHIEF: AXEL ALONSO
CHIEF CREATIVE OFFICER: JOE QUESADA
PUBLISHER: DAN BUCKLEY
EXECUTIVE PRODUCER: ALAN FINE

SHE-HULK VOL. 1: LAW AND DISORDER. Contains material originally published in magazine form as SHE-HULK #1-6. Second printing 2015. ISBN# 978-0-7851-9019-6. Published by MARVEL WORLDWIDE, INC., a subsidiary of MARVEL ENTERTAINMENT, LLC. OFFICE OF PUBLICATION: 135 West 50th Street, New York, NY 10020. Copyright © 2014 MARVEL. No similarity between any of the names, characters, persons, and/or institutions in this magazine with those of any living or dead person or institution is intended, and any such similarity which may exist is purely coincidental. Printed in Canada. ALAN FINE, President, Marvel Entertainment; DAN BUCKLEY, President, TV, Publishing and Brand Management; JOE QUESADA, Chief Creative Officer; TOM BREVOORT, SVP of Publishing; DAVID BOGART, SVP of Operations & Procurement, Publishing; C.B. CEBULSKI, VP of International Development & Brand Management; DAVID GABRIEL, SVP Print, Sales & Marketing; JIM O'KEEFE, VP of Operations & Logistics; DAN CARR, Executive Director of Publishing Technology; SUSAN CRESPI, Editorial Operations Manager; ALEX MORALES, Publishing Operations Manager; STAN LEE, Chairman Emeritus. For information regarding advertising in Marvel Comics or on Marvel.com, please contact Jonathan Rheingold, VP of Custom Solutions & Ad Sales, at jrheingold@marvel.com. For Marvel subscription inquiries, please call 800-217-9158. Manufactured between 7/8/2015 and 8/10/2015 by SOLISCO PRINTERS, SCOTT, QC, CANADA.

10987654321

Jennifer Walters was a shy attorney, good at her job and quiet in her life, when she found herself gunned down by a crime boss. With her life on the line, only one person was close enough to donate the blood she needed for a vital transfusion: her cousin, Dr. Bruce Banner, who was secretly the gamma-irradiated monster known as the Incredible Hulk.

Bruce's blood saved Jennifer's life...but gave her the power to turn into a superstrong, green-skinned bombshell. Unlike her cousin, Jennifer Walters has managed to maintain her sanity and control over her superhuman form and even continued her career as an attorney – while also doubling as a member of the Avengers, the Fantastic Four, and a super hero known the world over.

Wherever justice is threatened, you can bet on the gamma-powered gal with the brain and brawn to right some wrong, the Sensational...

SHE-HULK

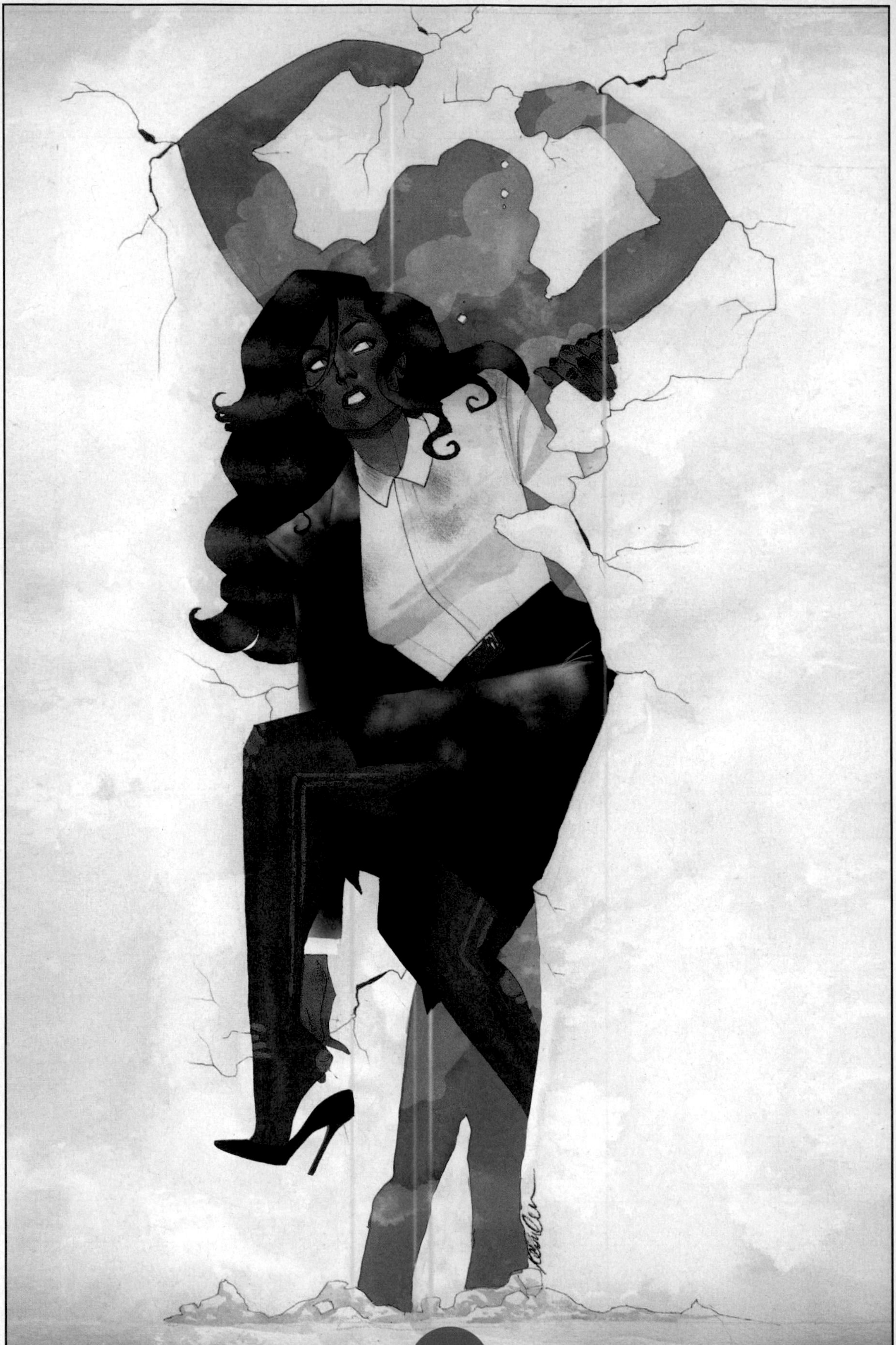

1

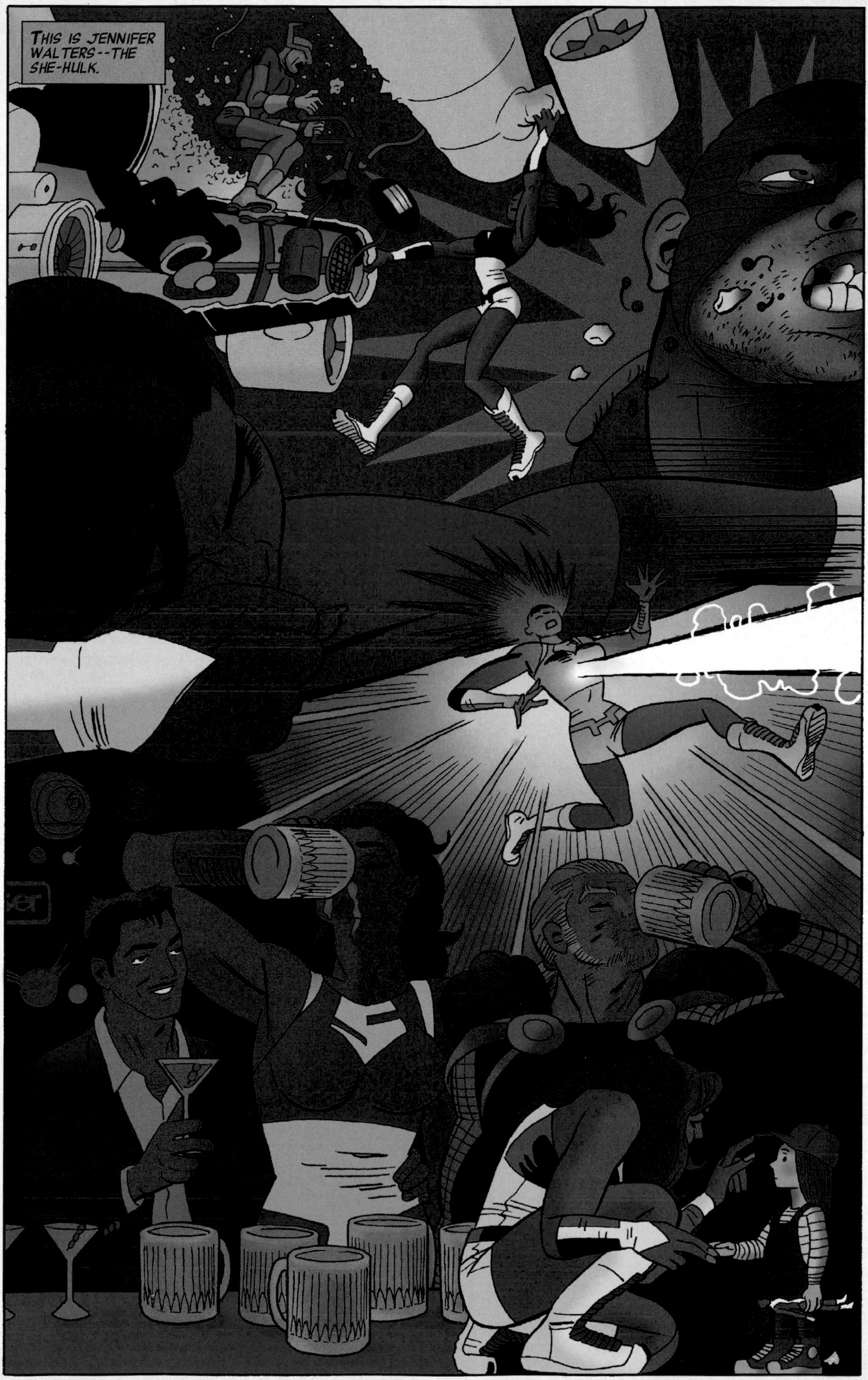
THIS IS JENNIFER WALTERS--THE SHE-HULK.

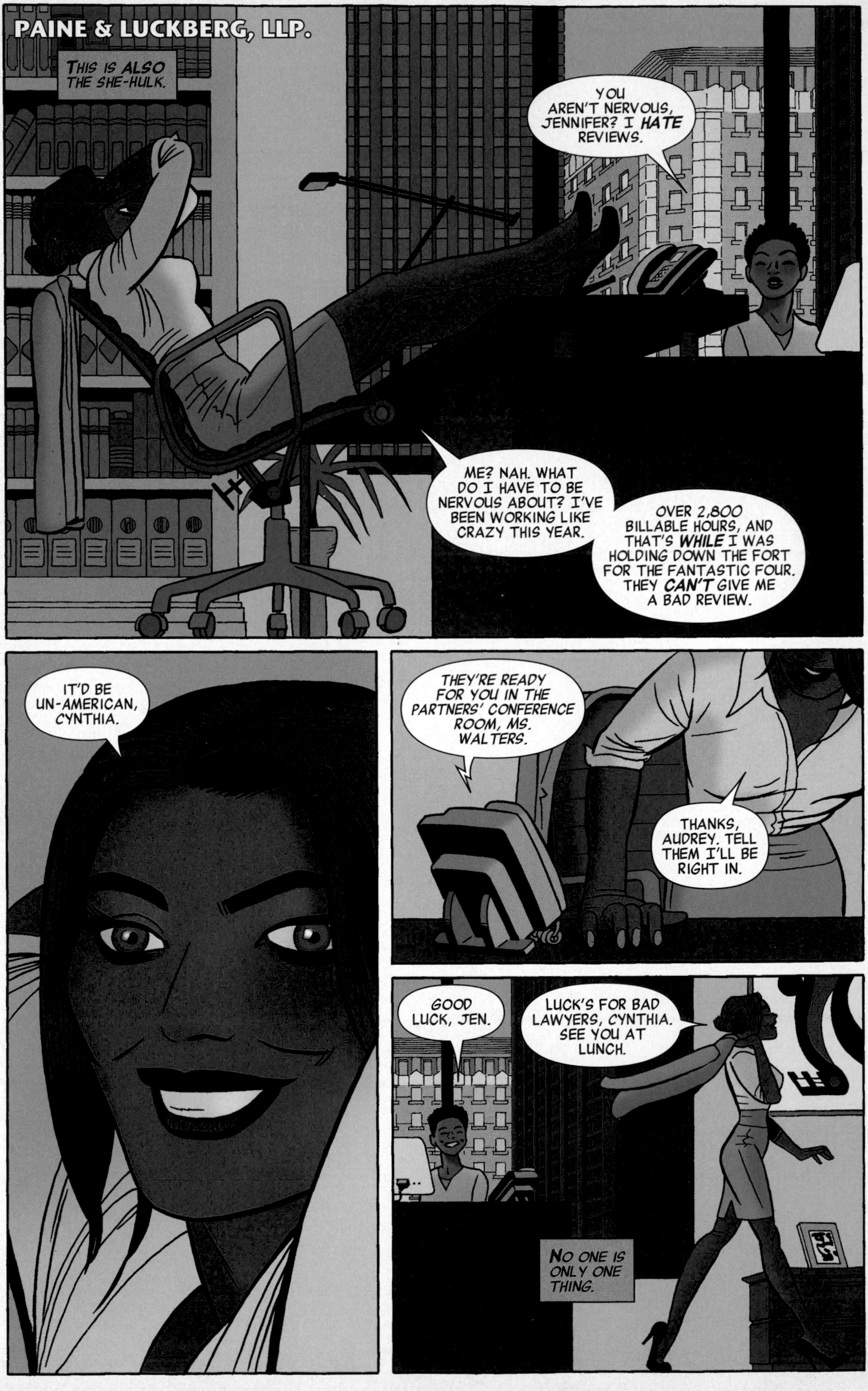

PAINE & LUCKBERG, LLP.
THIS IS ALSO THE SHE-HULK.
YOU AREN'T NERVOUS, JENNIFER? I HATE REVIEWS.
ME? NAH. WHAT DO I HAVE TO BE NERVOUS ABOUT? I'VE BEEN WORKING LIKE CRAZY THIS YEAR.
OVER 2,800 BILLABLE HOURS, AND THAT'S WHILE I WAS HOLDING DOWN THE FORT FOR THE FANTASTIC FOUR. THEY CAN'T GIVE ME A BAD REVIEW.
IT'D BE UN-AMERICAN, CYNTHIA.
THEY'RE READY FOR YOU IN THE PARTNERS' CONFERENCE ROOM, MS. WALTERS.
THANKS, AUDREY. TELL THEM I'LL BE RIGHT IN.
GOOD LUCK, JEN.
LUCK'S FOR BAD LAWYERS, CYNTHIA. SEE YOU AT LUNCH.
NO ONE IS ONLY ONE THING.

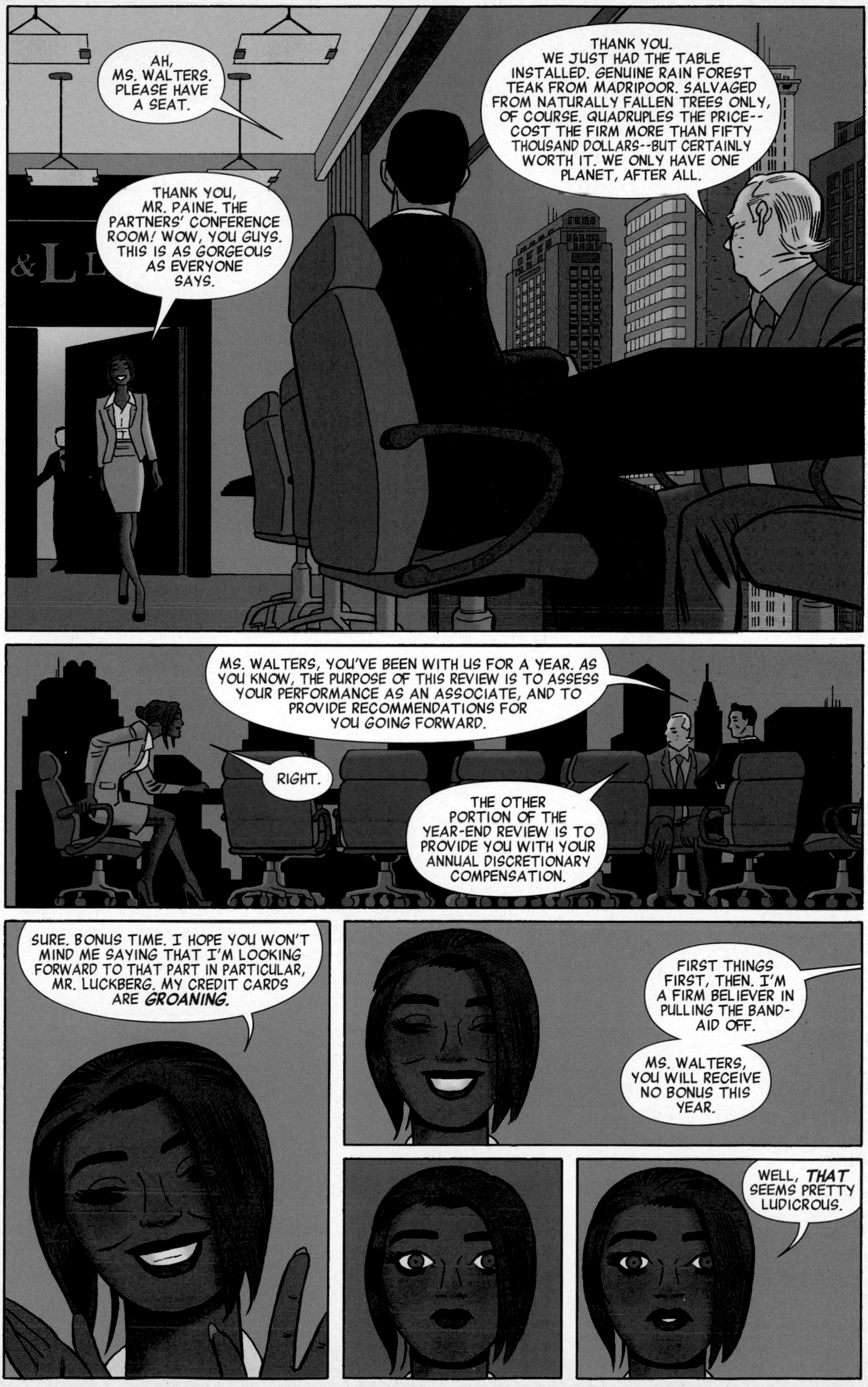
AH, MS. WALTERS. PLEASE HAVE A SEAT.
THANK YOU, MR. PAINE. THE PARTNERS' CONFERENCE ROOM! WOW, YOU GUYS. THIS IS AS GORGEOUS AS EVERYONE SAYS.
THANK YOU. WE JUST HAD THE TABLE INSTALLED. GENUINE RAIN FOREST TEAK FROM MADRIPOOR. SALVAGED FROM NATURALLY FALLEN TREES ONLY, OF COURSE. QUADRUPLES THE PRICE--COST THE FIRM MORE THAN FIFTY THOUSAND DOLLARS--BUT CERTAINLY WORTH IT. WE ONLY HAVE ONE PLANET, AFTER ALL.
MS. WALTERS, YOU'VE BEEN WITH US FOR A YEAR. AS YOU KNOW, THE PURPOSE OF THIS REVIEW IS TO ASSESS YOUR PERFORMANCE AS AN ASSOCIATE, AND TO PROVIDE RECOMMENDATIONS FOR YOU GOING FORWARD.
RIGHT.
THE OTHER PORTION OF THE YEAR-END REVIEW IS TO PROVIDE YOU WITH YOUR ANNUAL DISCRETIONARY COMPENSATION.
SURE. BONUS TIME. I HOPE YOU WON'T MIND ME SAYING THAT I'M LOOKING FORWARD TO THAT PART IN PARTICULAR, MR. LUCKBERG. MY CREDIT CARDS ARE ***GROANING.***
FIRST THINGS FIRST, THEN. I'M A FIRM BELIEVER IN PULLING THE BAND-AID OFF.
MS. WALTERS, YOU WILL RECEIVE NO BONUS THIS YEAR.
WELL, ***THAT*** SEEMS PRETTY LUDICROUS.

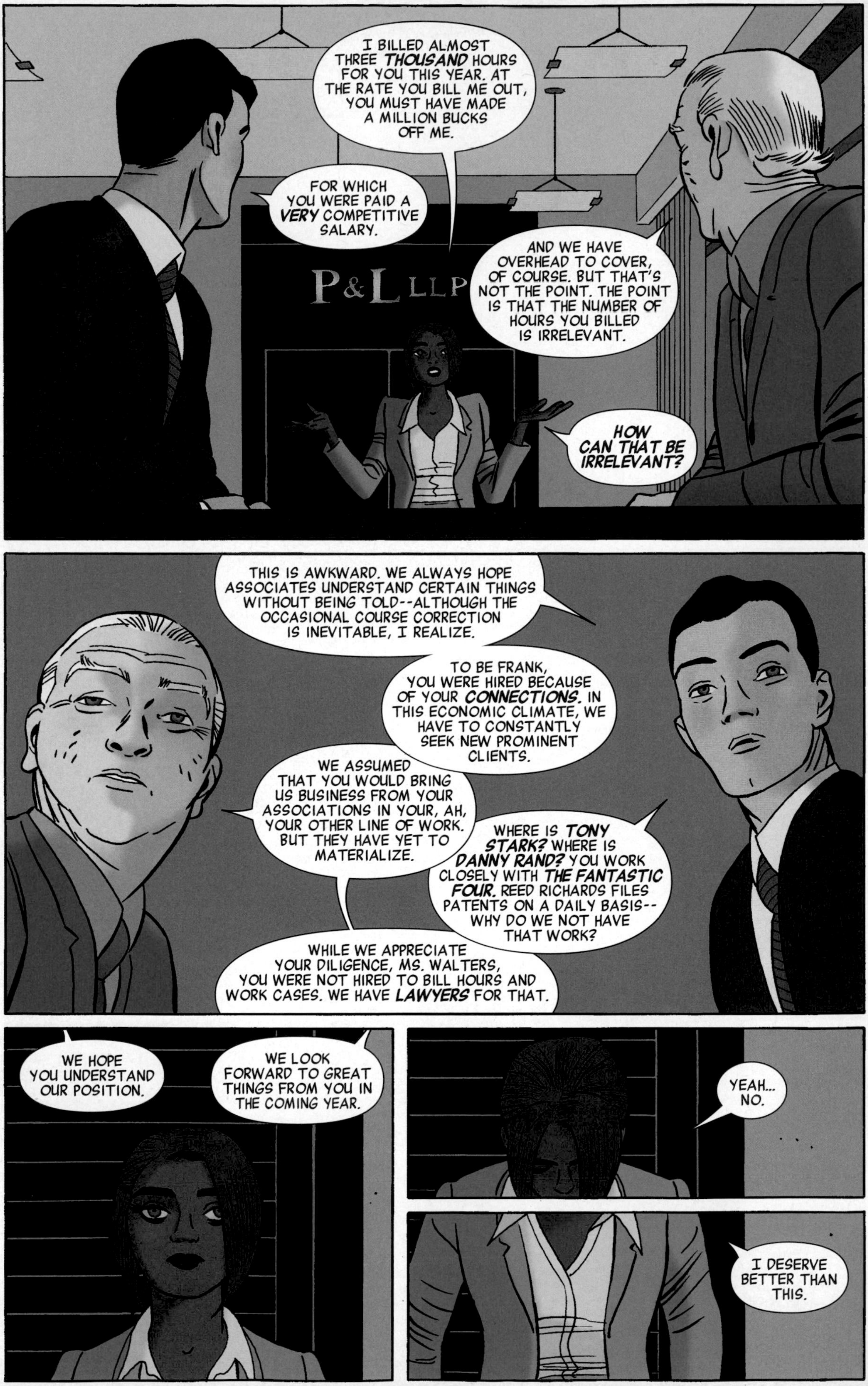
I BILLED ALMOST THREE THOUSAND HOURS FOR YOU THIS YEAR. AT THE RATE YOU BILL ME OUT, YOU MUST HAVE MADE A MILLION BUCKS OFF ME.
FOR WHICH YOU WERE PAID A VERY COMPETITIVE SALARY.
P&L LLP
AND WE HAVE OVERHEAD TO COVER, OF COURSE. BUT THAT'S NOT THE POINT. THE POINT IS THAT THE NUMBER OF HOURS YOU BILLED IS IRRELEVANT.
HOW CAN THAT BE IRRELEVANT?
THIS IS AWKWARD. WE ALWAYS HOPE ASSOCIATES UNDERSTAND CERTAIN THINGS WITHOUT BEING TOLD--ALTHOUGH THE OCCASIONAL COURSE CORRECTION IS INEVITABLE, I REALIZE.
TO BE FRANK, YOU WERE HIRED BECAUSE OF YOUR CONNECTIONS. IN THIS ECONOMIC CLIMATE, WE HAVE TO CONSTANTLY SEEK NEW PROMINENT CLIENTS.
WE ASSUMED THAT YOU WOULD BRING US BUSINESS FROM YOUR ASSOCIATIONS IN YOUR, AH, YOUR OTHER LINE OF WORK. BUT THEY HAVE YET TO MATERIALIZE.
WHERE IS TONY STARK? WHERE IS DANNY RAND? YOU WORK CLOSELY WITH THE FANTASTIC FOUR. REED RICHARDS FILES PATENTS ON A DAILY BASIS-- WHY DO WE NOT HAVE THAT WORK?
WHILE WE APPRECIATE YOUR DILIGENCE, MS. WALTERS, YOU WERE NOT HIRED TO BILL HOURS AND WORK CASES. WE HAVE LAWYERS FOR THAT.
WE HOPE YOU UNDERSTAND OUR POSITION.
WE LOOK FORWARD TO GREAT THINGS FROM YOU IN THE COMING YEAR.
YEAH... NO.
I DESERVE BETTER THAN THIS.

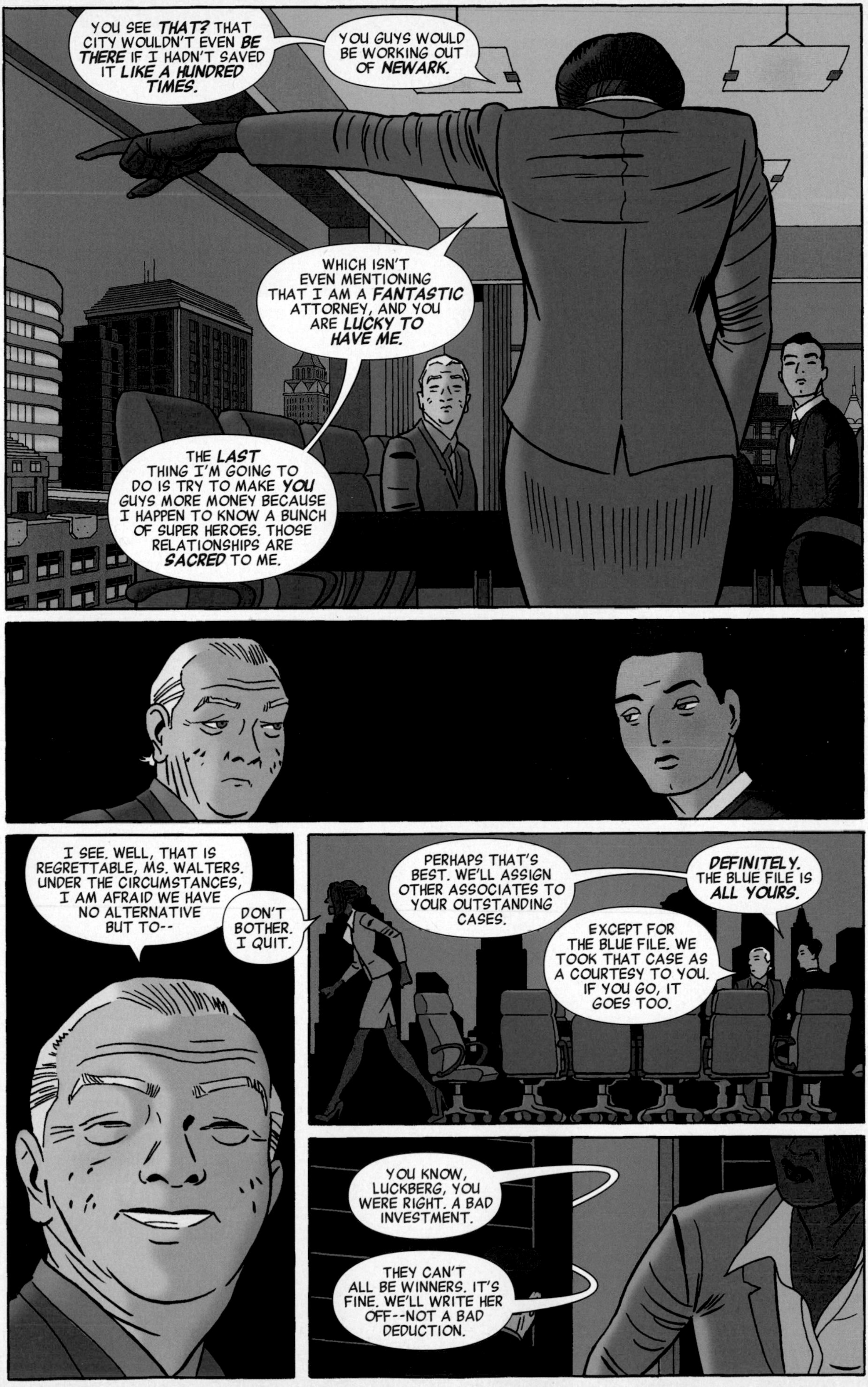
YOU SEE THAT? THAT CITY WOULDN'T EVEN BE THERE IF I HADN'T SAVED IT LIKE A HUNDRED TIMES.
YOU GUYS WOULD BE WORKING OUT OF NEWARK.
WHICH ISN'T EVEN MENTIONING THAT I AM A FANTASTIC ATTORNEY, AND YOU ARE LUCKY TO HAVE ME.
THE LAST THING I'M GOING TO DO IS TRY TO MAKE YOU GUYS MORE MONEY BECAUSE I HAPPEN TO KNOW A BUNCH OF SUPER HEROES. THOSE RELATIONSHIPS ARE SACRED TO ME.
I SEE. WELL, THAT IS REGRETTABLE, MS. WALTERS. UNDER THE CIRCUMSTANCES, I AM AFRAID WE HAVE NO ALTERNATIVE BUT TO--
DON'T BOTHER. I QUIT.
PERHAPS THAT'S BEST. WE'LL ASSIGN OTHER ASSOCIATES TO YOUR OUTSTANDING CASES.
DEFINITELY. THE BLUE FILE IS ALL YOURS.
EXCEPT FOR THE BLUE FILE. WE TOOK THAT CASE AS A COURTESY TO YOU. IF YOU GO, IT GOES TOO.
YOU KNOW, LUCKBERG, YOU WERE RIGHT. A BAD INVESTMENT.
THEY CAN'T ALL BE WINNERS. IT'S FINE. WE'LL WRITE HER OFF--NOT A BAD DEDUCTION.

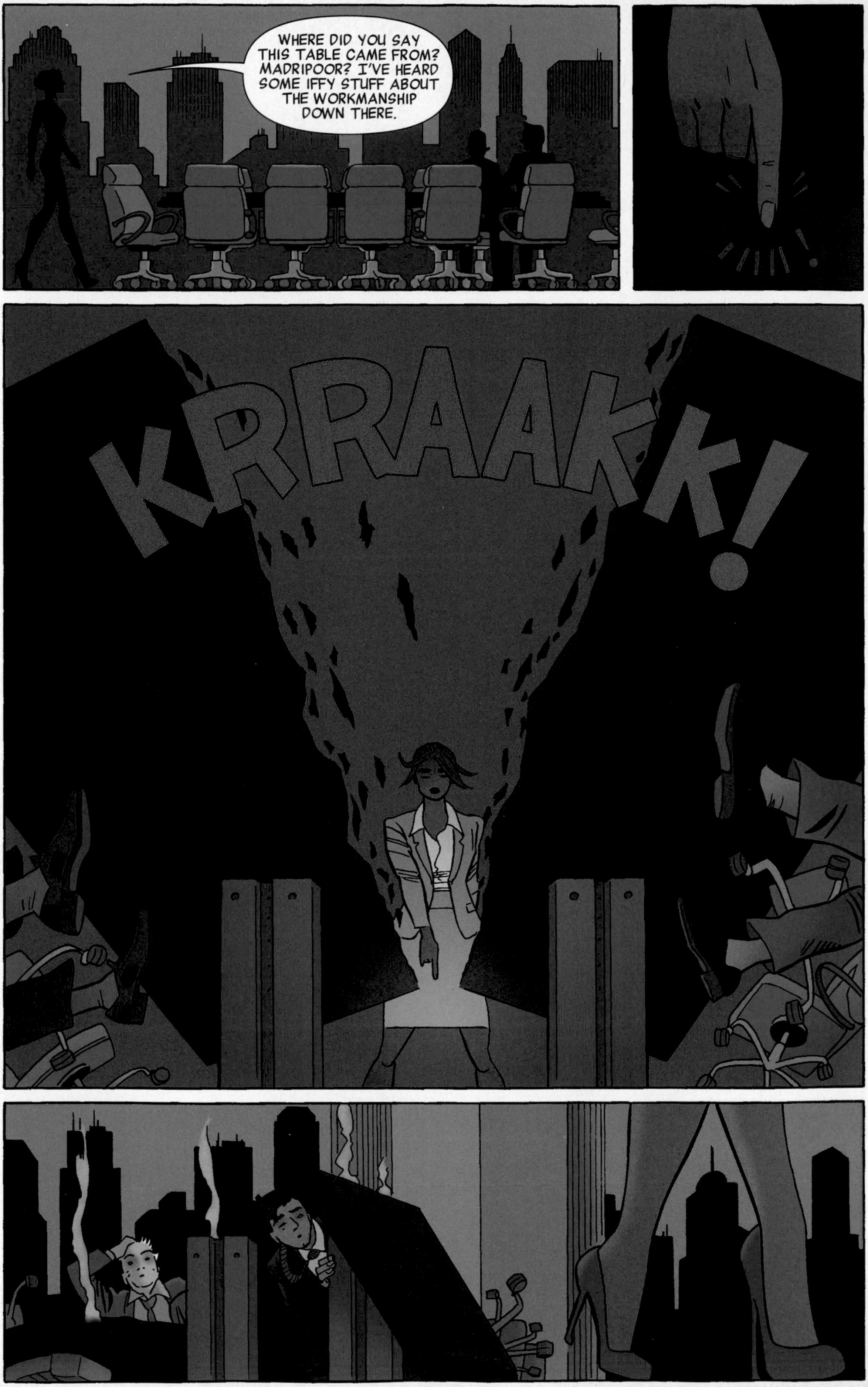
WHERE DID YOU SAY THIS TABLE CAME FROM? MADRIPOOR? I'VE HEARD SOME IFFY STUFF ABOUT THE WORKMANSHIP DOWN THERE.
KRRAAKK!

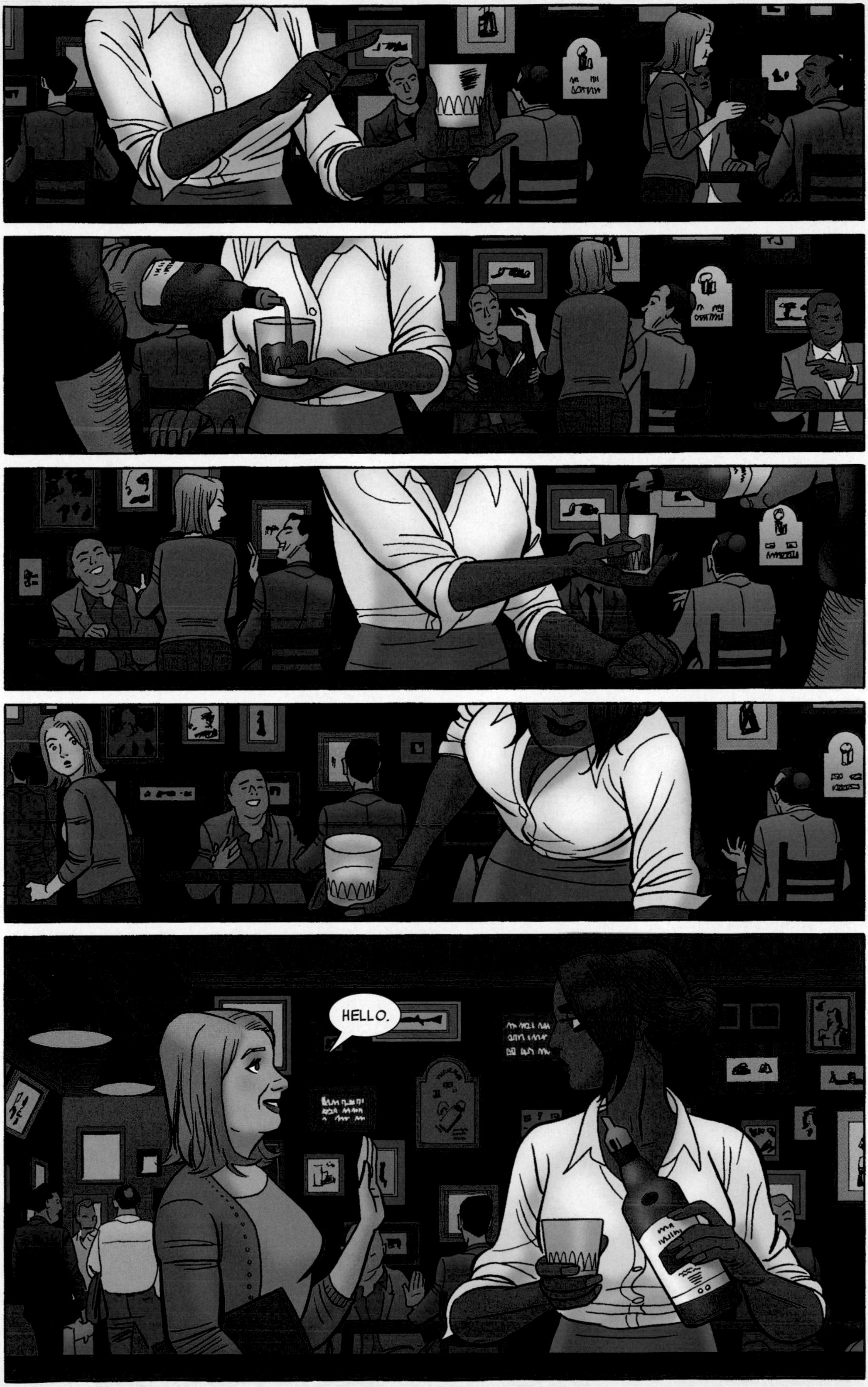
HELLO.

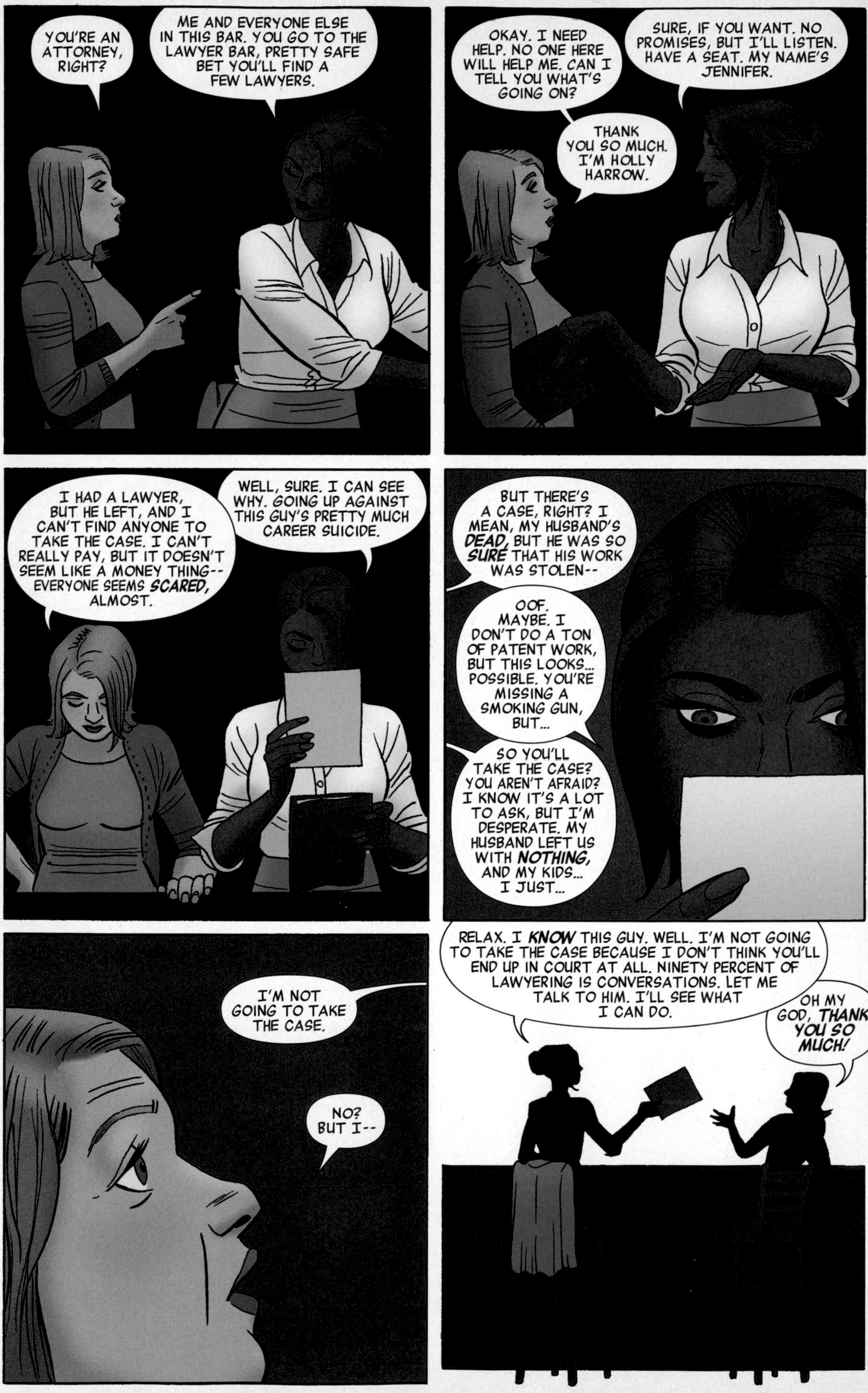
YOU'RE AN ATTORNEY, RIGHT?
ME AND EVERYONE ELSE IN THIS BAR. YOU GO TO THE LAWYER BAR, PRETTY SAFE BET YOU'LL FIND A FEW LAWYERS.
OKAY. I NEED HELP. NO ONE HERE WILL HELP ME. CAN I TELL YOU WHAT'S GOING ON?
SURE, IF YOU WANT. NO PROMISES, BUT I'LL LISTEN. HAVE A SEAT. MY NAME'S JENNIFER.
THANK YOU SO MUCH. I'M HOLLY HARROW.
I HAD A LAWYER, BUT HE LEFT, AND I CAN'T FIND ANYONE TO TAKE THE CASE. I CAN'T REALLY PAY, BUT IT DOESN'T SEEM LIKE A MONEY THING-- EVERYONE SEEMS SCARED, ALMOST.
WELL, SURE. I CAN SEE WHY. GOING UP AGAINST THIS GUY'S PRETTY MUCH CAREER SUICIDE.
BUT THERE'S A CASE, RIGHT? I MEAN, MY HUSBAND'S DEAD, BUT HE WAS SO SURE THAT HIS WORK WAS STOLEN--
OOF. MAYBE. I DON'T DO A TON OF PATENT WORK, BUT THIS LOOKS... POSSIBLE. YOU'RE MISSING A SMOKING GUN, BUT...
SO YOU'LL TAKE THE CASE? YOU AREN'T AFRAID? I KNOW IT'S A LOT TO ASK, BUT I'M DESPERATE. MY HUSBAND LEFT US WITH NOTHING, AND MY KIDS... I JUST...
I'M NOT GOING TO TAKE THE CASE.
NO? BUT I--
RELAX. I KNOW THIS GUY. WELL. I'M NOT GOING TO TAKE THE CASE BECAUSE I DON'T THINK YOU'LL END UP IN COURT AT ALL. NINETY PERCENT OF LAWYERING IS CONVERSATIONS. LET ME TALK TO HIM. I'LL SEE WHAT I CAN DO.
OH MY GOD, THANK YOU SO MUCH!

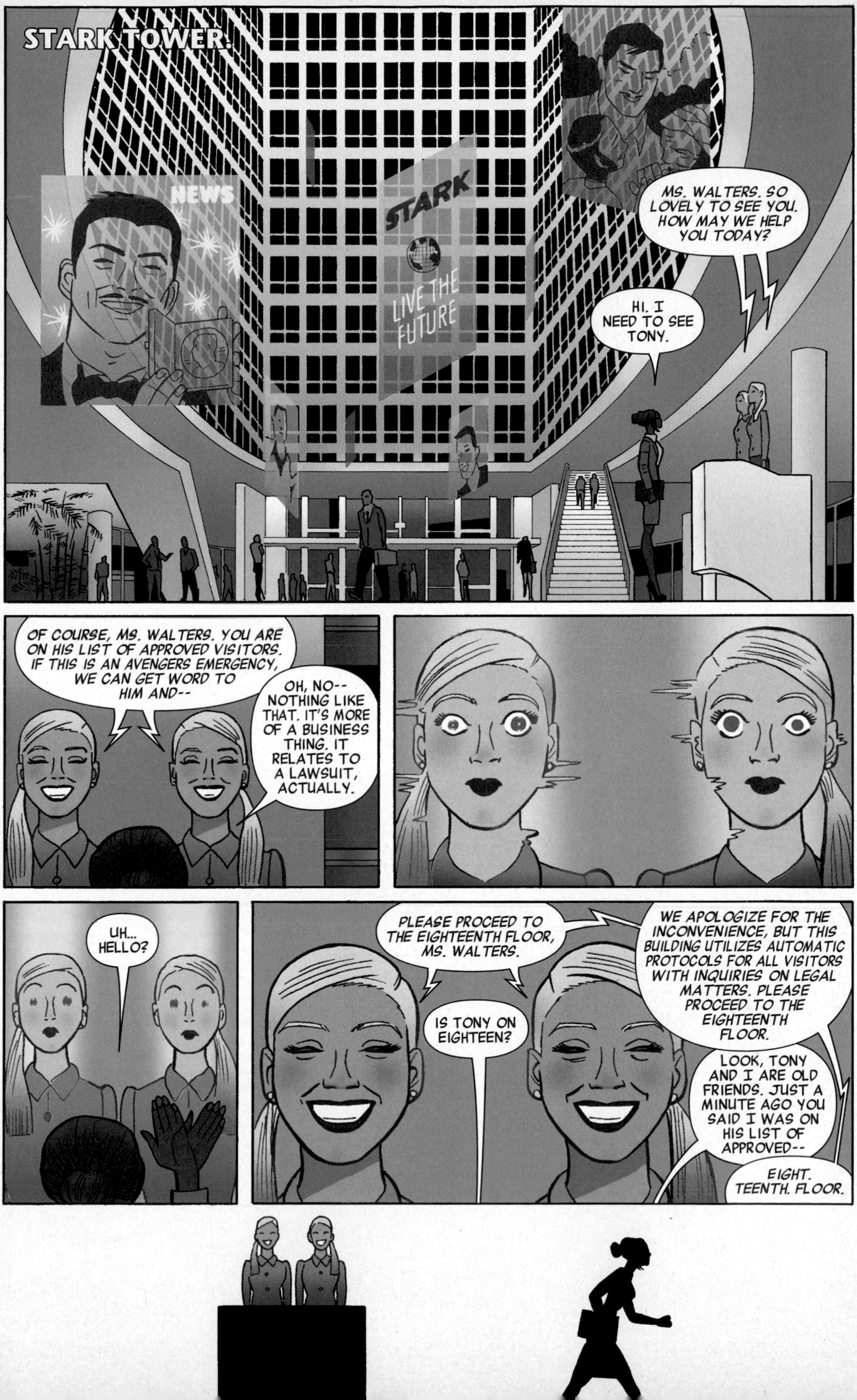
STARK TOWER.
NEWS
STARK
LIVE THE FUTURE
MS. WALTERS. SO LOVELY TO SEE YOU. HOW MAY WE HELP YOU TODAY?
HI. I NEED TO SEE TONY.
OF COURSE, MS. WALTERS. YOU ARE ON HIS LIST OF APPROVED VISITORS. IF THIS IS AN AVENGERS EMERGENCY, WE CAN GET WORD TO HIM AND--
OH, NO-- NOTHING LIKE THAT. IT'S MORE OF A BUSINESS THING. IT RELATES TO A LAWSUIT, ACTUALLY.
UH... HELLO?
PLEASE PROCEED TO THE EIGHTEENTH FLOOR, MS. WALTERS.
IS TONY ON EIGHTEEN?
WE APOLOGIZE FOR THE INCONVENIENCE, BUT THIS BUILDING UTILIZES AUTOMATIC PROTOCOLS FOR ALL VISITORS WITH INQUIRIES ON LEGAL MATTERS. PLEASE PROCEED TO THE EIGHTEENTH FLOOR.
LOOK, TONY AND I ARE OLD FRIENDS. JUST A MINUTE AGO YOU SAID I WAS ON HIS LIST OF APPROVED--
EIGHT. TEENTH. FLOOR.

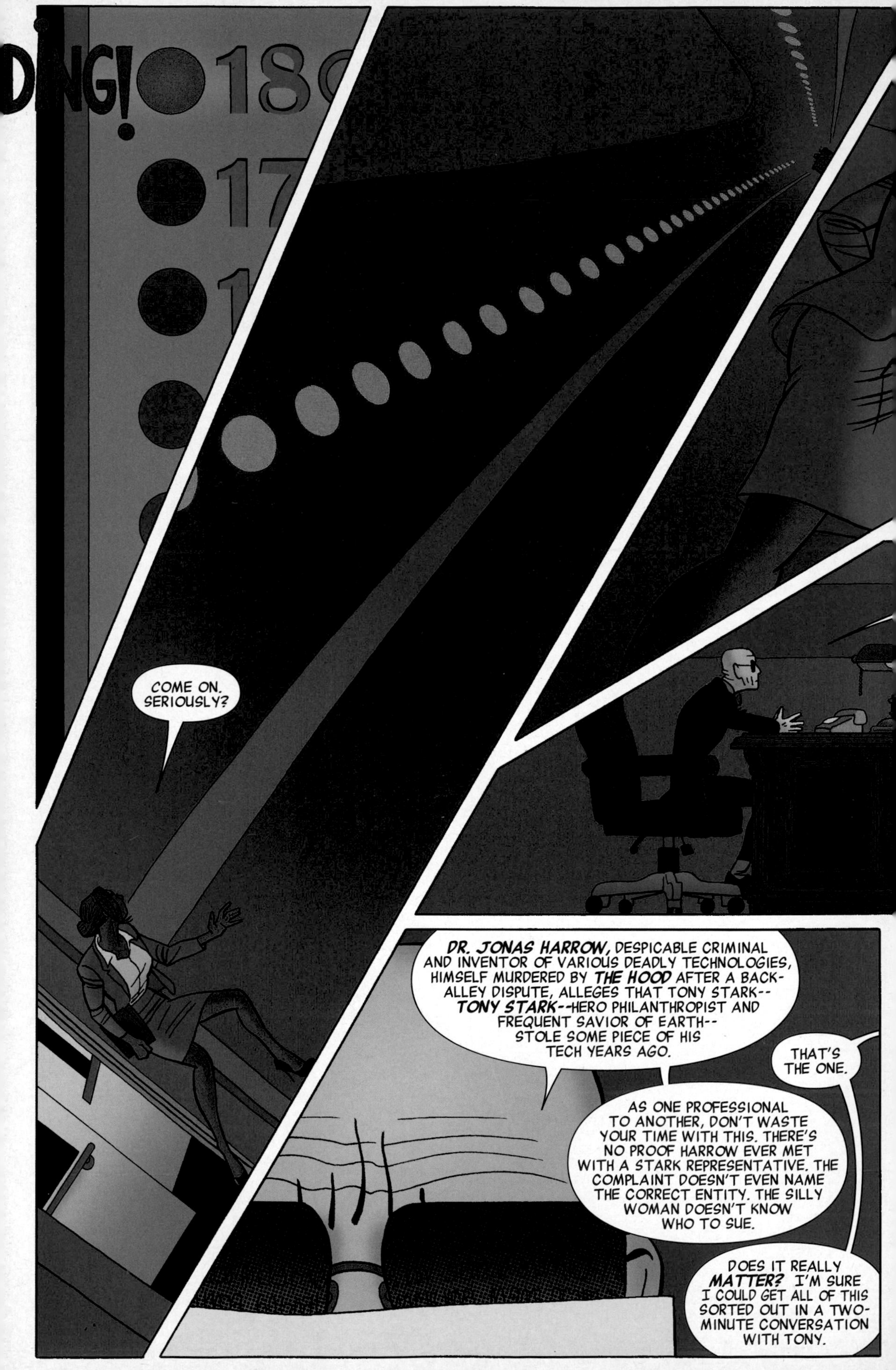
DING!
18
17
COME ON. SERIOUSLY?
DR. JONAS HARROW, DESPICABLE CRIMINAL AND INVENTOR OF VARIOUS DEADLY TECHNOLOGIES, HIMSELF MURDERED BY THE HOOD AFTER A BACK-ALLEY DISPUTE, ALLEGES THAT TONY STARK-- TONY STARK--HERO PHILANTHROPIST AND FREQUENT SAVIOR OF EARTH-- STOLE SOME PIECE OF HIS TECH YEARS AGO.
THAT'S THE ONE.
AS ONE PROFESSIONAL TO ANOTHER, DON'T WASTE YOUR TIME WITH THIS. THERE'S NO PROOF HARROW EVER MET WITH A STARK REPRESENTATIVE. THE COMPLAINT DOESN'T EVEN NAME THE CORRECT ENTITY. THE SILLY WOMAN DOESN'T KNOW WHO TO SUE.
DOES IT REALLY MATTER? I'M SURE I COULD GET ALL OF THIS SORTED OUT IN A TWO-MINUTE CONVERSATION WITH TONY.

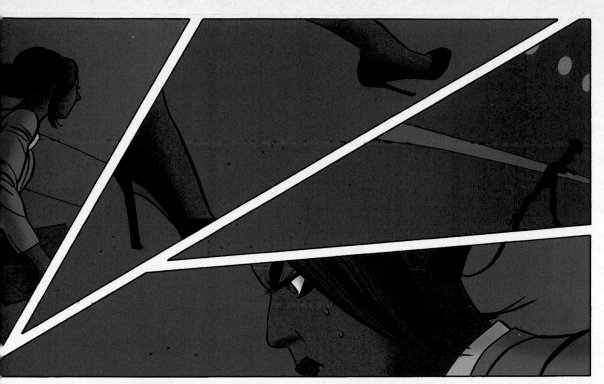

GOOD AFTERNOON, MS. WALTERS. I AM LEGAL.

THE LEGAL *DEPARTMENT,* OR...

NO. SIMPLY LEGAL. I AM EMPLOYED BY MR. STARK TO ASSESS INQUIRIES OF A LITIGATIONAL NATURE, TO DETERMINE WHICH, IF ANY, MERIT HIS ATTENTION.

THEY RARELY DO. WHICH IS HOW WE BOTH PREFER THINGS, FRANKLY.

NOW, WHO IS THE PARTY ADVERSE TO MR. STARK? IS IT YOU?

NO. IT'S A WOMAN NAMED HOLLY HARROW. SHE'S ALLEGING--

AH, YES. THE *HARROW* MATTER.

DOES IT *MATTER?* MADAM, MR. STARK'S ORIGINAL COMPANY WAS *STARK INDUSTRIES,* CEDED TO MR. JAMES RHODEY AND RENAMED *STARK INTERNATIONAL.* THAT ENTITY WAS ITSELF SUBJECT TO HOSTILE TAKEOVER BY OBADIAH STANE AND RENAMED *STANE INTERNATIONAL.* UPON MR. STARK'S BUYOUT OF STANE INTERNATIONAL, THE PRIMARY OPERATING ENTITY WAS REORGANIZED UNDER THE NAME STARK ENTERPRISES.

AFTER A CHANGE IN BUSINESS DIRECTION, MR. STARK'S PRIMARY ENTITY WAS STARK RESILIENT, BUT HE GAVE THAT COMPANY TO HIS LADY FRIEND TO RUN NOT LONG AGO.

MR. STARK DIED NOT LONG AFTER THIS POINT, AND THE COMPANY WAS MERGED WITH FUJIKAWA INDUSTRIES, AN ASIAN CONCERN, TO BECOME STARK FUJIKAWA. ONCE MR. STARK CEASED BEING DEAD, HE FOUNDED STARK SOLUTIONS, WHICH WAS DISSOLVED AFTER IMPROPRIETIES BEST NOT MENTIONED, PAVING THE WAY FOR THE REVIVAL OF BOTH STARK INDUSTRIES *AND* STARK INTERNATIONAL, ALTHOUGH THOSE ENTITIES WERE A GERMAN GMBH AND A CAYMAN ISLANDS LIMITED PARTNERSHIP, RESPECTIVELY.

SO YOU CAN SEE, IT CERTAINLY *DOES* MATTER. FEEL FREE TO RETURN ONCE YOU HAVE *PROPERLY* REVIEWED THE FILE. PERHAPS THEN WE CAN SEE ABOUT BRINGING THE ISSUE TO MR. STARK'S ATTENTION.

FORGET IT. SELL THE RUNAROUND SOMEWHERE ELSE. I'LL JUST SEE YOU IN COURT.

CERTAINLY. PLEASE EXIT THE BUILDING PROMPTLY, MS. WALTERS. IN FIVE MINUTES, I WILL ALERT BUILDING SECURITY THAT AN ADVERSE PARTY IS LOOSE IN THE TOWER.

YOU'RE THE WORST.

I AM NEITHER BAD NOR GOOD. I AM SIMPLY LEGAL.

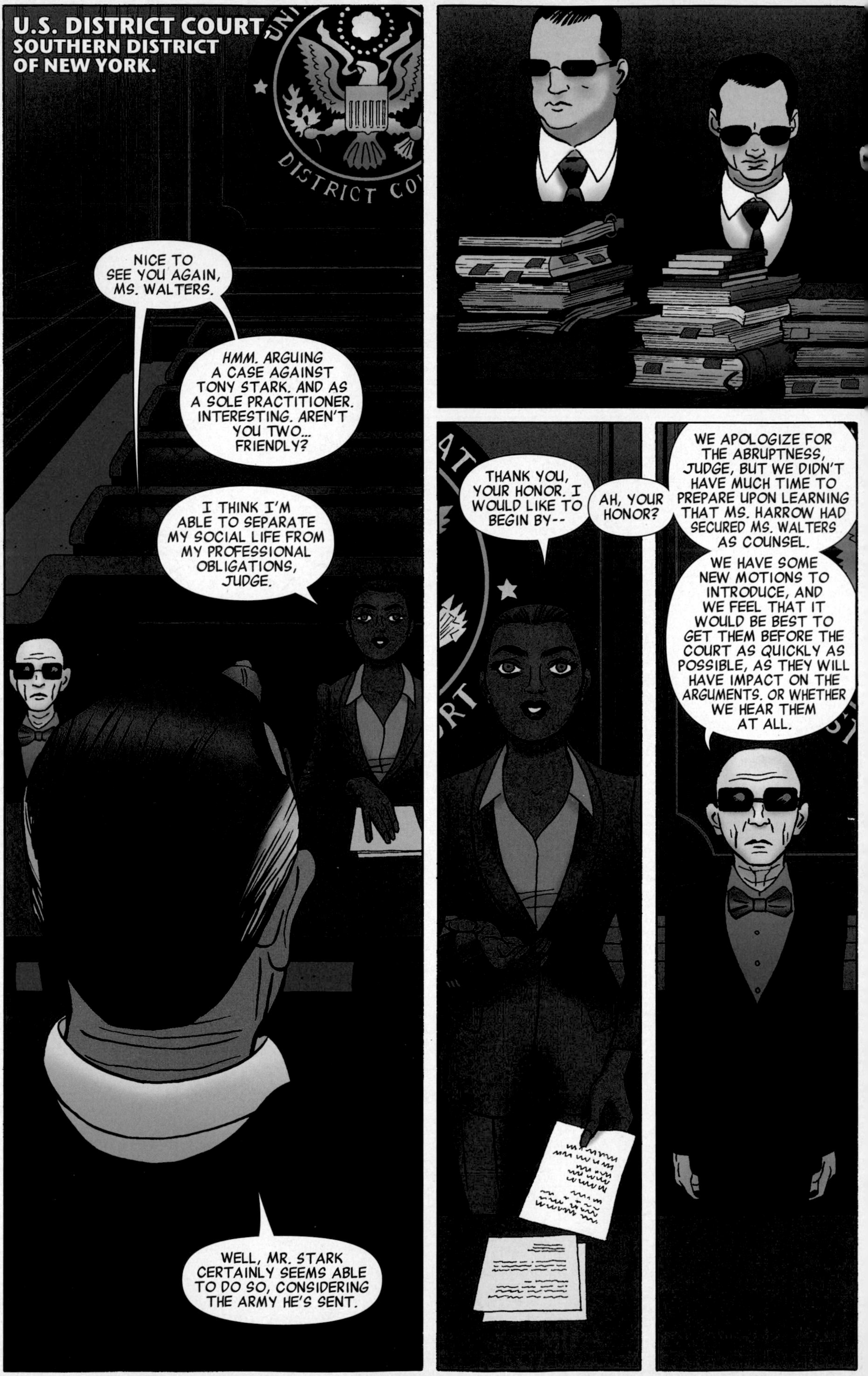
U.S. DISTRICT COURT SOUTHERN DISTRICT OF NEW YORK.
DISTRICT CO
NICE TO SEE YOU AGAIN, MS. WALTERS.
HMM. ARGUING A CASE AGAINST TONY STARK. AND AS A SOLE PRACTITIONER. INTERESTING. AREN'T YOU TWO... FRIENDLY?
I THINK I'M ABLE TO SEPARATE MY SOCIAL LIFE FROM MY PROFESSIONAL OBLIGATIONS, JUDGE.
WELL, MR. STARK CERTAINLY SEEMS ABLE TO DO SO, CONSIDERING THE ARMY HE'S SENT.
THANK YOU, YOUR HONOR. I WOULD LIKE TO BEGIN BY--
AH, YOUR HONOR?
WE APOLOGIZE FOR THE ABRUPTNESS, JUDGE, BUT WE DIDN'T HAVE MUCH TIME TO PREPARE UPON LEARNING THAT MS. HARROW HAD SECURED MS. WALTERS AS COUNSEL.
WE HAVE SOME NEW MOTIONS TO INTRODUCE, AND WE FEEL THAT IT WOULD BE BEST TO GET THEM BEFORE THE COURT AS QUICKLY AS POSSIBLE, AS THEY WILL HAVE IMPACT ON THE ARGUMENTS. OR WHETHER WE HEAR THEM AT ALL.

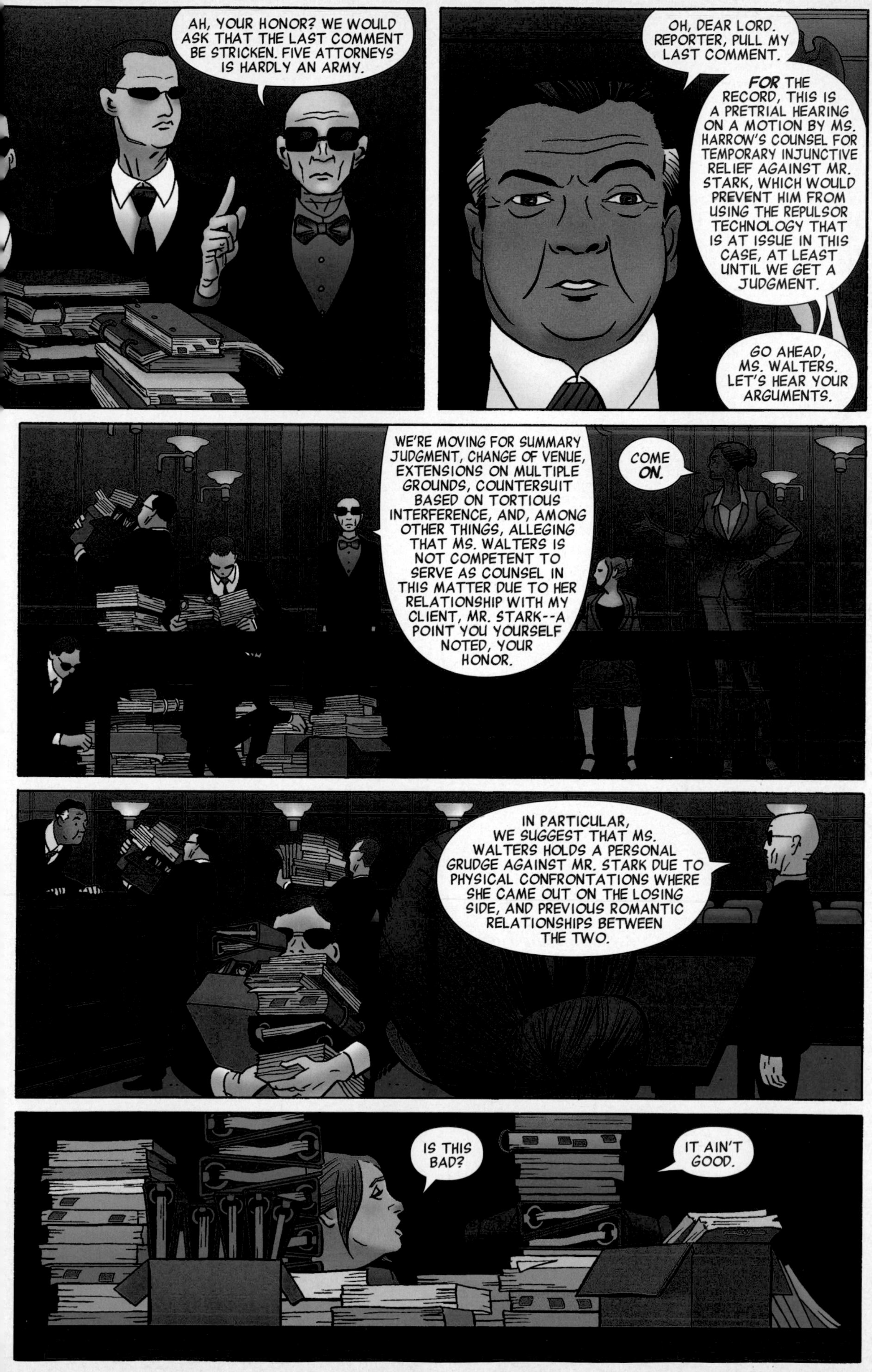
AH, YOUR HONOR? WE WOULD ASK THAT THE LAST COMMENT BE STRICKEN. FIVE ATTORNEYS IS HARDLY AN ARMY.
OH, DEAR LORD. REPORTER, PULL MY LAST COMMENT.
FOR THE RECORD, THIS IS A PRETRIAL HEARING ON A MOTION BY MS. HARROW'S COUNSEL FOR TEMPORARY INJUNCTIVE RELIEF AGAINST MR. STARK, WHICH WOULD PREVENT HIM FROM USING THE REPULSOR TECHNOLOGY THAT IS AT ISSUE IN THIS CASE, AT LEAST UNTIL WE GET A JUDGMENT.
GO AHEAD, MS. WALTERS. LET'S HEAR YOUR ARGUMENTS.
WE'RE MOVING FOR SUMMARY JUDGMENT, CHANGE OF VENUE, EXTENSIONS ON MULTIPLE GROUNDS, COUNTERSUIT BASED ON TORTIOUS INTERFERENCE, AND, AMONG OTHER THINGS, ALLEGING THAT MS. WALTERS IS NOT COMPETENT TO SERVE AS COUNSEL IN THIS MATTER DUE TO HER RELATIONSHIP WITH MY CLIENT, MR. STARK--A POINT YOU YOURSELF NOTED, YOUR HONOR.
COME ON.
IN PARTICULAR, WE SUGGEST THAT MS. WALTERS HOLDS A PERSONAL GRUDGE AGAINST MR. STARK DUE TO PHYSICAL CONFRONTATIONS WHERE SHE CAME OUT ON THE LOSING SIDE, AND PREVIOUS ROMANTIC RELATIONSHIPS BETWEEN THE TWO.
IS THIS BAD?
IT AIN'T GOOD.

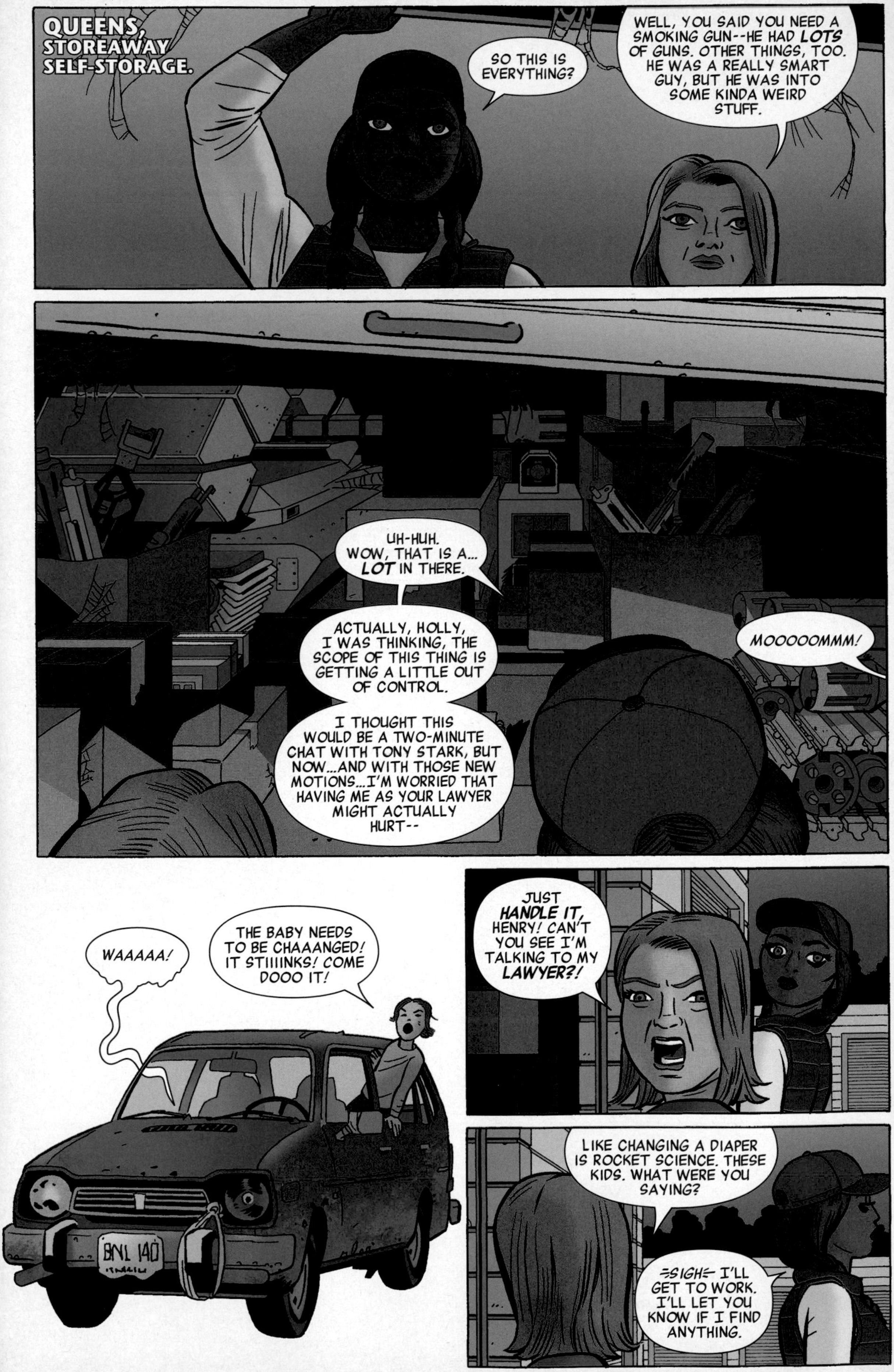
QUEENS, STOREAWAY SELF-STORAGE.
SO THIS IS EVERYTHING?
WELL, YOU SAID YOU NEED A SMOKING GUN--HE HAD LOTS OF GUNS. OTHER THINGS, TOO. HE WAS A REALLY SMART GUY, BUT HE WAS INTO SOME KINDA WEIRD STUFF.
UH-HUH. WOW, THAT IS A... LOT IN THERE.
ACTUALLY, HOLLY, I WAS THINKING, THE SCOPE OF THIS THING IS GETTING A LITTLE OUT OF CONTROL.
I THOUGHT THIS WOULD BE A TWO-MINUTE CHAT WITH TONY STARK, BUT NOW...AND WITH THOSE NEW MOTIONS...I'M WORRIED THAT HAVING ME AS YOUR LAWYER MIGHT ACTUALLY HURT--
MOOOOOMMM!
WAAAAA!
THE BABY NEEDS TO BE CHAAANGED! IT STIIIINKS! COME DOOO IT!
BNL 140
JUST HANDLE IT, HENRY! CAN'T YOU SEE I'M TALKING TO MY LAWYER?!
LIKE CHANGING A DIAPER IS ROCKET SCIENCE. THESE KIDS. WHAT WERE YOU SAYING?
=SIGH= I'LL GET TO WORK. I'LL LET YOU KNOW IF I FIND ANYTHING.

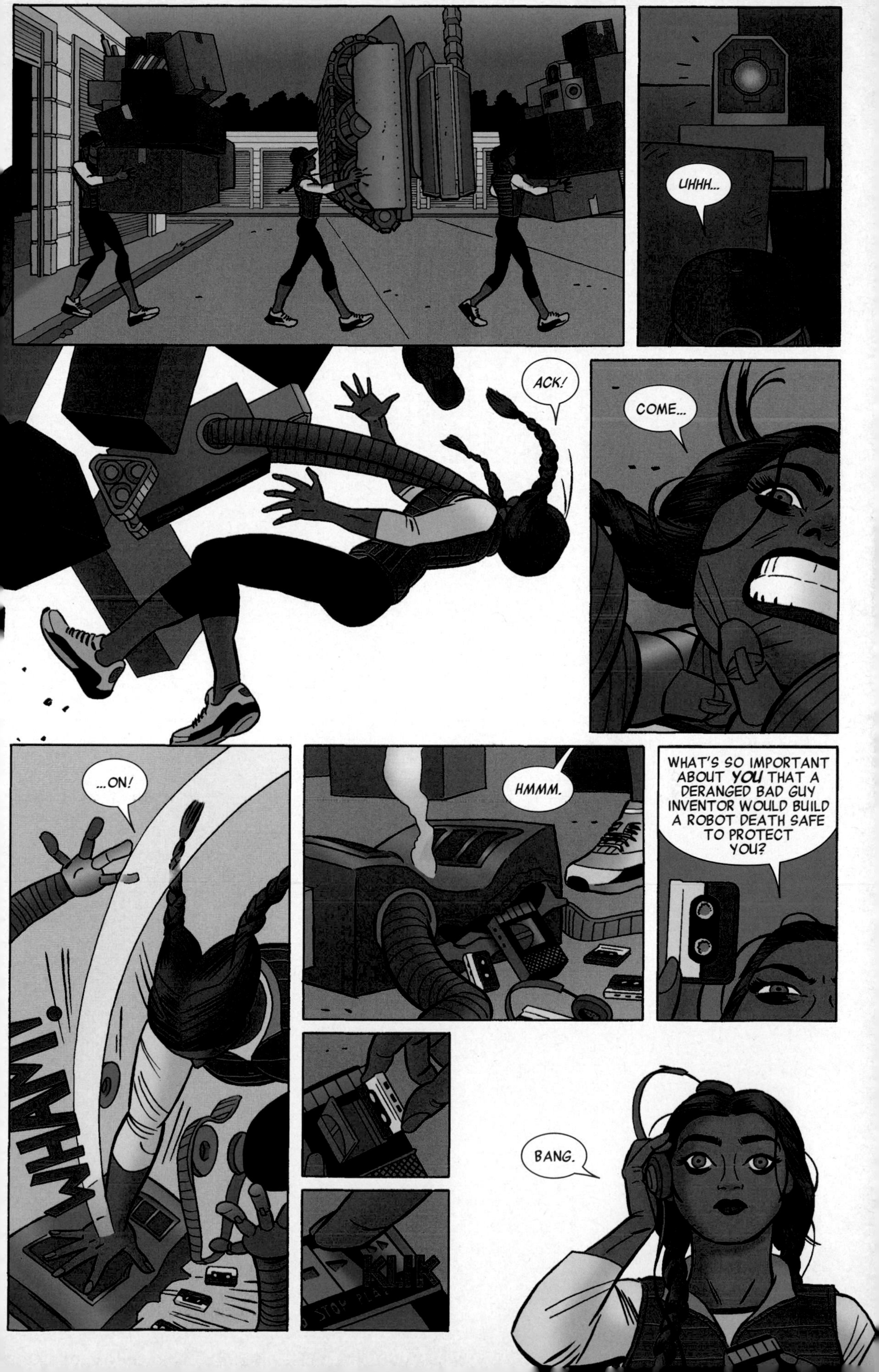
UHHH...
ACK!
COME...
...ON!
WHAM!!
HMMM.
WHAT'S SO IMPORTANT ABOUT YOU THAT A DERANGED BAD GUY INVENTOR WOULD BUILD A ROBOT DEATH SAFE TO PROTECT YOU?
KLIK
BANG.

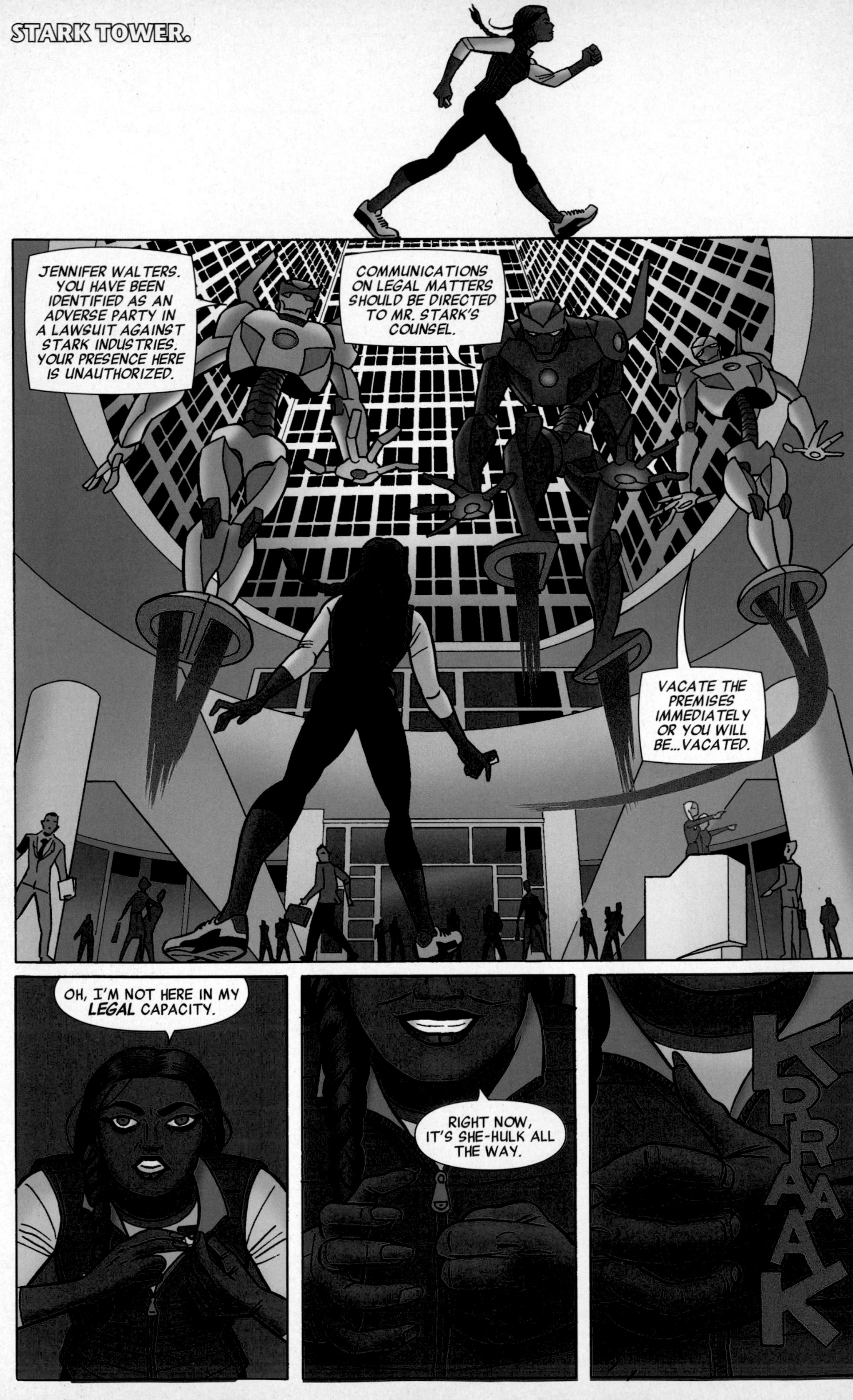
STARK TOWER.
JENNIFER WALTERS. YOU HAVE BEEN IDENTIFIED AS AN ADVERSE PARTY IN A LAWSUIT AGAINST STARK INDUSTRIES. YOUR PRESENCE HERE IS UNAUTHORIZED.
COMMUNICATIONS ON LEGAL MATTERS SHOULD BE DIRECTED TO MR. STARK'S COUNSEL.
VACATE THE PREMISES IMMEDIATELY OR YOU WILL BE...VACATED.
OH, I'M NOT HERE IN MY LEGAL CAPACITY.
RIGHT NOW, IT'S SHE-HULK ALL THE WAY.
KRRAAAK

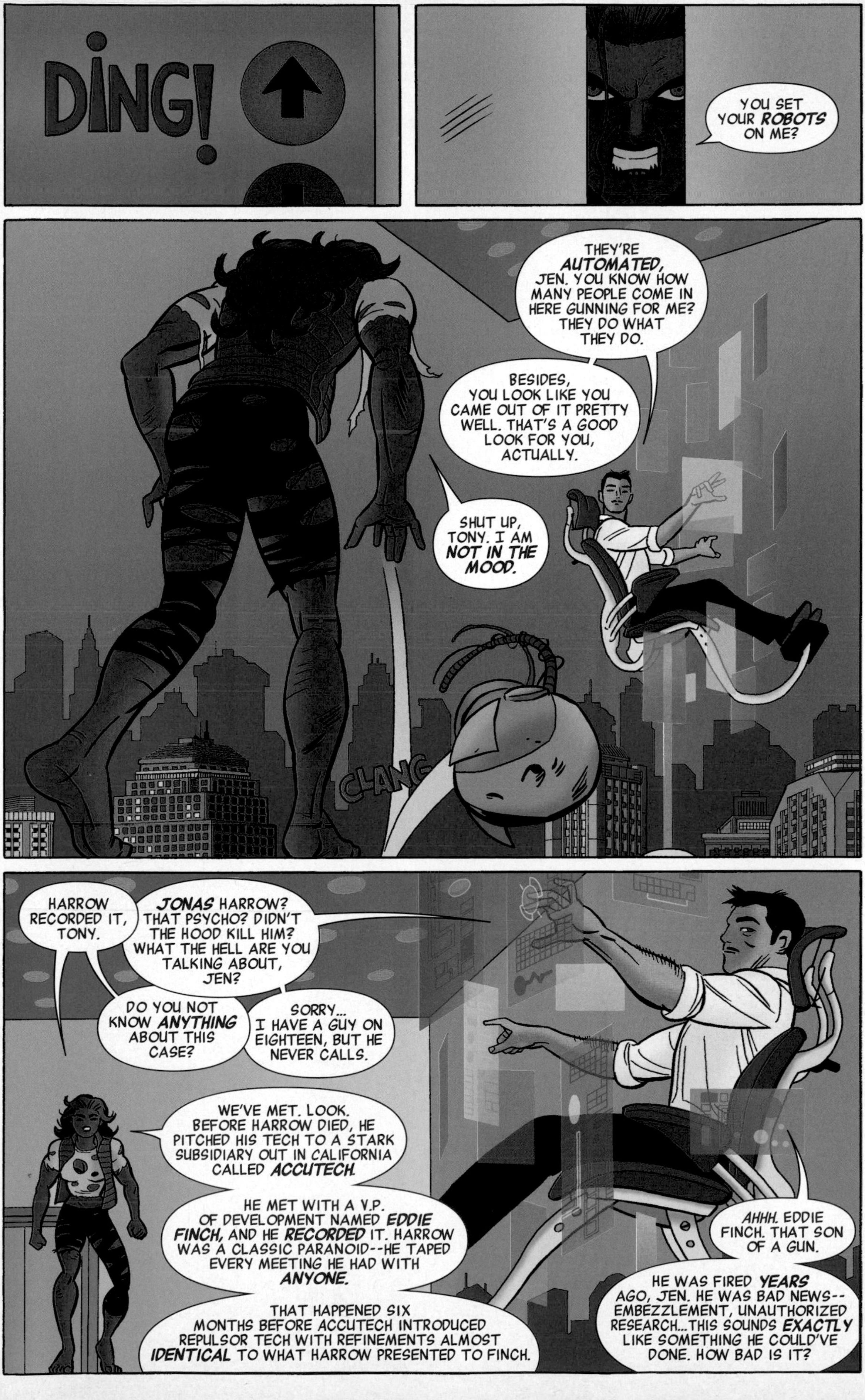
DING!
YOU SET YOUR ROBOTS ON ME?
THEY'RE AUTOMATED, JEN. YOU KNOW HOW MANY PEOPLE COME IN HERE GUNNING FOR ME? THEY DO WHAT THEY DO.
BESIDES, YOU LOOK LIKE YOU CAME OUT OF IT PRETTY WELL. THAT'S A GOOD LOOK FOR YOU, ACTUALLY.
SHUT UP, TONY. I AM NOT IN THE MOOD.
CLANG
HARROW RECORDED IT, TONY.
JONAS HARROW? THAT PSYCHO? DIDN'T THE HOOD KILL HIM? WHAT THE HELL ARE YOU TALKING ABOUT, JEN?
DO YOU NOT KNOW ANYTHING ABOUT THIS CASE?
SORRY... I HAVE A GUY ON EIGHTEEN, BUT HE NEVER CALLS.
WE'VE MET. LOOK. BEFORE HARROW DIED, HE PITCHED HIS TECH TO A STARK SUBSIDIARY OUT IN CALIFORNIA CALLED ACCUTECH.
HE MET WITH A V.P. OF DEVELOPMENT NAMED EDDIE FINCH, AND HE RECORDED IT. HARROW WAS A CLASSIC PARANOID--HE TAPED EVERY MEETING HE HAD WITH ANYONE.
THAT HAPPENED SIX MONTHS BEFORE ACCUTECH INTRODUCED REPULSOR TECH WITH REFINEMENTS ALMOST IDENTICAL TO WHAT HARROW PRESENTED TO FINCH.
AHHH. EDDIE FINCH. THAT SON OF A GUN.
HE WAS FIRED YEARS AGO, JEN. HE WAS BAD NEWS--EMBEZZLEMENT, UNAUTHORIZED RESEARCH...THIS SOUNDS EXACTLY LIKE SOMETHING HE COULD'VE DONE. HOW BAD IS IT?

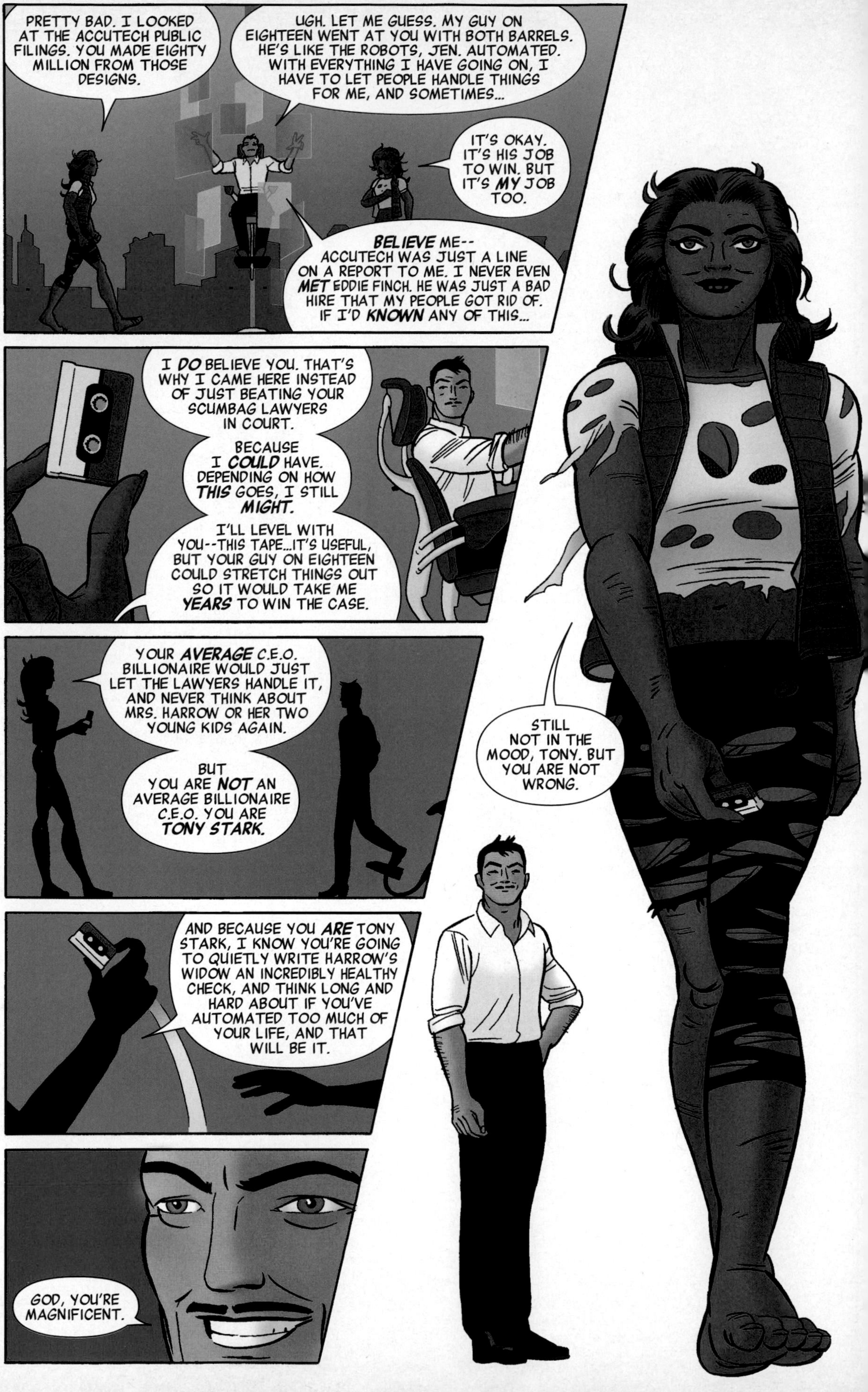
PRETTY BAD. I LOOKED AT THE ACCUTECH PUBLIC FILINGS. YOU MADE EIGHTY MILLION FROM THOSE DESIGNS.
UGH. LET ME GUESS. MY GUY ON EIGHTEEN WENT AT YOU WITH BOTH BARRELS. HE'S LIKE THE ROBOTS, JEN. AUTOMATED. WITH EVERYTHING I HAVE GOING ON, I HAVE TO LET PEOPLE HANDLE THINGS FOR ME, AND SOMETIMES...
IT'S OKAY. IT'S HIS JOB TO WIN. BUT IT'S MY JOB TOO.
BELIEVE ME-- ACCUTECH WAS JUST A LINE ON A REPORT TO ME. I NEVER EVEN MET EDDIE FINCH. HE WAS JUST A BAD HIRE THAT MY PEOPLE GOT RID OF. IF I'D KNOWN ANY OF THIS...
I DO BELIEVE YOU. THAT'S WHY I CAME HERE INSTEAD OF JUST BEATING YOUR SCUMBAG LAWYERS IN COURT.
BECAUSE I COULD HAVE. DEPENDING ON HOW THIS GOES, I STILL MIGHT.
I'LL LEVEL WITH YOU--THIS TAPE...IT'S USEFUL, BUT YOUR GUY ON EIGHTEEN COULD STRETCH THINGS OUT SO IT WOULD TAKE ME YEARS TO WIN THE CASE.
YOUR AVERAGE C.E.O. BILLIONAIRE WOULD JUST LET THE LAWYERS HANDLE IT, AND NEVER THINK ABOUT MRS. HARROW OR HER TWO YOUNG KIDS AGAIN.
BUT YOU ARE NOT AN AVERAGE BILLIONAIRE C.E.O. YOU ARE TONY STARK.
AND BECAUSE YOU ARE TONY STARK, I KNOW YOU'RE GOING TO QUIETLY WRITE HARROW'S WIDOW AN INCREDIBLY HEALTHY CHECK, AND THINK LONG AND HARD ABOUT IF YOU'VE AUTOMATED TOO MUCH OF YOUR LIFE, AND THAT WILL BE IT.
GOD, YOU'RE MAGNIFICENT.
STILL NOT IN THE MOOD, TONY. BUT YOU ARE NOT WRONG.

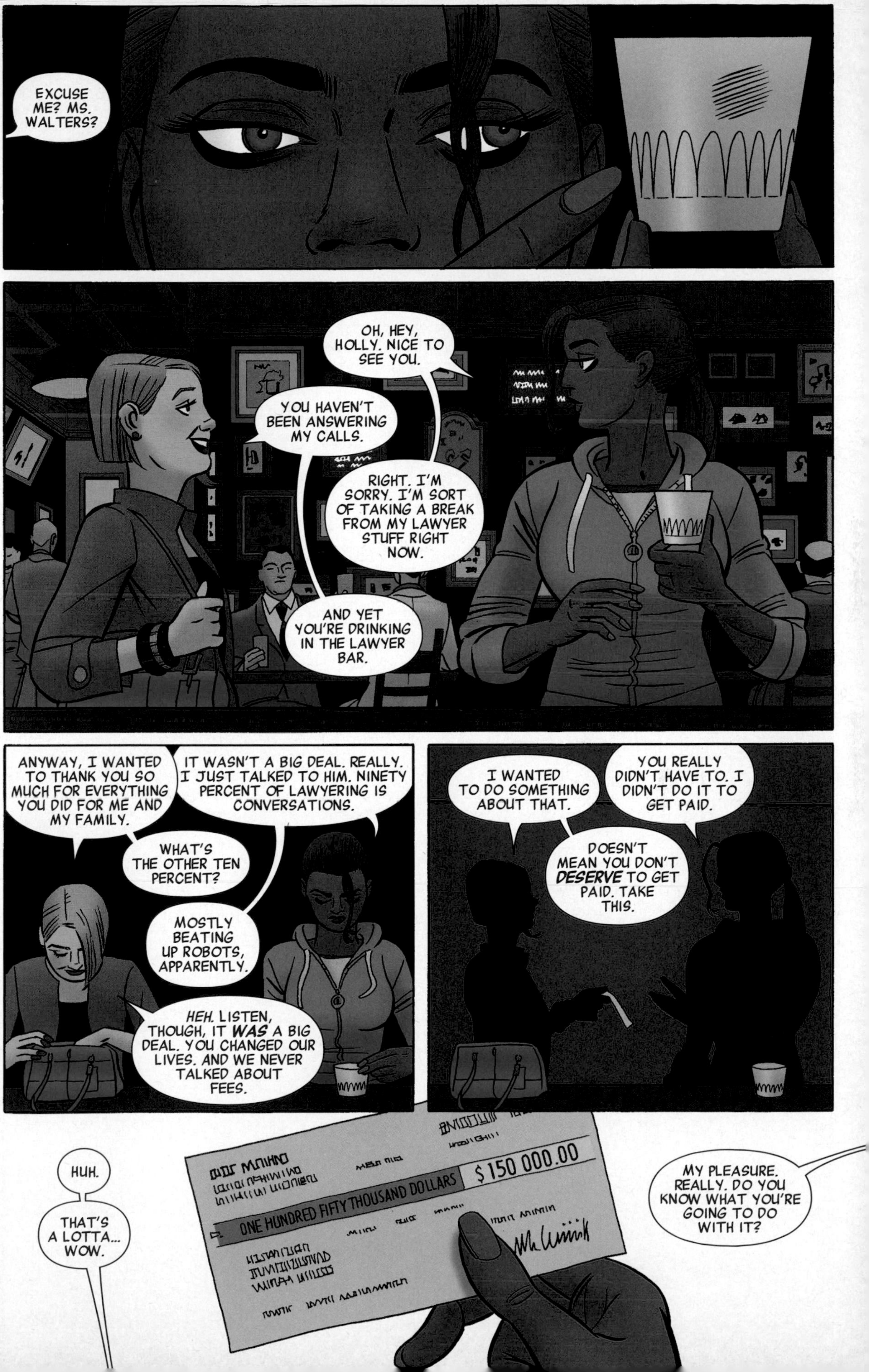
EXCUSE ME? MS. WALTERS?
OH, HEY, HOLLY. NICE TO SEE YOU.
YOU HAVEN'T BEEN ANSWERING MY CALLS.
RIGHT. I'M SORRY. I'M SORT OF TAKING A BREAK FROM MY LAWYER STUFF RIGHT NOW.
AND YET YOU'RE DRINKING IN THE LAWYER BAR.
ANYWAY, I WANTED TO THANK YOU SO MUCH FOR EVERYTHING YOU DID FOR ME AND MY FAMILY.
IT WASN'T A BIG DEAL. REALLY. I JUST TALKED TO HIM. NINETY PERCENT OF LAWYERING IS CONVERSATIONS.
WHAT'S THE OTHER TEN PERCENT?
MOSTLY BEATING UP ROBOTS, APPARENTLY.
HEH. LISTEN, THOUGH, IT WAS A BIG DEAL. YOU CHANGED OUR LIVES. AND WE NEVER TALKED ABOUT FEES.
I WANTED TO DO SOMETHING ABOUT THAT.
YOU REALLY DIDN'T HAVE TO. I DIDN'T DO IT TO GET PAID.
DOESN'T MEAN YOU DON'T DESERVE TO GET PAID. TAKE THIS.
$ 150 000.00
ONE HUNDRED FIFTY THOUSAND DOLLARS
HUH.
THAT'S A LOTTA... WOW.
MY PLEASURE. REALLY. DO YOU KNOW WHAT YOU'RE GOING TO DO WITH IT?

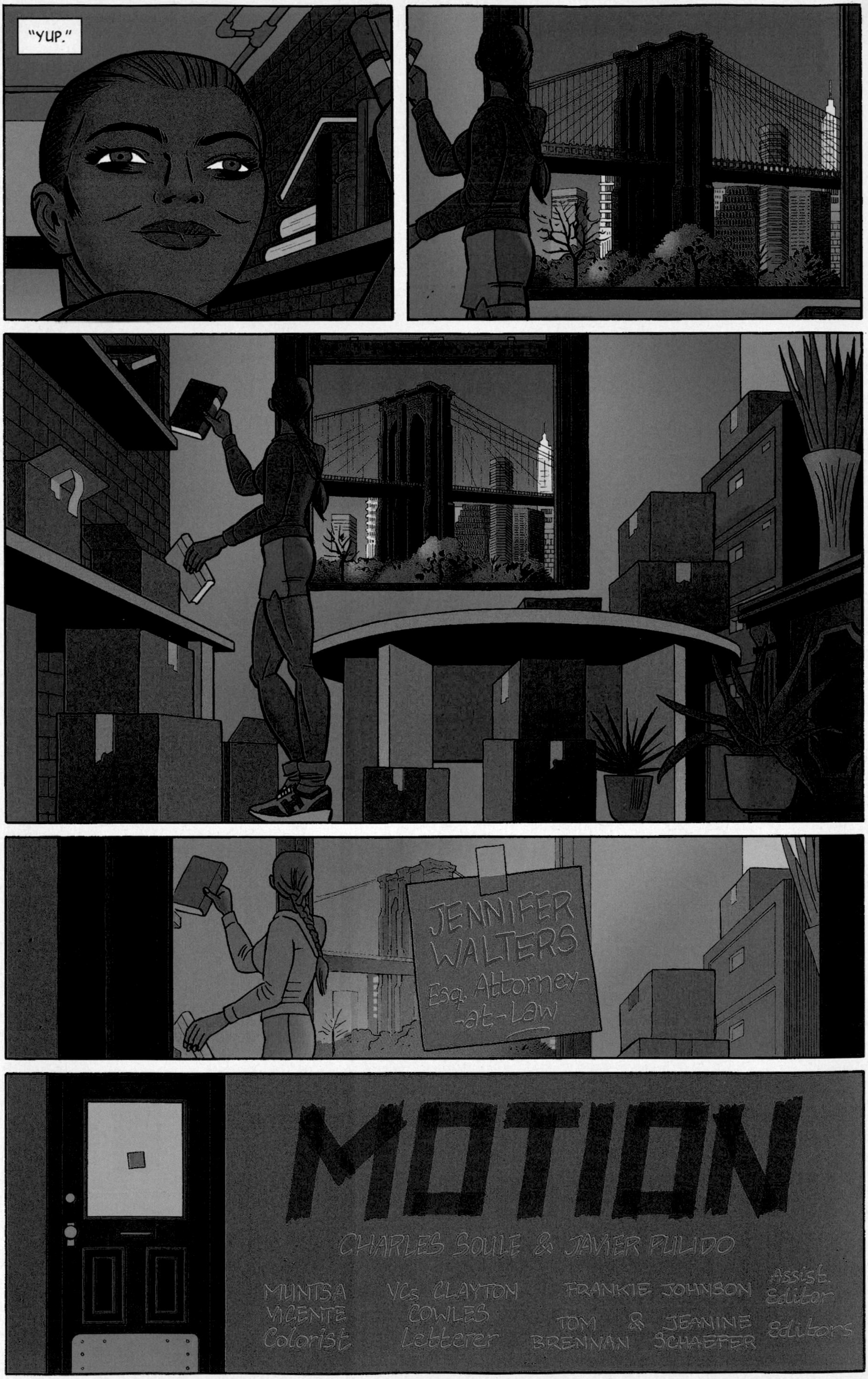
"YUP."
JENNIFER WALTERS Esq. Attorney-at-Law
MOTION
CHARLES SOULE & JAVIER PULIDO
MUNTSA VICENTE Colorist
VC's CLAYTON COWLES Letterer
FRANKIE JOHNSON Assist. Editor
TOM BRENNAN & JEANINE SCHAEFER Editors

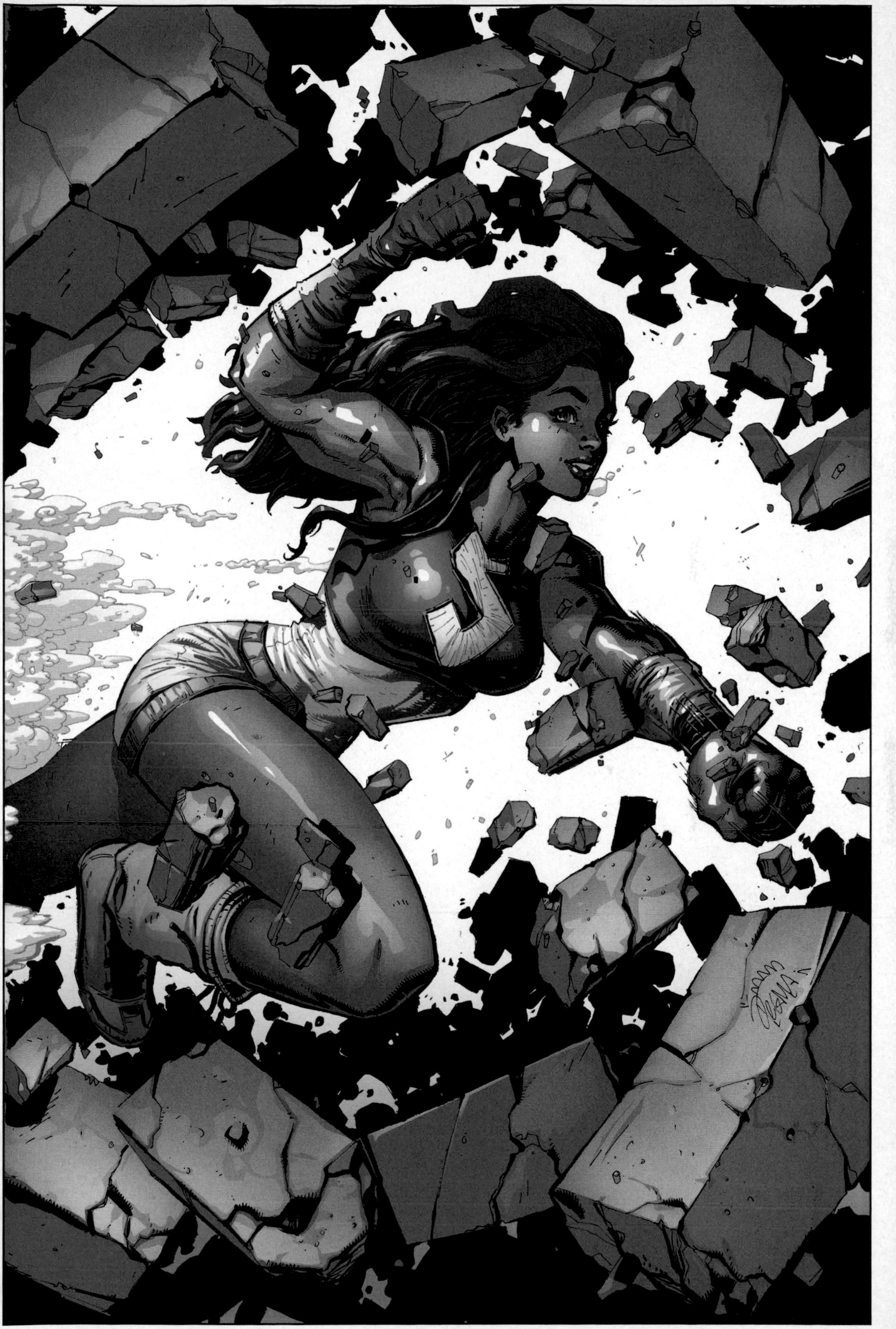

SHE-HULK #1 VARIANT BY RYAN STEGMAN & EDGAR DELGADO

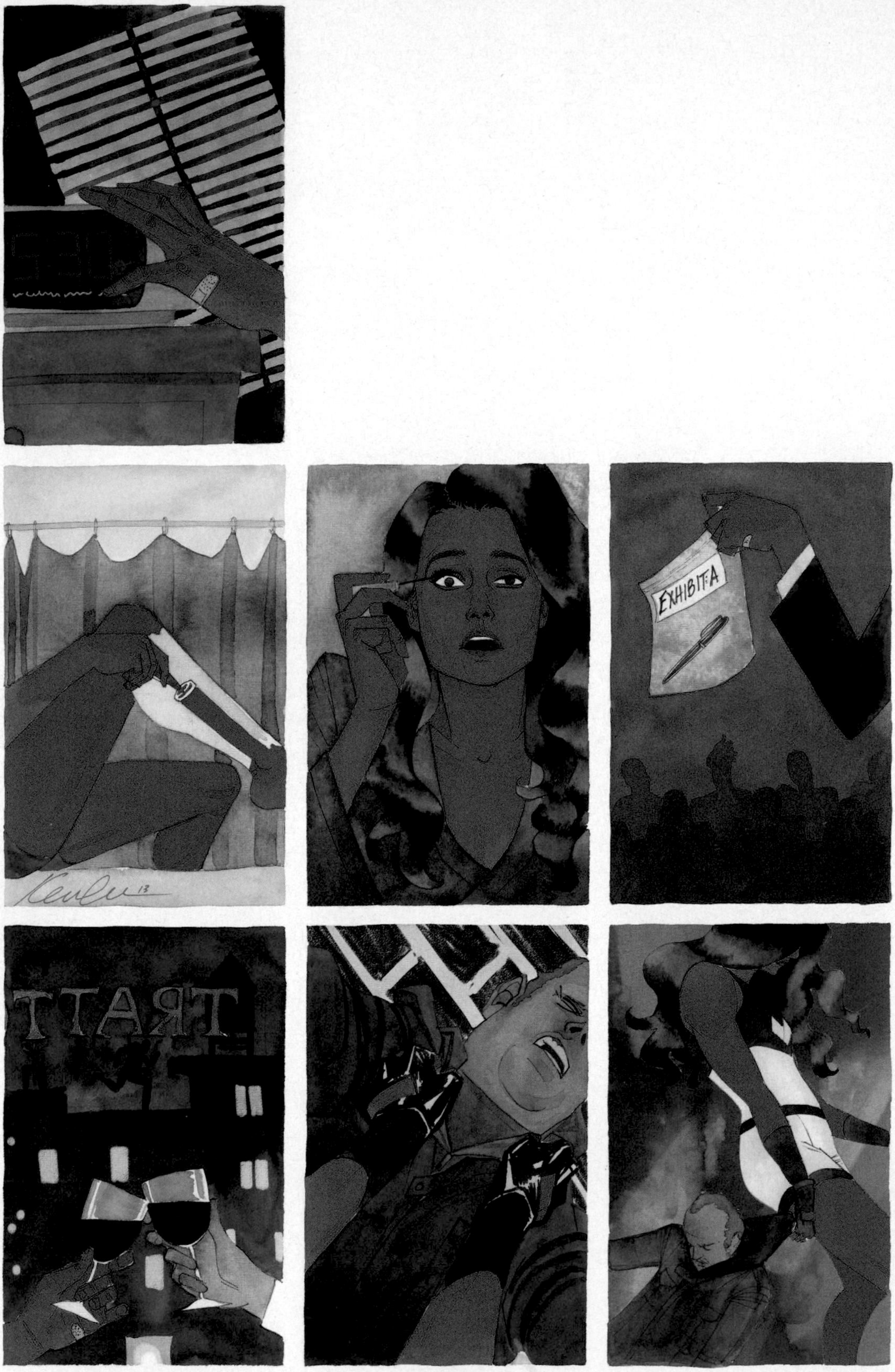
EXHIBIT A

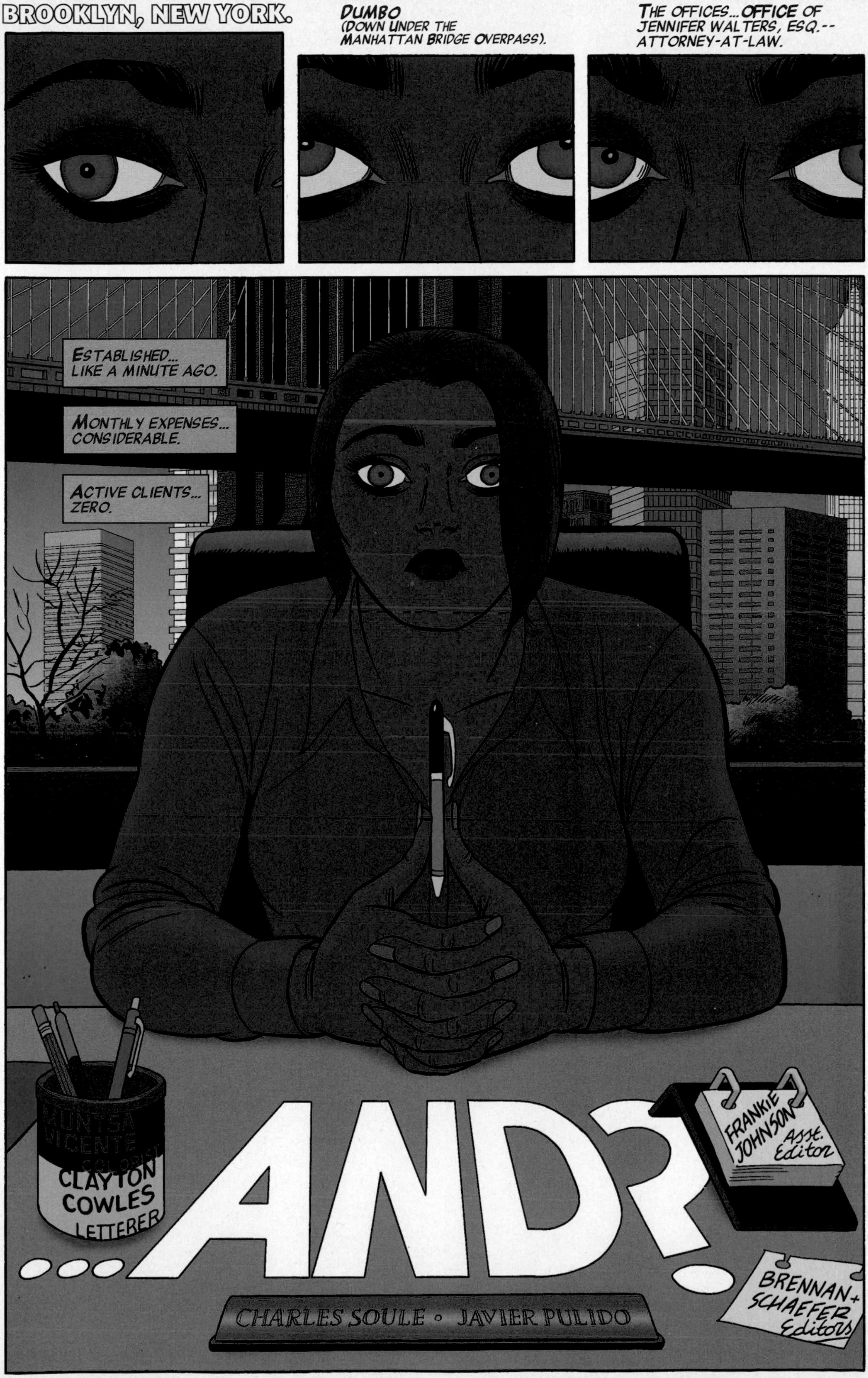

BROOKLYN, NEW YORK.
DUMBO (DOWN UNDER THE MANHATTAN BRIDGE OVERPASS).
THE OFFICES...OFFICE OF JENNIFER WALTERS, ESQ.-- ATTORNEY-AT-LAW.
ESTABLISHED... LIKE A MINUTE AGO.
MONTHLY EXPENSES... CONSIDERABLE.
ACTIVE CLIENTS... ZERO.
...AND?
CHARLES SOULE • JAVIER PULIDO
MUNTSA VICENTE COLORIST
CLAYTON COWLES LETTERER
FRANKIE JOHNSON Asst. Editor
BRENNAN + SCHAEFER Editors

ACTIVE CASES...

...ONE.

=SIGH.=

UNFORTUNATELY.

HMMM...

STATE OF NORTH DAKOTA COURT
COUNTY OF DIVIDE
478206

FILED

GEORGE SAYWITZ,
Plaintiff

VS.

ANTHONY LUDGATE DRUID;
GREER GRANT NELSON;
MONICA RAMBEAU;
HERMAN SCHULTZ;
KEVIN TRENCH;
ALTON VIBREAUX;
JENNIFER WALTERS; and
WYATT WINGFOOT,
Defendants

MOTION FOR CHANGE OF VENUE

Comes plaintiff George Saywitz, representing himself pro se before this court, for his Motion for Change of Venue, states:

1. Plaintiff seeks damages and other forms of judicial relief in this matter from Defendants Anthony Ludgate Druid, Greer Grant Nelson, Monica Rambeau, Herman Schultz, Kevin Trench, Alton Vibreaux, Jennifer Walters and Wyatt Wingfoot, as previously stated in the original complaint, as amended, filed with this court.

Plaintiff seeks a change of venue in this matter from Divide County to another suitable county within the State of North Dakota.

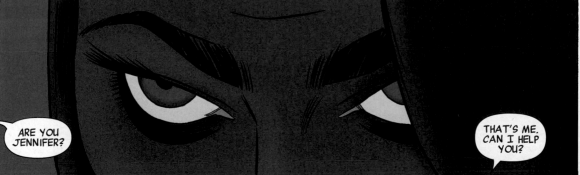

ARE YOU JENNIFER?

THAT'S ME. CAN I HELP YOU?

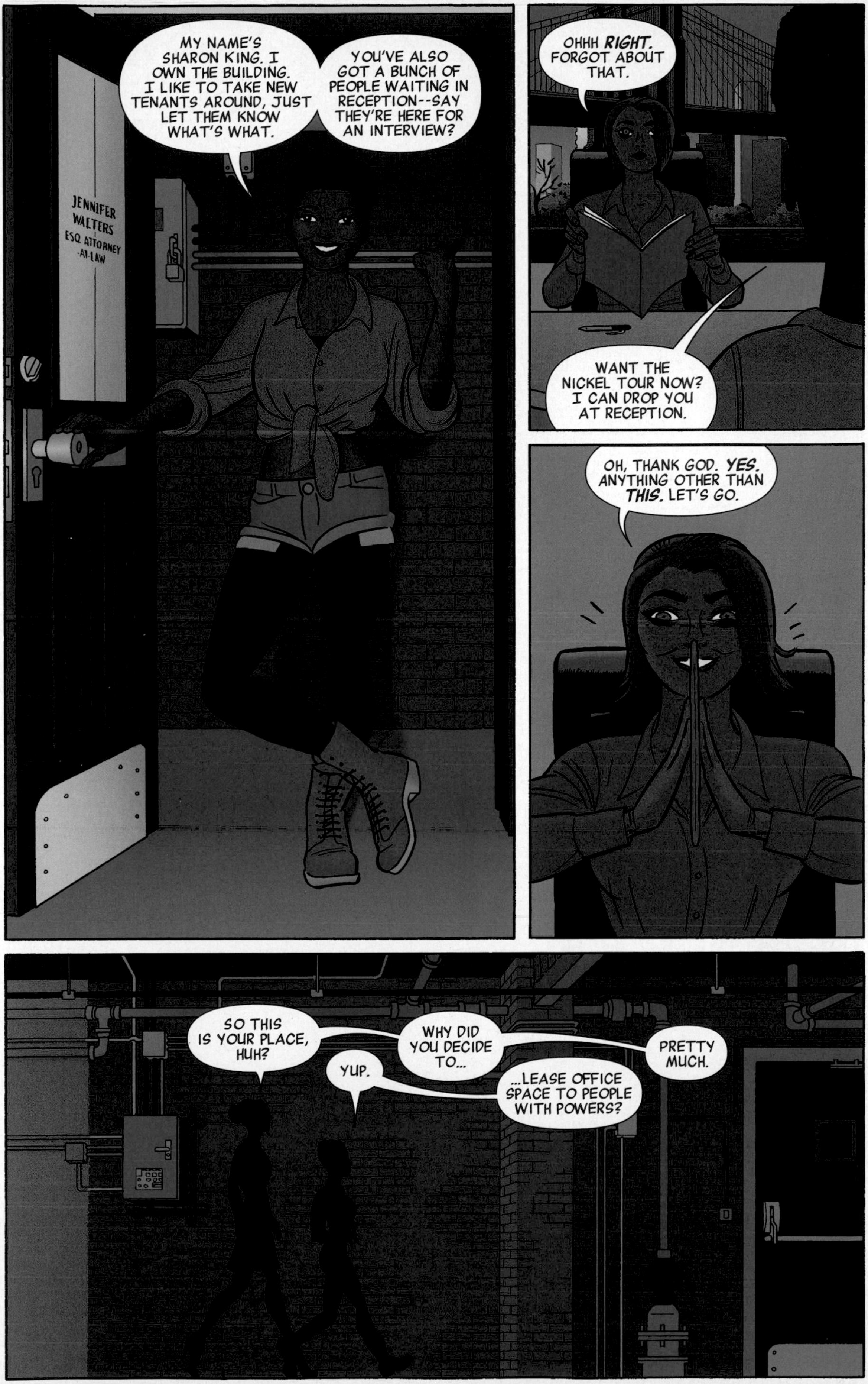

MY NAME'S SHARON KING. I OWN THE BUILDING. I LIKE TO TAKE NEW TENANTS AROUND, JUST LET THEM KNOW WHAT'S WHAT.
YOU'VE ALSO GOT A BUNCH OF PEOPLE WAITING IN RECEPTION--SAY THEY'RE HERE FOR AN INTERVIEW?
JENNIFER WALTERS ESQ. ATTORNEY -AT-LAW
OHHH RIGHT. FORGOT ABOUT THAT.
WANT THE NICKEL TOUR NOW? I CAN DROP YOU AT RECEPTION.
OH, THANK GOD. YES. ANYTHING OTHER THAN THIS. LET'S GO.
SO THIS IS YOUR PLACE, HUH?
YUP.
WHY DID YOU DECIDE TO...
...LEASE OFFICE SPACE TO PEOPLE WITH POWERS?
PRETTY MUCH.

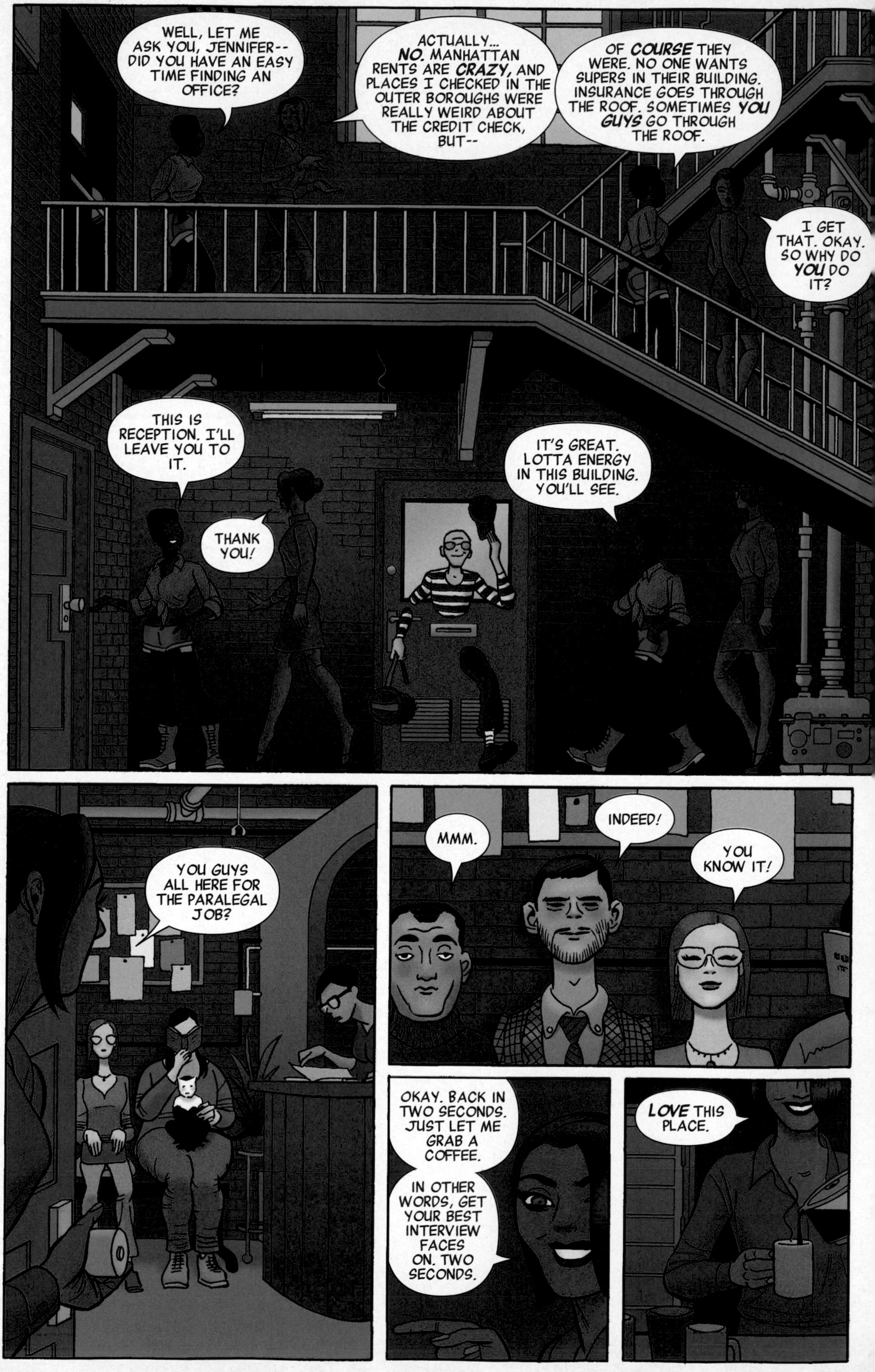
WELL, LET ME ASK YOU, JENNIFER-- DID YOU HAVE AN EASY TIME FINDING AN OFFICE?
ACTUALLY... NO. MANHATTAN RENTS ARE CRAZY, AND PLACES I CHECKED IN THE OUTER BOROUGHS WERE REALLY WEIRD ABOUT THE CREDIT CHECK, BUT--
OF COURSE THEY WERE. NO ONE WANTS SUPERS IN THEIR BUILDING. INSURANCE GOES THROUGH THE ROOF. SOMETIMES YOU GUYS GO THROUGH THE ROOF.
I GET THAT. OKAY. SO WHY DO YOU DO IT?
THIS IS RECEPTION. I'LL LEAVE YOU TO IT.
THANK YOU!
IT'S GREAT. LOTTA ENERGY IN THIS BUILDING. YOU'LL SEE.
YOU GUYS ALL HERE FOR THE PARALEGAL JOB?
MMM.
INDEED!
YOU KNOW IT!
OKAY. BACK IN TWO SECONDS. JUST LET ME GRAB A COFFEE.
IN OTHER WORDS, GET YOUR BEST INTERVIEW FACES ON. TWO SECONDS.
LOVE THIS PLACE.

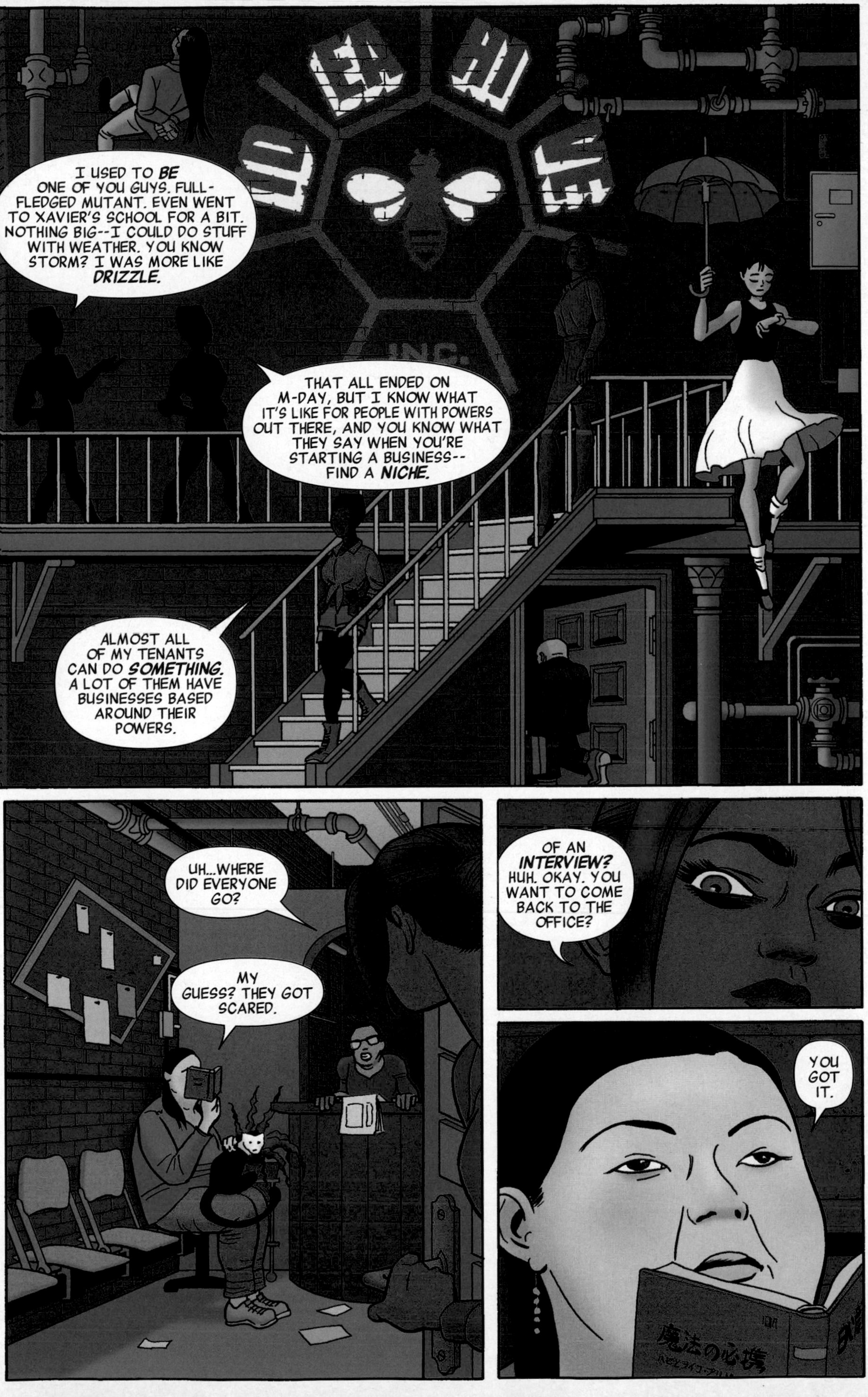

I USED TO BE ONE OF YOU GUYS. FULL-FLEDGED MUTANT. EVEN WENT TO XAVIER'S SCHOOL FOR A BIT. NOTHING BIG--I COULD DO STUFF WITH WEATHER. YOU KNOW STORM? I WAS MORE LIKE DRIZZLE.
INC.
THAT ALL ENDED ON M-DAY, BUT I KNOW WHAT IT'S LIKE FOR PEOPLE WITH POWERS OUT THERE, AND YOU KNOW WHAT THEY SAY WHEN YOU'RE STARTING A BUSINESS--FIND A NICHE.
ALMOST ALL OF MY TENANTS CAN DO SOMETHING. A LOT OF THEM HAVE BUSINESSES BASED AROUND THEIR POWERS.
UH...WHERE DID EVERYONE GO?
MY GUESS? THEY GOT SCARED.
OF AN INTERVIEW? HUH. OKAY. YOU WANT TO COME BACK TO THE OFFICE?
YOU GOT IT.
魔法の必携

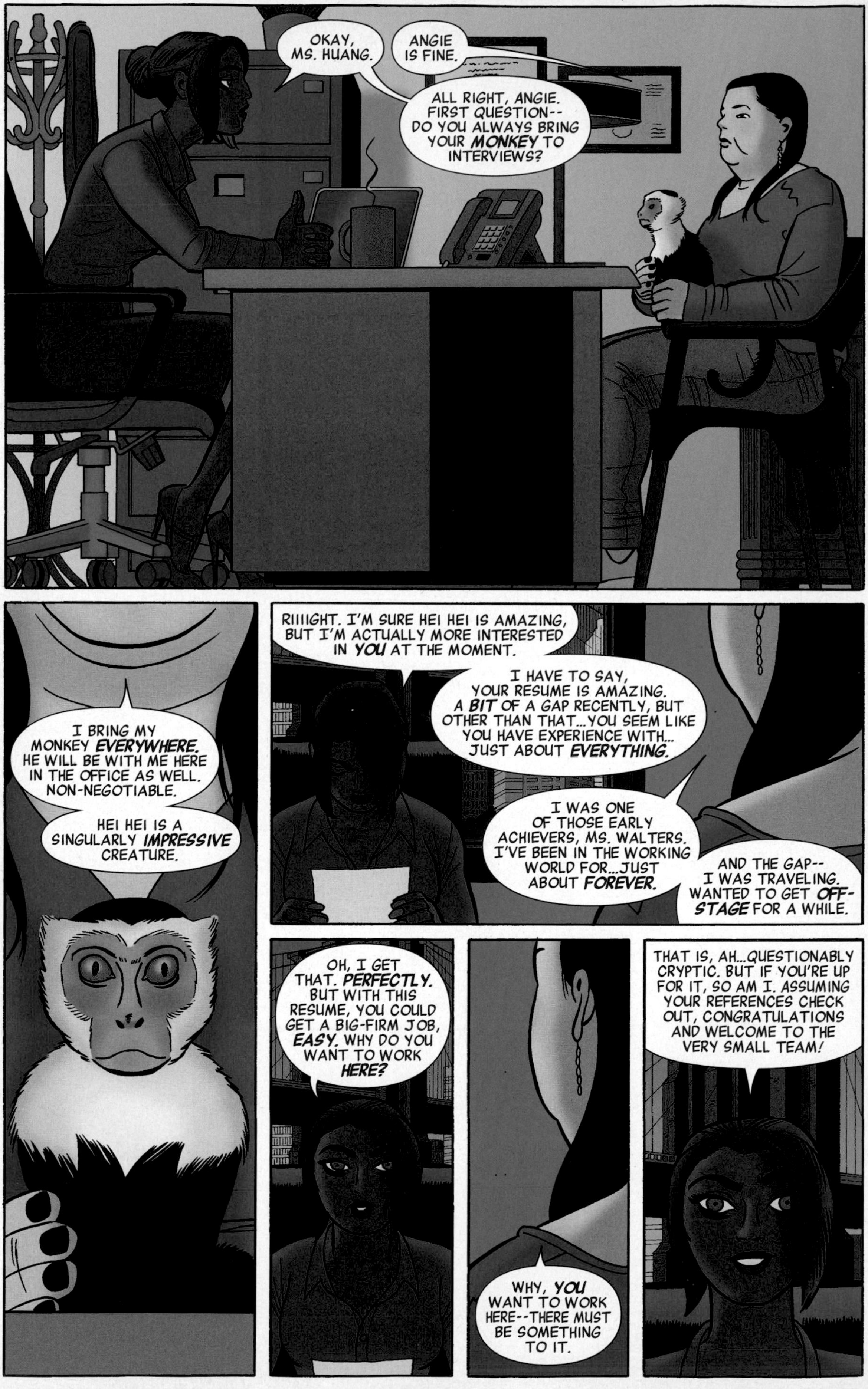
OKAY, MS. HUANG.
ANGIE IS FINE.
ALL RIGHT, ANGIE. FIRST QUESTION-- DO YOU ALWAYS BRING YOUR MONKEY TO INTERVIEWS?
I BRING MY MONKEY EVERYWHERE. HE WILL BE WITH ME HERE IN THE OFFICE AS WELL. NON-NEGOTIABLE.
HEI HEI IS A SINGULARLY IMPRESSIVE CREATURE.
RIIIIGHT. I'M SURE HEI HEI IS AMAZING, BUT I'M ACTUALLY MORE INTERESTED IN YOU AT THE MOMENT.
I HAVE TO SAY, YOUR RESUME IS AMAZING. A BIT OF A GAP RECENTLY, BUT OTHER THAN THAT...YOU SEEM LIKE YOU HAVE EXPERIENCE WITH... JUST ABOUT EVERYTHING.
I WAS ONE OF THOSE EARLY ACHIEVERS, MS. WALTERS. I'VE BEEN IN THE WORKING WORLD FOR...JUST ABOUT FOREVER.
AND THE GAP-- I WAS TRAVELING. WANTED TO GET OFF-STAGE FOR A WHILE.
OH, I GET THAT. PERFECTLY. BUT WITH THIS RESUME, YOU COULD GET A BIG-FIRM JOB, EASY. WHY DO YOU WANT TO WORK HERE?
WHY, YOU WANT TO WORK HERE--THERE MUST BE SOMETHING TO IT.
THAT IS, AH...QUESTIONABLY CRYPTIC. BUT IF YOU'RE UP FOR IT, SO AM I. ASSUMING YOUR REFERENCES CHECK OUT, CONGRATULATIONS AND WELCOME TO THE VERY SMALL TEAM!

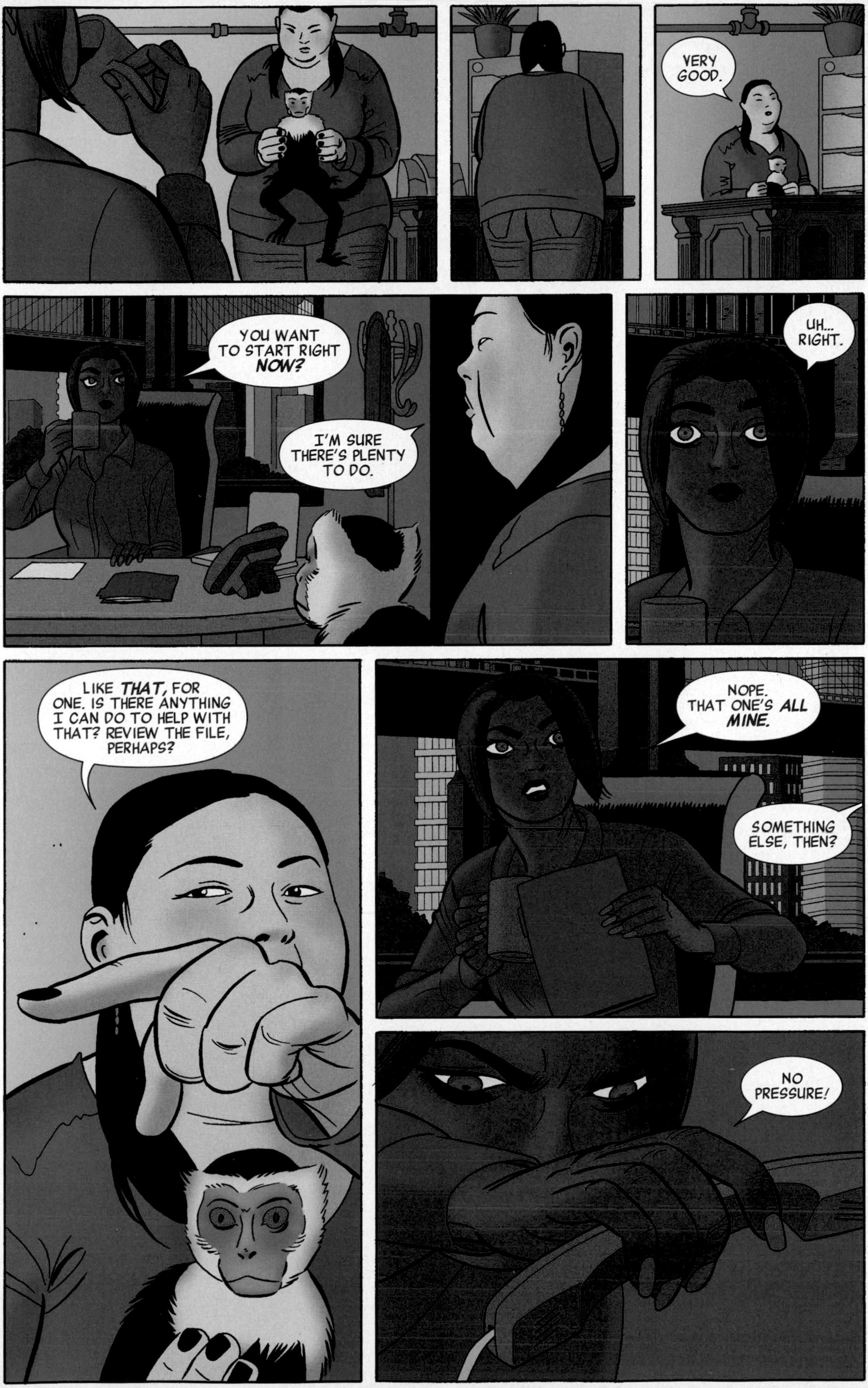
VERY GOOD.
YOU WANT TO START RIGHT NOW?
I'M SURE THERE'S PLENTY TO DO.
UH... RIGHT.
LIKE THAT, FOR ONE. IS THERE ANYTHING I CAN DO TO HELP WITH THAT? REVIEW THE FILE, PERHAPS?
NOPE. THAT ONE'S ALL MINE.
SOMETHING ELSE, THEN?
NO PRESSURE!

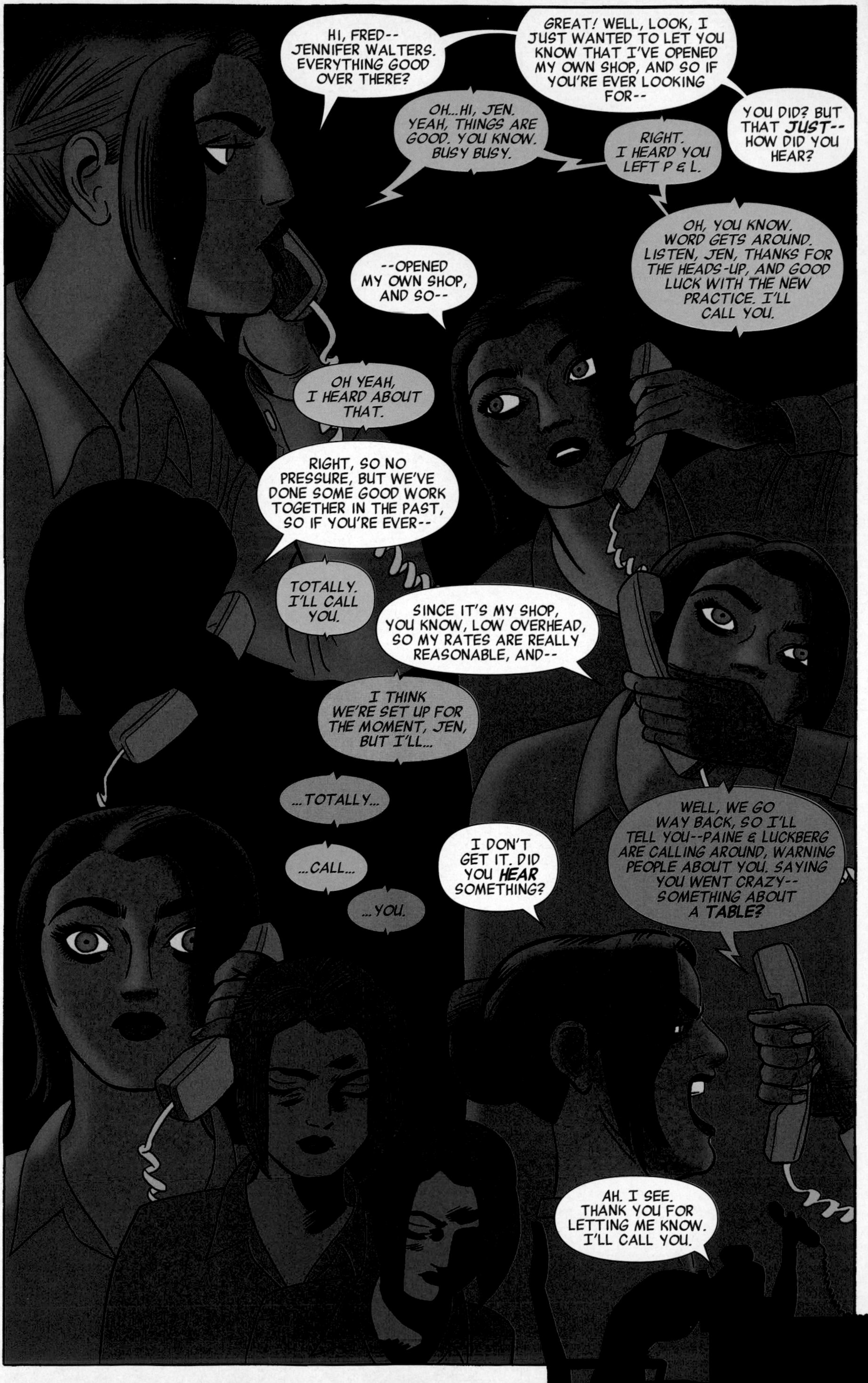
HI, FRED-- JENNIFER WALTERS. EVERYTHING GOOD OVER THERE?
OH...HI, JEN. YEAH, THINGS ARE GOOD. YOU KNOW. BUSY BUSY.
GREAT! WELL, LOOK, I JUST WANTED TO LET YOU KNOW THAT I'VE OPENED MY OWN SHOP, AND SO IF YOU'RE EVER LOOKING FOR--
RIGHT. I HEARD YOU LEFT P & L.
YOU DID? BUT THAT JUST-- HOW DID YOU HEAR?
OH, YOU KNOW. WORD GETS AROUND. LISTEN, JEN, THANKS FOR THE HEADS-UP, AND GOOD LUCK WITH THE NEW PRACTICE. I'LL CALL YOU.
--OPENED MY OWN SHOP, AND SO--
OH YEAH, I HEARD ABOUT THAT.
RIGHT, SO NO PRESSURE, BUT WE'VE DONE SOME GOOD WORK TOGETHER IN THE PAST, SO IF YOU'RE EVER--
TOTALLY. I'LL CALL YOU.
SINCE IT'S MY SHOP, YOU KNOW, LOW OVERHEAD, SO MY RATES ARE REALLY REASONABLE, AND--
I THINK WE'RE SET UP FOR THE MOMENT, JEN, BUT I'LL...
...TOTALLY...
...CALL...
...YOU.
I DON'T GET IT. DID YOU HEAR SOMETHING?
WELL, WE GO WAY BACK, SO I'LL TELL YOU--PAINE & LUCKBERG ARE CALLING AROUND, WARNING PEOPLE ABOUT YOU. SAYING YOU WENT CRAZY-- SOMETHING ABOUT A TABLE?
AH. I SEE. THANK YOU FOR LETTING ME KNOW. I'LL CALL YOU.

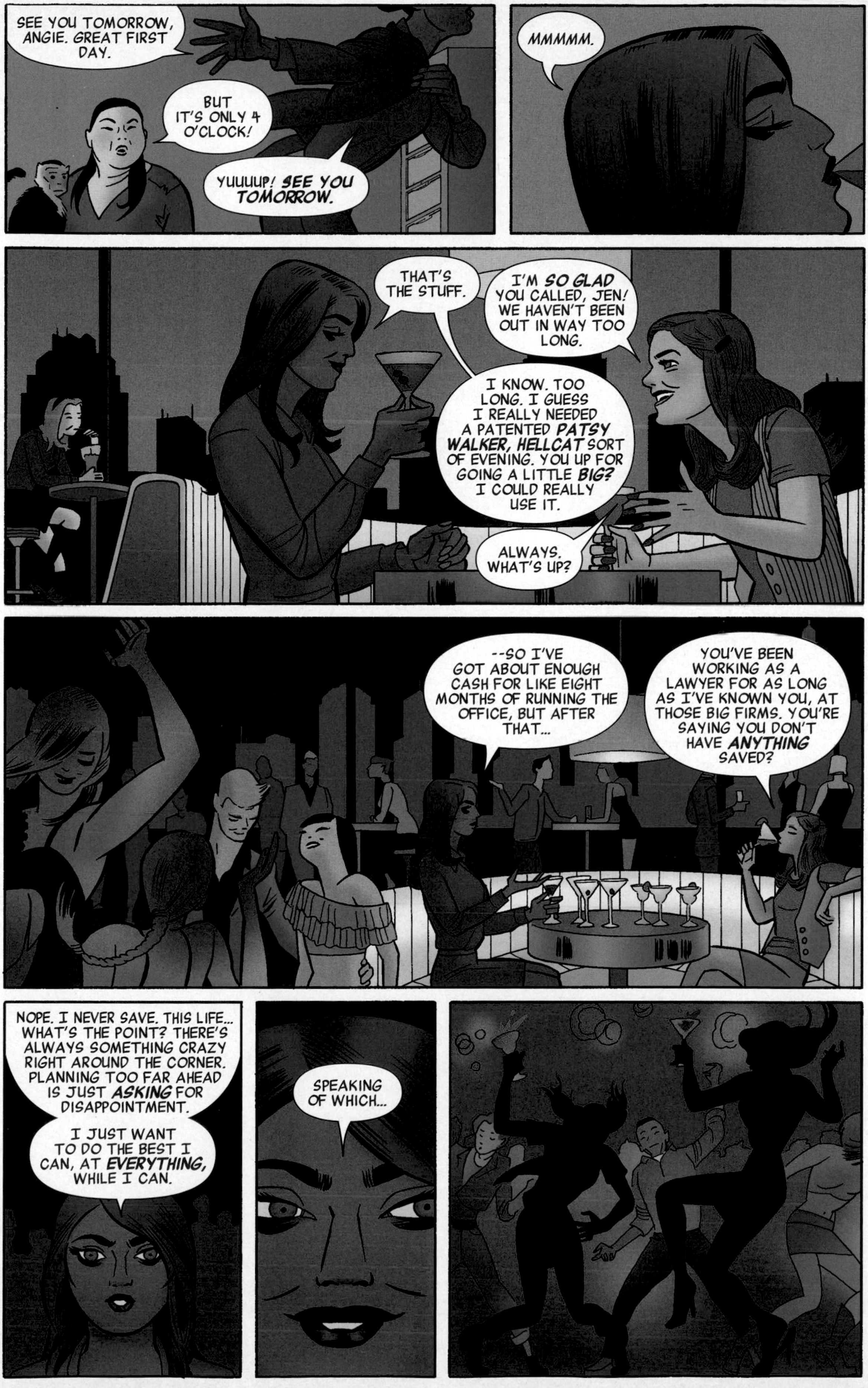
SEE YOU TOMORROW, ANGIE. GREAT FIRST DAY.
BUT IT'S ONLY 4 O'CLOCK!
YUUUUP! SEE YOU TOMORROW.
MMMMM.
THAT'S THE STUFF.
I'M SO GLAD YOU CALLED, JEN! WE HAVEN'T BEEN OUT IN WAY TOO LONG.
I KNOW. TOO LONG. I GUESS I REALLY NEEDED A PATENTED PATSY WALKER, HELLCAT SORT OF EVENING. YOU UP FOR GOING A LITTLE BIG? I COULD REALLY USE IT.
ALWAYS. WHAT'S UP?
--SO I'VE GOT ABOUT ENOUGH CASH FOR LIKE EIGHT MONTHS OF RUNNING THE OFFICE, BUT AFTER THAT...
YOU'VE BEEN WORKING AS A LAWYER FOR AS LONG AS I'VE KNOWN YOU, AT THOSE BIG FIRMS. YOU'RE SAYING YOU DON'T HAVE ANYTHING SAVED?
NOPE. I NEVER SAVE. THIS LIFE... WHAT'S THE POINT? THERE'S ALWAYS SOMETHING CRAZY RIGHT AROUND THE CORNER. PLANNING TOO FAR AHEAD IS JUST ASKING FOR DISAPPOINTMENT.
I JUST WANT TO DO THE BEST I CAN, AT EVERYTHING, WHILE I CAN.
SPEAKING OF WHICH...

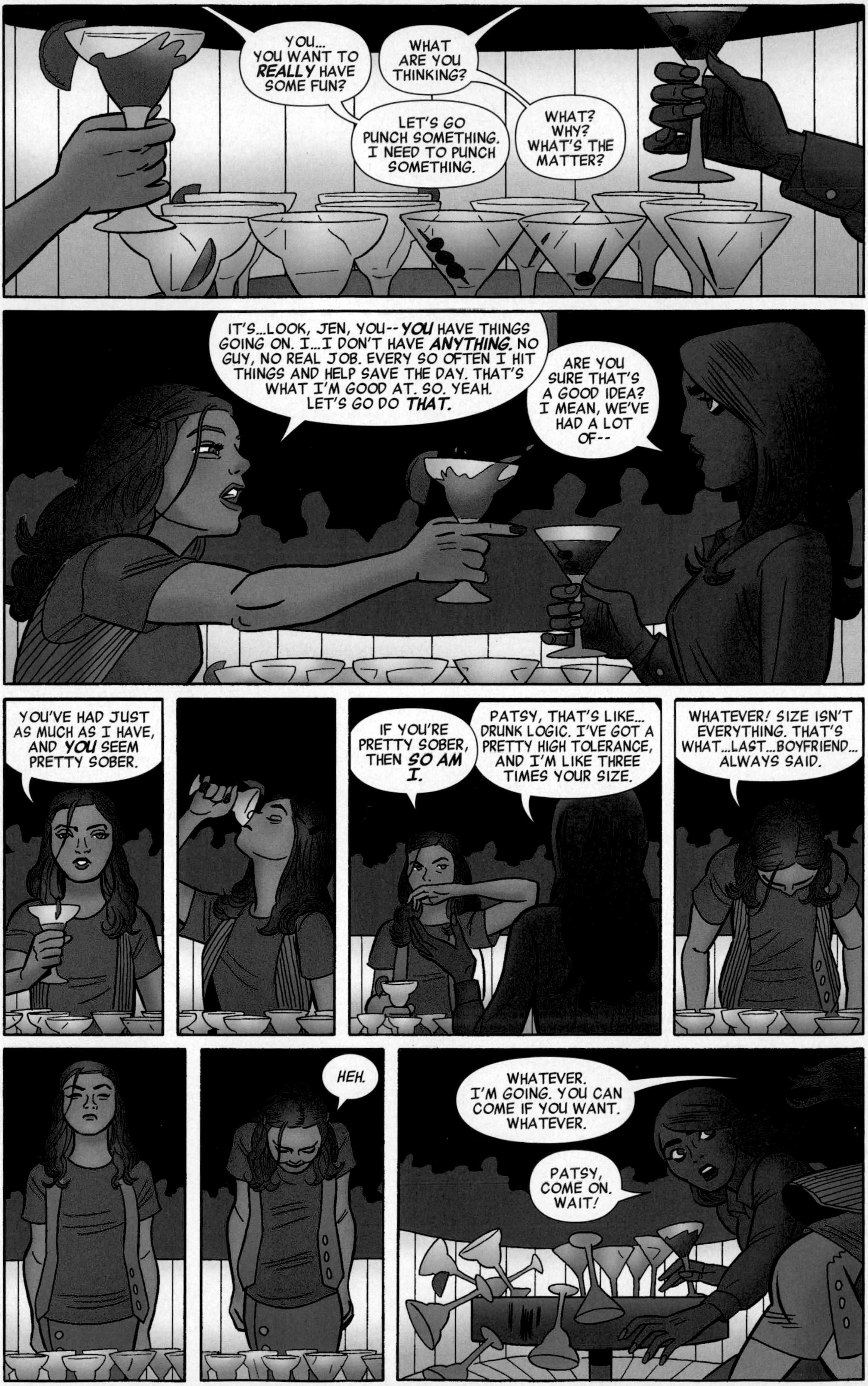
YOU... YOU WANT TO REALLY HAVE SOME FUN?
WHAT ARE YOU THINKING?
LET'S GO PUNCH SOMETHING. I NEED TO PUNCH SOMETHING.
WHAT? WHY? WHAT'S THE MATTER?
IT'S...LOOK, JEN, YOU-- YOU HAVE THINGS GOING ON. I...I DON'T HAVE ANYTHING. NO GUY, NO REAL JOB. EVERY SO OFTEN I HIT THINGS AND HELP SAVE THE DAY. THAT'S WHAT I'M GOOD AT. SO. YEAH. LET'S GO DO THAT.
ARE YOU SURE THAT'S A GOOD IDEA? I MEAN, WE'VE HAD A LOT OF--
YOU'VE HAD JUST AS MUCH AS I HAVE, AND YOU SEEM PRETTY SOBER.
IF YOU'RE PRETTY SOBER, THEN SO AM I.
PATSY, THAT'S LIKE... DRUNK LOGIC. I'VE GOT A PRETTY HIGH TOLERANCE, AND I'M LIKE THREE TIMES YOUR SIZE.
WHATEVER! SIZE ISN'T EVERYTHING. THAT'S WHAT...LAST...BOYFRIEND... ALWAYS SAID.
HEH.
WHATEVER. I'M GOING. YOU CAN COME IF YOU WANT. WHATEVER.
PATSY, COME ON. WAIT!

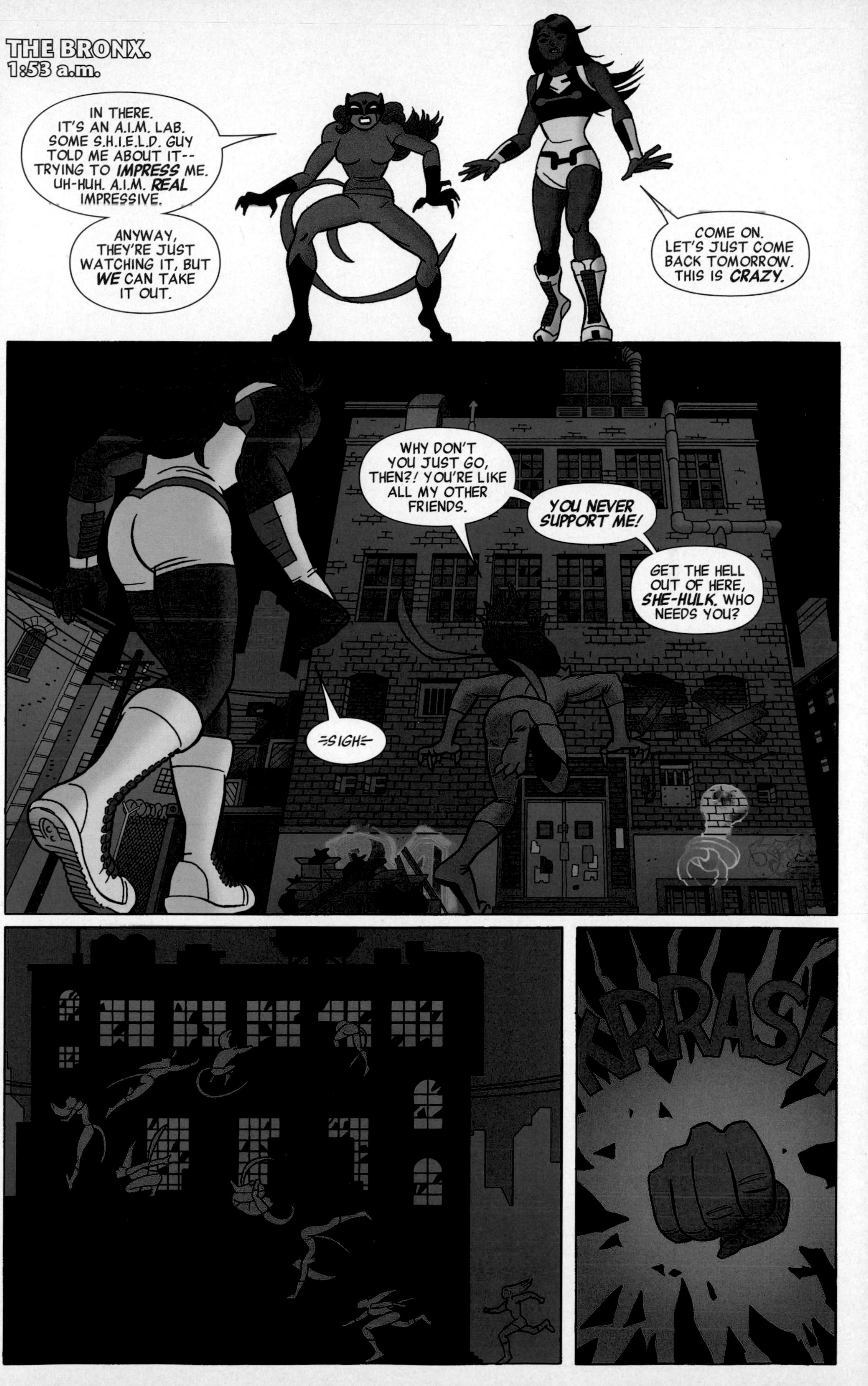
THE BRONX. 1:53 a.m.
IN THERE. IT'S AN A.I.M. LAB. SOME S.H.I.E.L.D. GUY TOLD ME ABOUT IT-- TRYING TO IMPRESS ME. UH-HUH. A.I.M. REAL IMPRESSIVE.
ANYWAY, THEY'RE JUST WATCHING IT, BUT WE CAN TAKE IT OUT.
COME ON. LET'S JUST COME BACK TOMORROW. THIS IS CRAZY.
WHY DON'T YOU JUST GO, THEN?! YOU'RE LIKE ALL MY OTHER FRIENDS.
YOU NEVER SUPPORT ME!
GET THE HELL OUT OF HERE, SHE-HULK. WHO NEEDS YOU?
SIGH
KRRASH

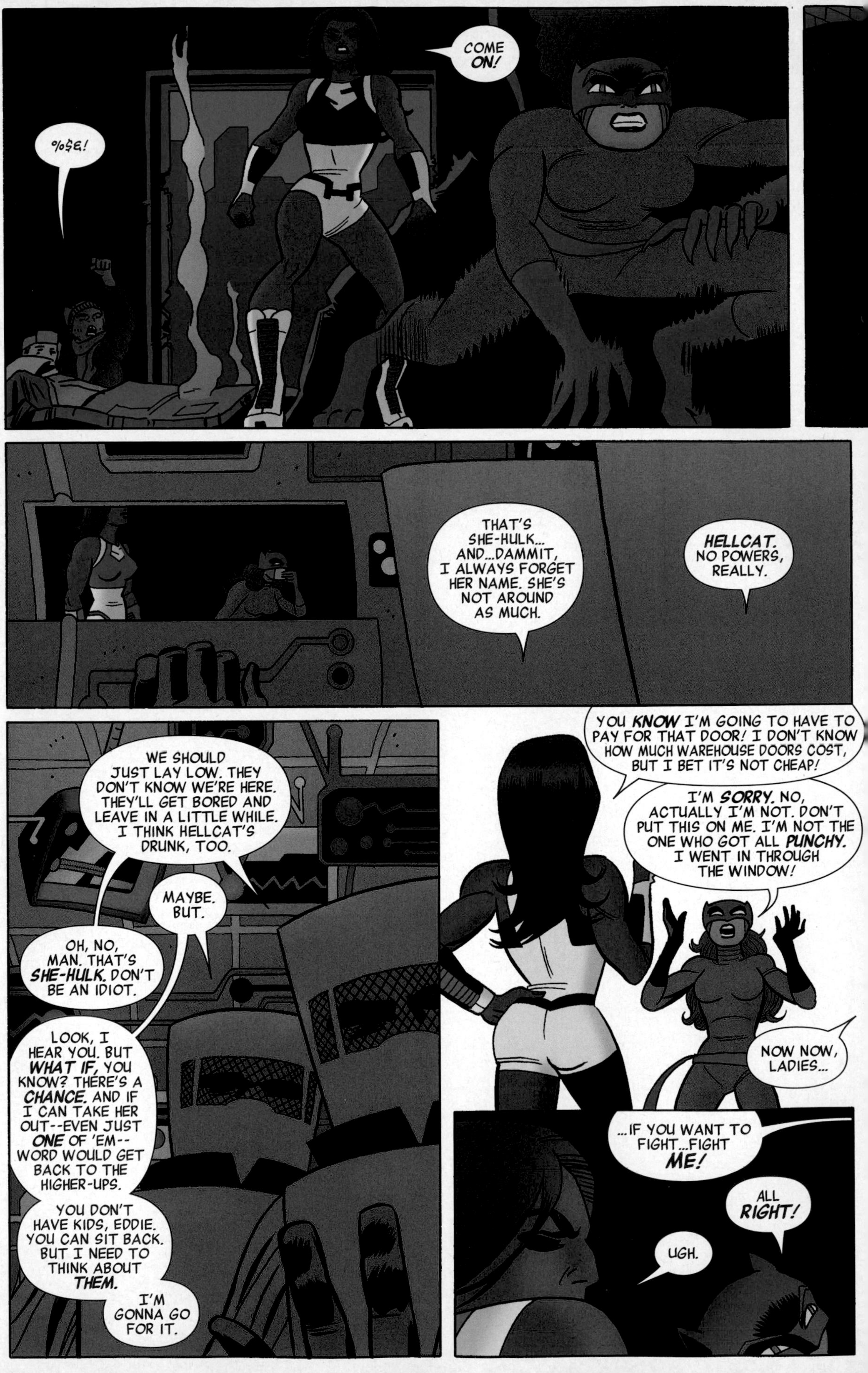
COME ON!
%$&!
THAT'S SHE-HULK... AND...DAMMIT, I ALWAYS FORGET HER NAME. SHE'S NOT AROUND AS MUCH.
HELLCAT. NO POWERS, REALLY.
WE SHOULD JUST LAY LOW. THEY DON'T KNOW WE'RE HERE. THEY'LL GET BORED AND LEAVE IN A LITTLE WHILE. I THINK HELLCAT'S DRUNK, TOO.
MAYBE. BUT.
OH, NO, MAN. THAT'S SHE-HULK. DON'T BE AN IDIOT.
LOOK, I HEAR YOU. BUT WHAT IF, YOU KNOW? THERE'S A CHANCE. AND IF I CAN TAKE HER OUT--EVEN JUST ONE OF 'EM--WORD WOULD GET BACK TO THE HIGHER-UPS.
YOU DON'T HAVE KIDS, EDDIE. YOU CAN SIT BACK. BUT I NEED TO THINK ABOUT THEM.
I'M GONNA GO FOR IT.
YOU KNOW I'M GOING TO HAVE TO PAY FOR THAT DOOR! I DON'T KNOW HOW MUCH WAREHOUSE DOORS COST, BUT I BET IT'S NOT CHEAP!
I'M SORRY. NO, ACTUALLY I'M NOT. DON'T PUT THIS ON ME. I'M NOT THE ONE WHO GOT ALL PUNCHY. I WENT IN THROUGH THE WINDOW!
NOW NOW, LADIES...
...IF YOU WANT TO FIGHT...FIGHT ME!
ALL RIGHT!
UGH.

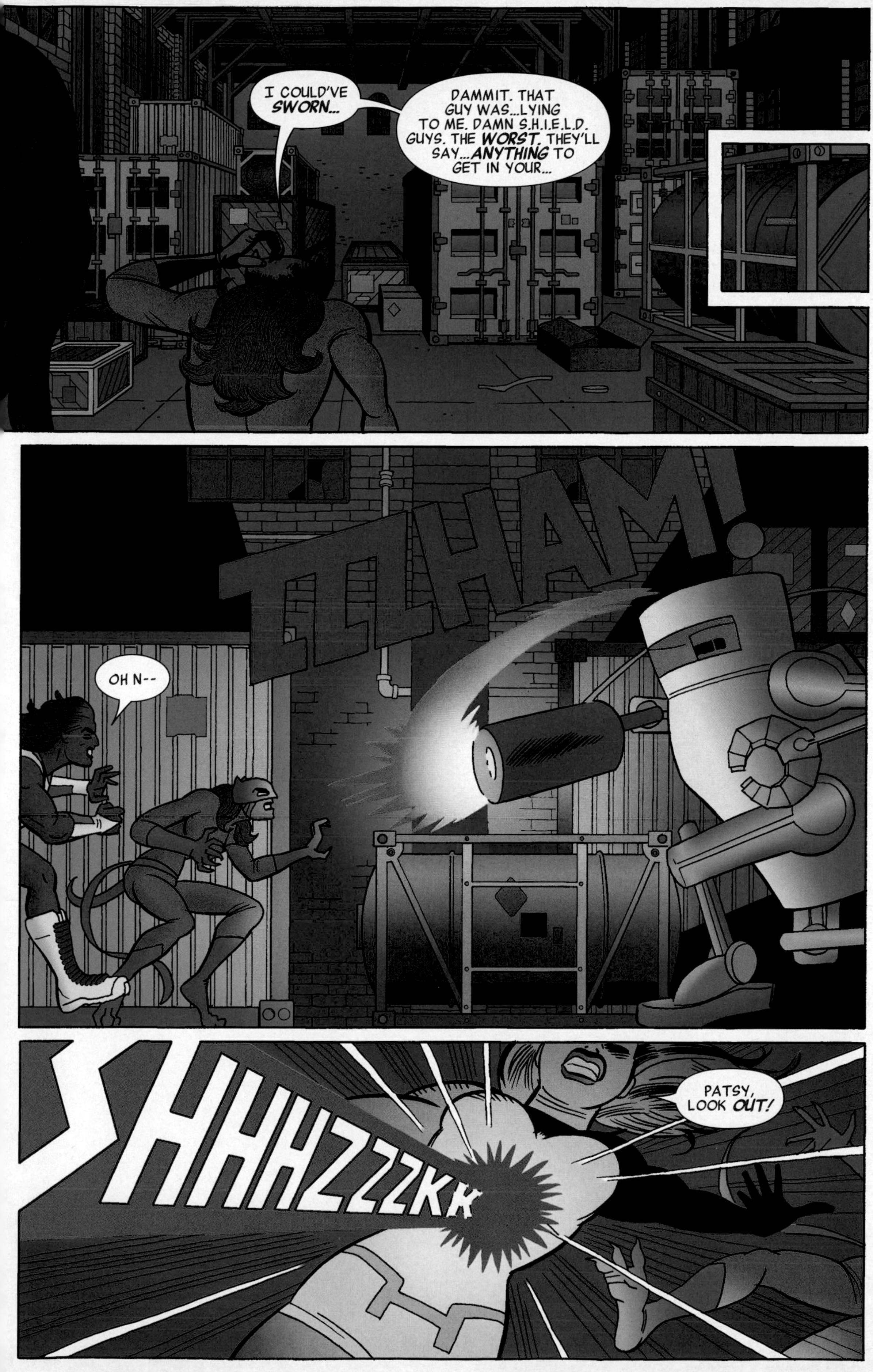
I COULD'VE SWORN...
DAMMIT. THAT GUY WAS...LYING TO ME. DAMN S.H.I.E.L.D. GUYS. THE WORST. THEY'LL SAY...ANYTHING TO GET IN YOUR...
ZZHAM!
OH N--
SHHHZZZKR
PATSY, LOOK OUT!

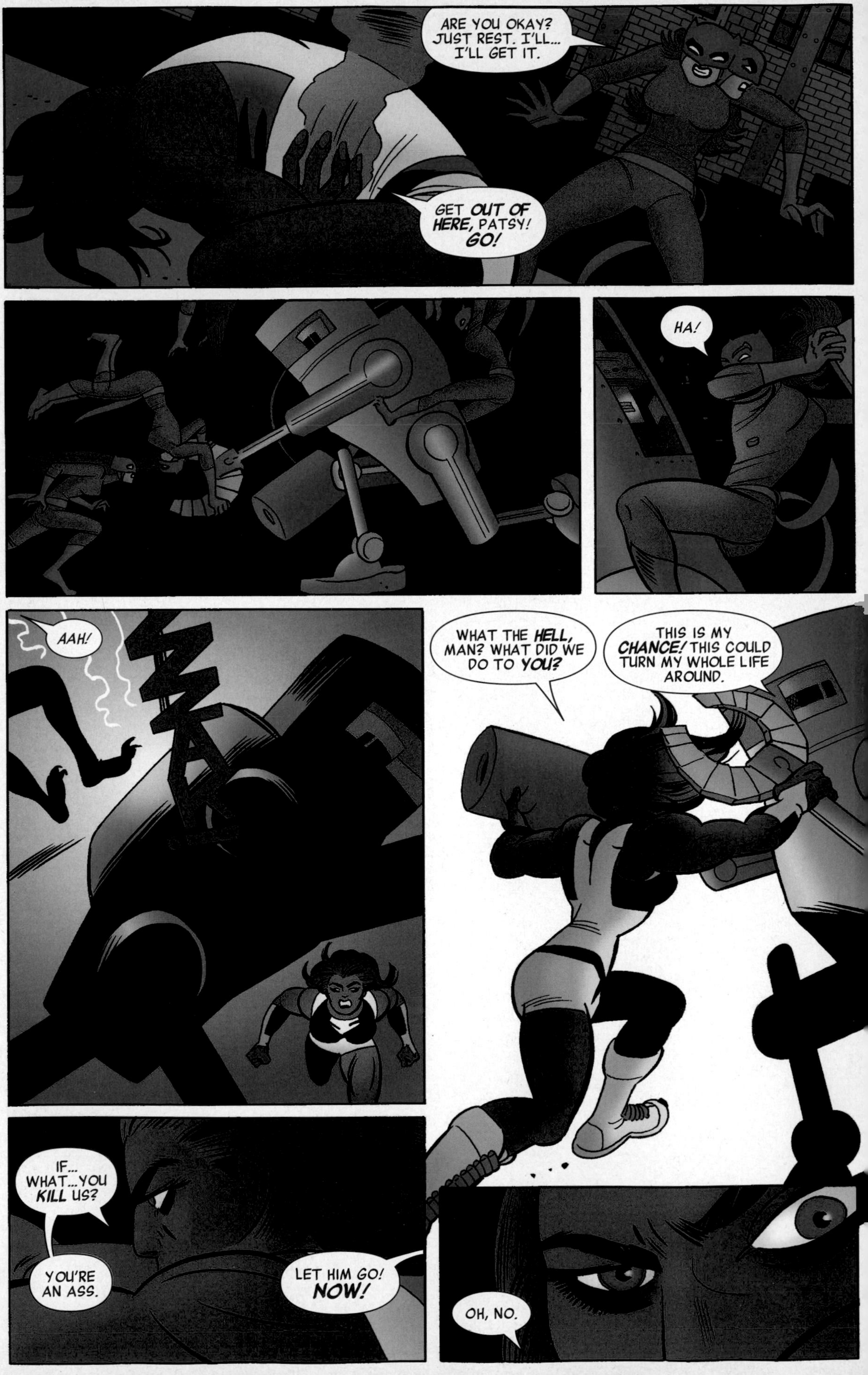

ARE YOU OKAY? JUST REST. I'LL... I'LL GET IT.
GET OUT OF HERE, PATSY! GO!
HA!
AAH!
WHAT THE HELL, MAN? WHAT DID WE DO TO YOU?
THIS IS MY CHANCE! THIS COULD TURN MY WHOLE LIFE AROUND.
IF... WHAT...YOU KILL US?
YOU'RE AN ASS.
LET HIM GO! NOW!
OH, NO.

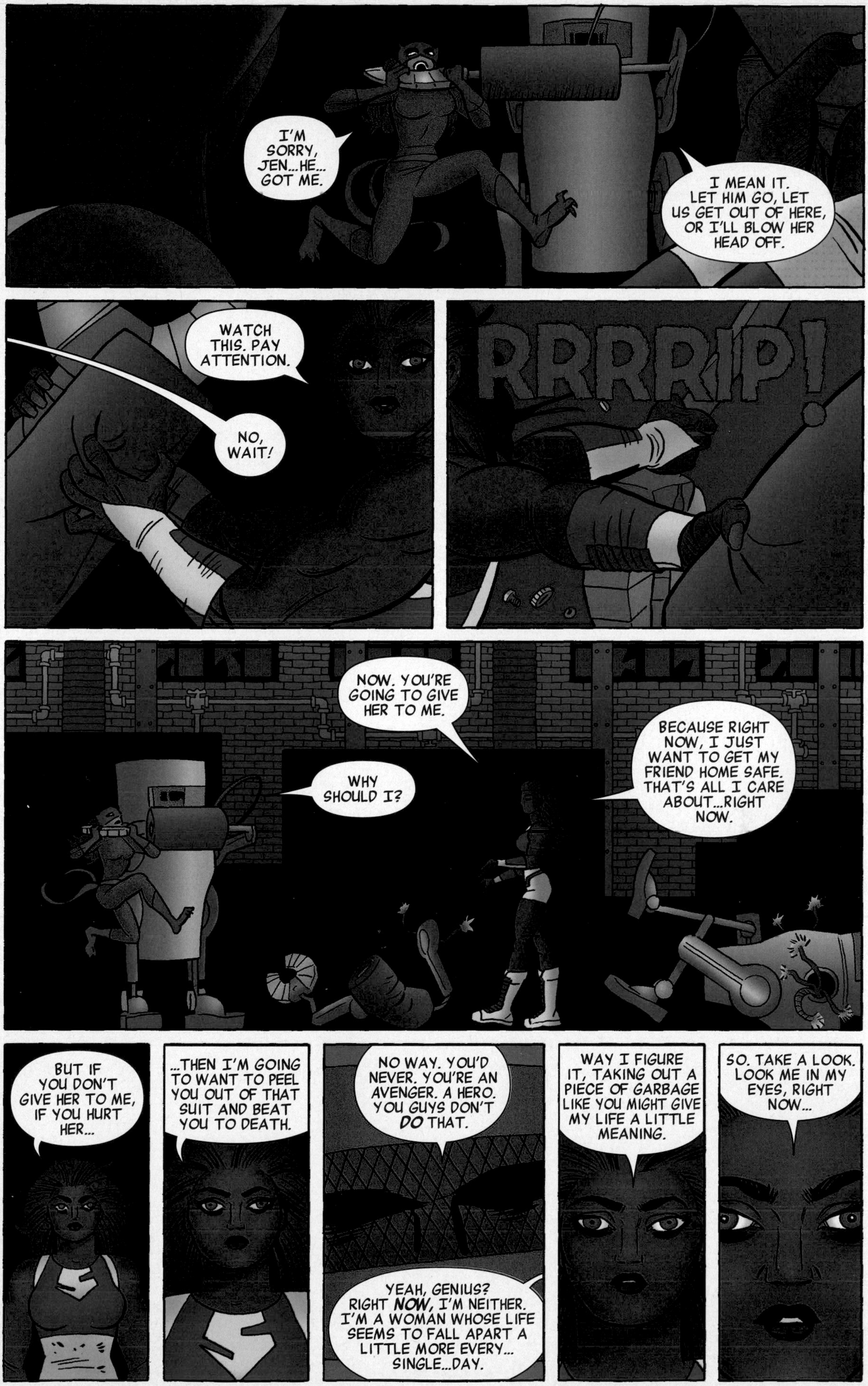
I'M SORRY, JEN...HE... GOT ME.
I MEAN IT. LET HIM GO, LET US GET OUT OF HERE, OR I'LL BLOW HER HEAD OFF.
WATCH THIS. PAY ATTENTION.
NO, WAIT!
RRRRRIP!
NOW. YOU'RE GOING TO GIVE HER TO ME.
WHY SHOULD I?
BECAUSE RIGHT NOW, I JUST WANT TO GET MY FRIEND HOME SAFE. THAT'S ALL I CARE ABOUT...RIGHT NOW.
BUT IF YOU DON'T GIVE HER TO ME, IF YOU HURT HER...
...THEN I'M GOING TO WANT TO PEEL YOU OUT OF THAT SUIT AND BEAT YOU TO DEATH.
NO WAY. YOU'D NEVER. YOU'RE AN AVENGER. A HERO. YOU GUYS DON'T *DO* THAT.
YEAH, GENIUS? RIGHT **NOW**, I'M NEITHER. I'M A WOMAN WHOSE LIFE SEEMS TO FALL APART A LITTLE MORE EVERY... SINGLE...DAY.
WAY I FIGURE IT, TAKING OUT A PIECE OF GARBAGE LIKE YOU MIGHT GIVE MY LIFE A LITTLE MEANING.
SO. TAKE A LOOK. LOOK ME IN MY EYES, RIGHT NOW...

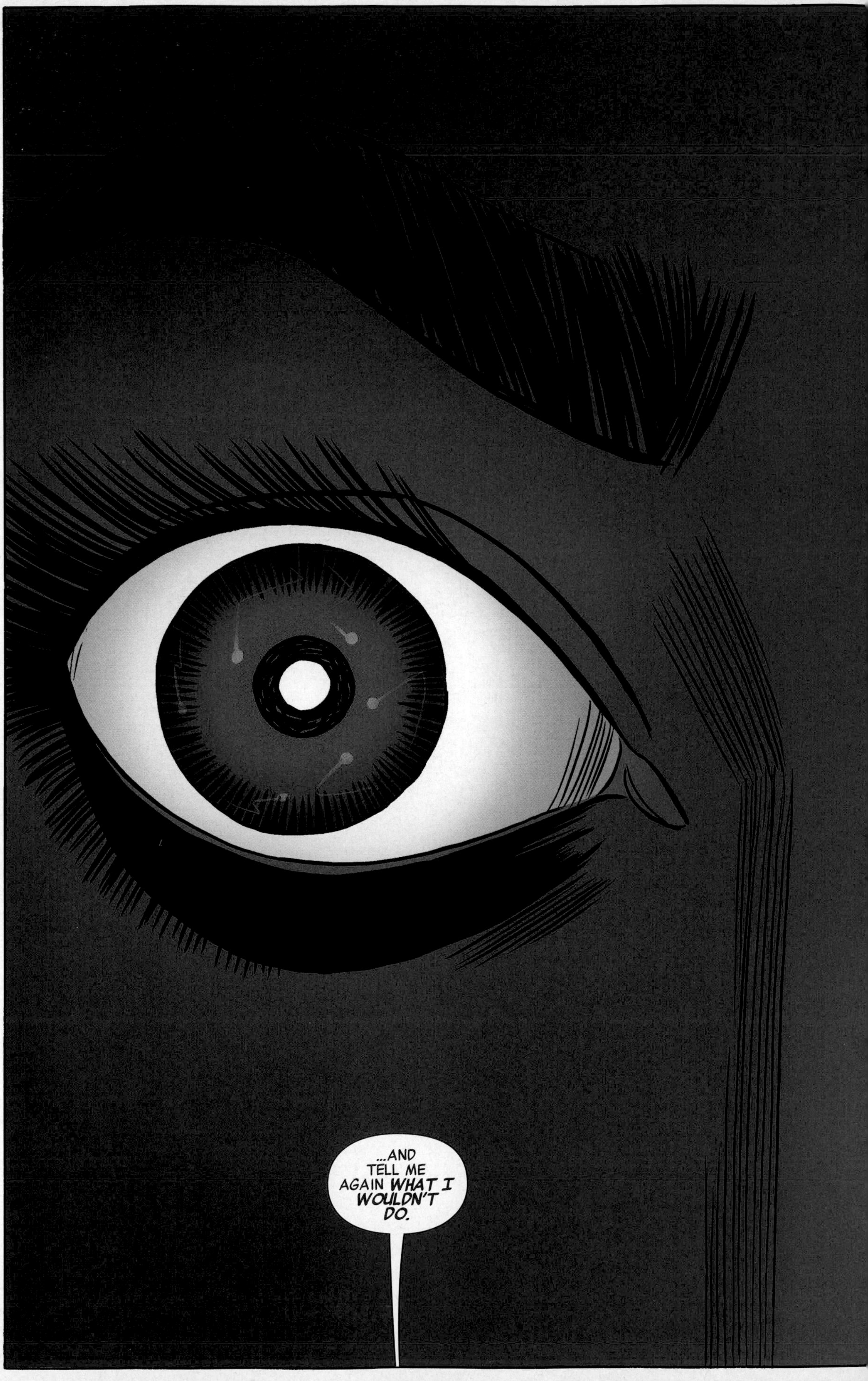
...AND TELL ME AGAIN WHAT I WOULDN'T DO.

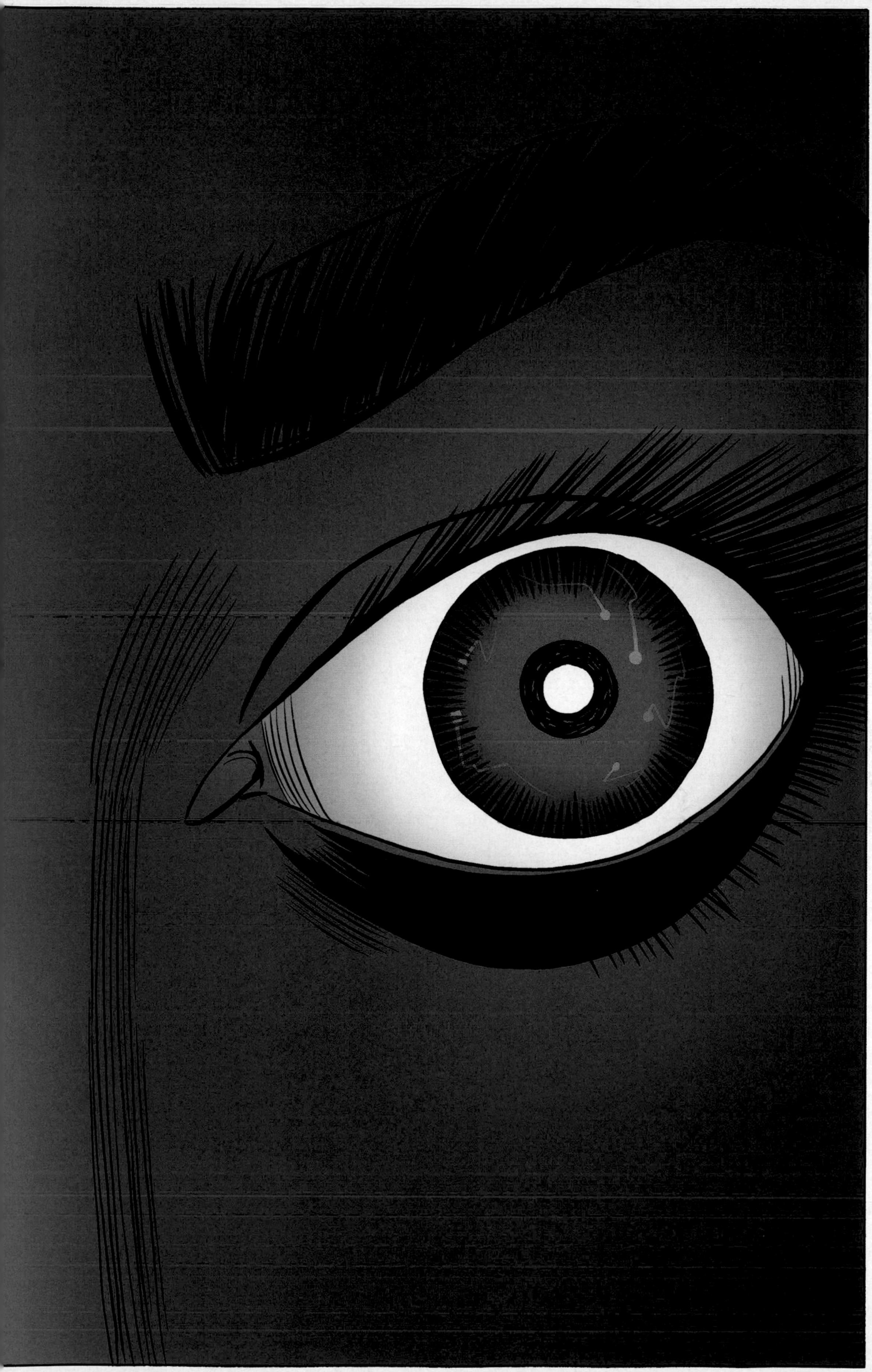

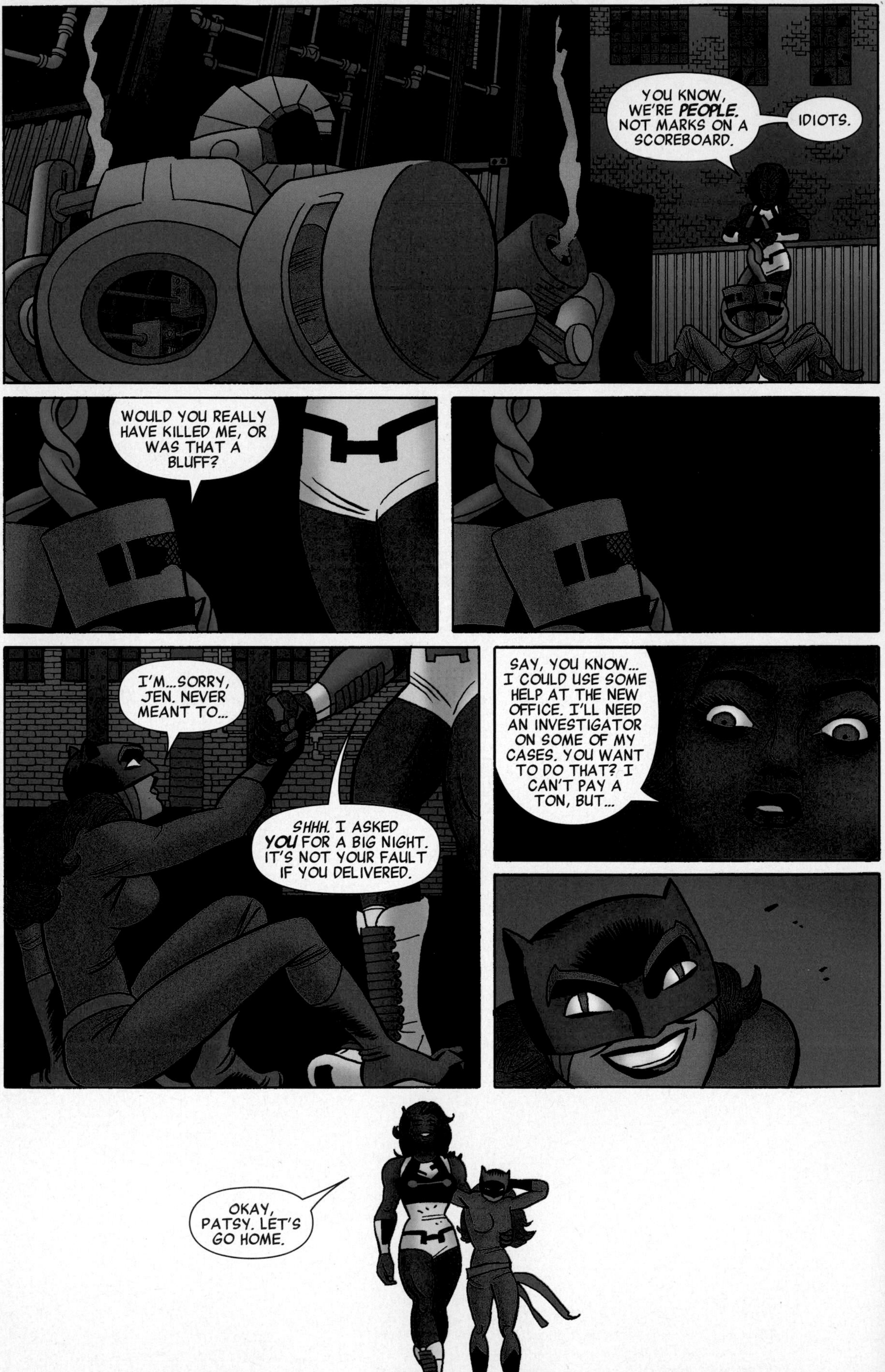
YOU KNOW, WE'RE PEOPLE. NOT MARKS ON A SCOREBOARD.
IDIOTS.
WOULD YOU REALLY HAVE KILLED ME, OR WAS THAT A BLUFF?
I'M...SORRY, JEN. NEVER MEANT TO...
SHHH. I ASKED YOU FOR A BIG NIGHT. IT'S NOT YOUR FAULT IF YOU DELIVERED.
SAY, YOU KNOW... I COULD USE SOME HELP AT THE NEW OFFICE. I'LL NEED AN INVESTIGATOR ON SOME OF MY CASES. YOU WANT TO DO THAT? I CAN'T PAY A TON, BUT...
OKAY, PATSY. LET'S GO HOME.

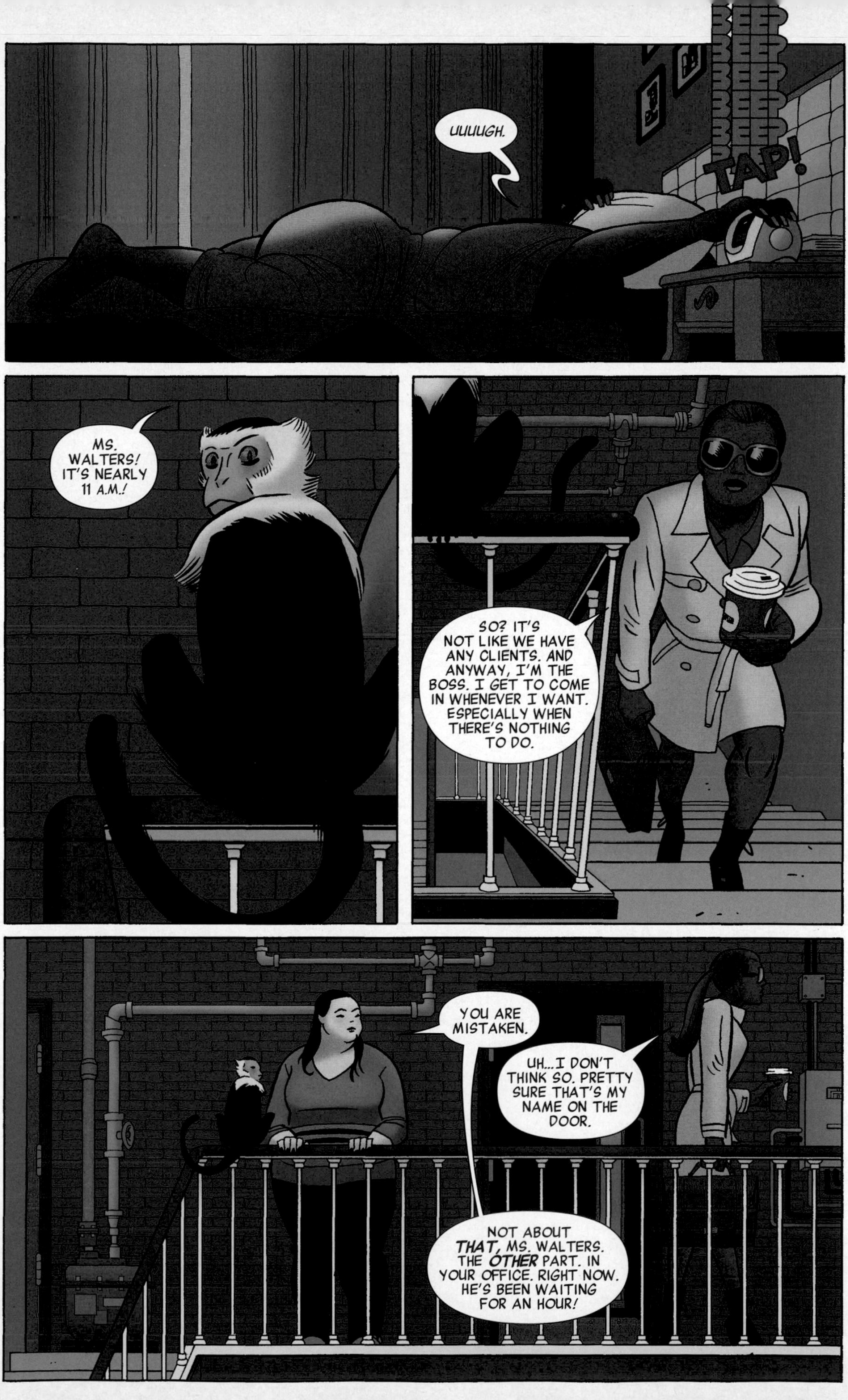

BEEP BEEP BEEP BEEP BEEP BEEP
UUUUGH.
TAP!
MS. WALTERS! IT'S NEARLY 11 A.M.!
SO? IT'S NOT LIKE WE HAVE ANY CLIENTS. AND ANYWAY, I'M THE BOSS. I GET TO COME IN WHENEVER I WANT. ESPECIALLY WHEN THERE'S NOTHING TO DO.
YOU ARE MISTAKEN.
UH...I DON'T THINK SO. PRETTY SURE THAT'S MY NAME ON THE DOOR.
NOT ABOUT *THAT,* MS. WALTERS. THE *OTHER* PART. IN YOUR OFFICE. RIGHT NOW. HE'S BEEN WAITING FOR AN HOUR!

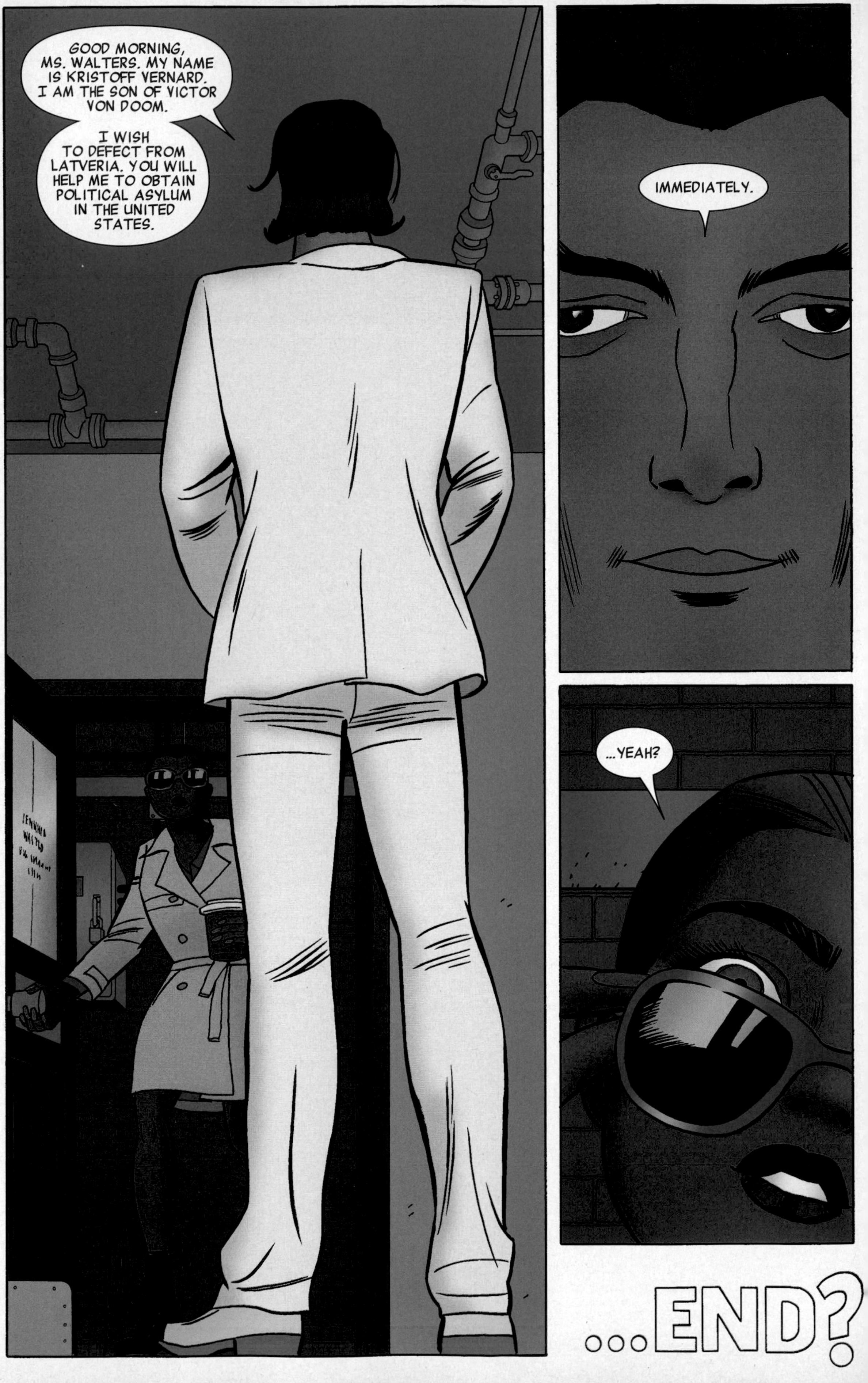
GOOD MORNING, MS. WALTERS. MY NAME IS KRISTOFF VERNARD. I AM THE SON OF VICTOR VON DOOM.
I WISH TO DEFECT FROM LATVERIA. YOU WILL HELP ME TO OBTAIN POLITICAL ASYLUM IN THE UNITED STATES.
IMMEDIATELY.
...YEAH?
...END?

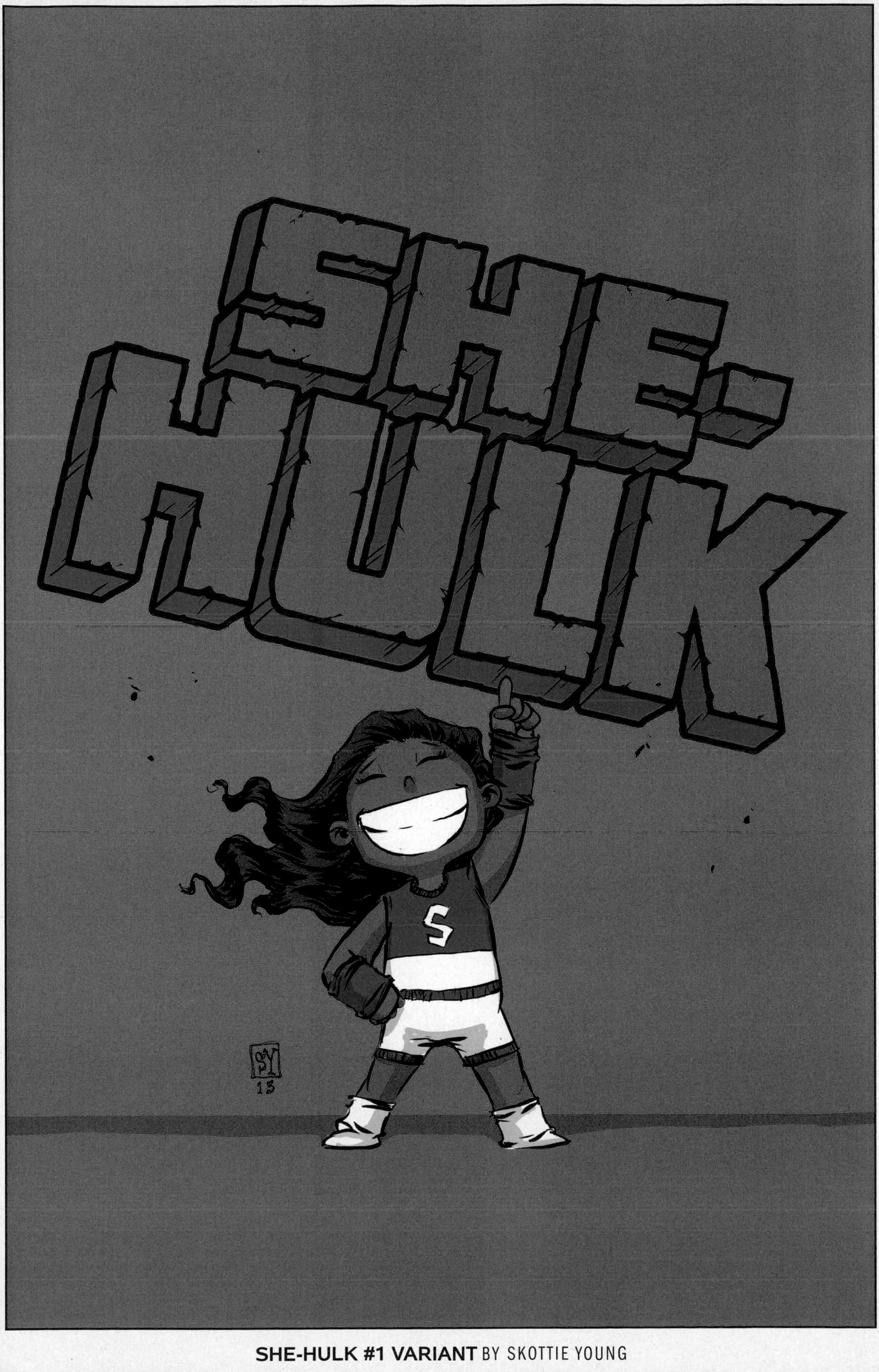
SHE-HULK
S
SY
13

SHE-HULK #1 VARIANT BY SKOTTIE YOUNG

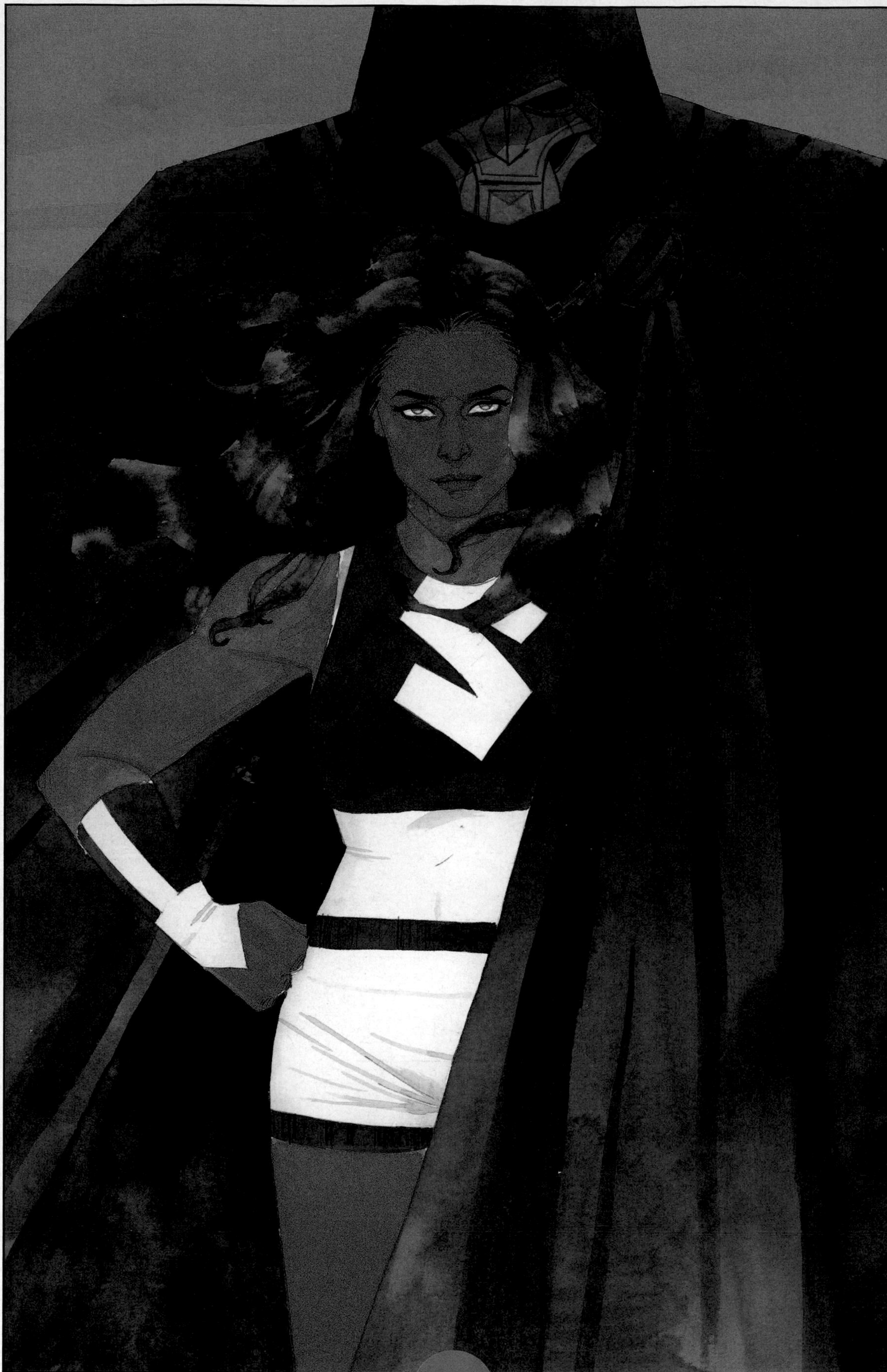

3

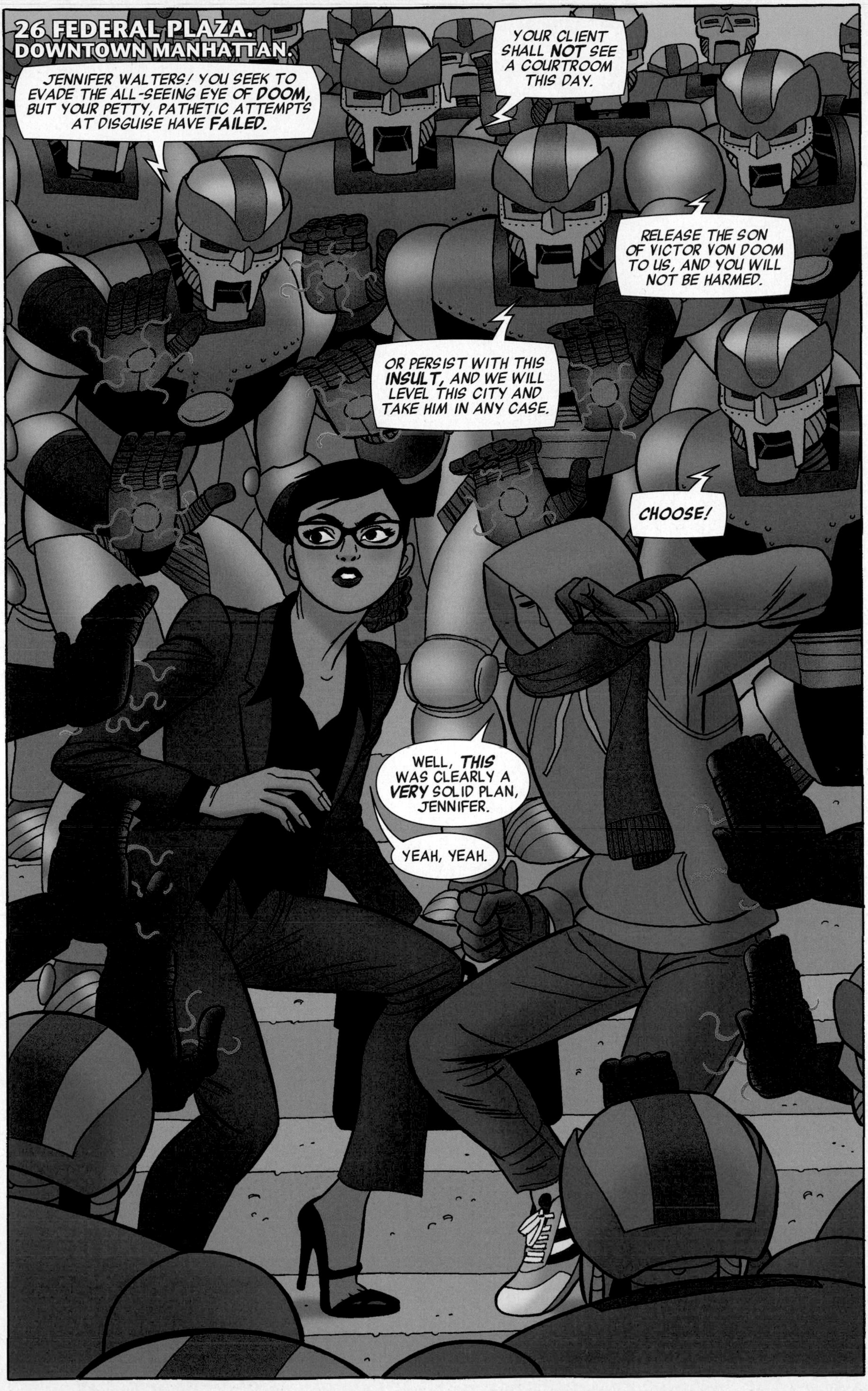
26 FEDERAL PLAZA. DOWNTOWN MANHATTAN.
JENNIFER WALTERS! YOU SEEK TO EVADE THE ALL-SEEING EYE OF DOOM, BUT YOUR PETTY, PATHETIC ATTEMPTS AT DISGUISE HAVE FAILED.
YOUR CLIENT SHALL NOT SEE A COURTROOM THIS DAY.
RELEASE THE SON OF VICTOR VON DOOM TO US, AND YOU WILL NOT BE HARMED.
OR PERSIST WITH THIS INSULT, AND WE WILL LEVEL THIS CITY AND TAKE HIM IN ANY CASE.
CHOOSE!
WELL, THIS WAS CLEARLY A VERY SOLID PLAN, JENNIFER.
YEAH, YEAH.

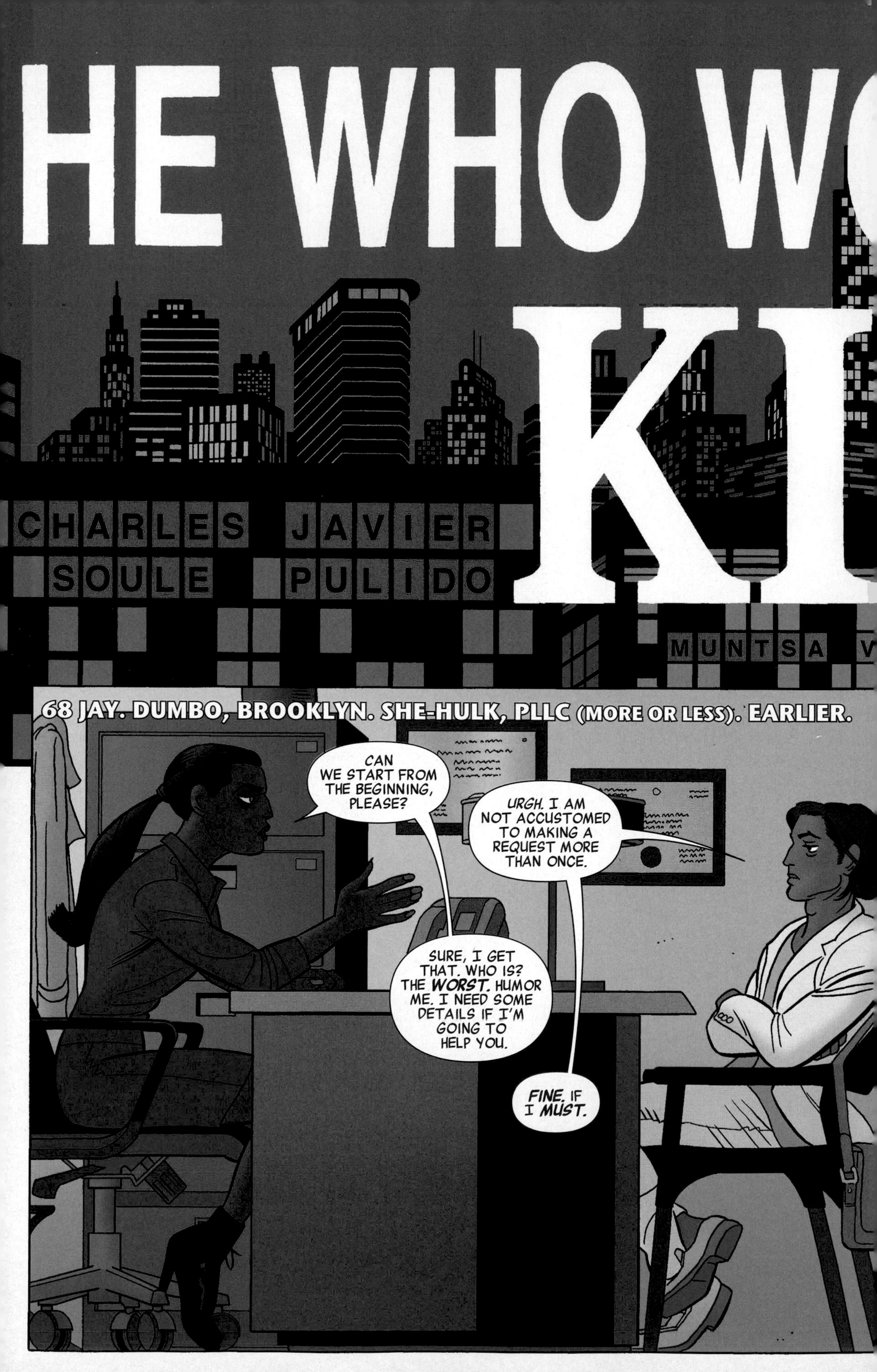
HE WHO W
KI
CHARLES SOULE
JAVIER PULIDO
MUNTSA V
68 JAY. DUMBO, BROOKLYN. SHE-HULK, PLLC (MORE OR LESS). EARLIER.
CAN WE START FROM THE BEGINNING, PLEASE?
URGH. I AM NOT ACCUSTOMED TO MAKING A REQUEST MORE THAN ONCE.
SURE, I GET THAT. WHO IS? THE WORST. HUMOR ME. I NEED SOME DETAILS IF I'M GOING TO HELP YOU.
FINE. IF I MUST.

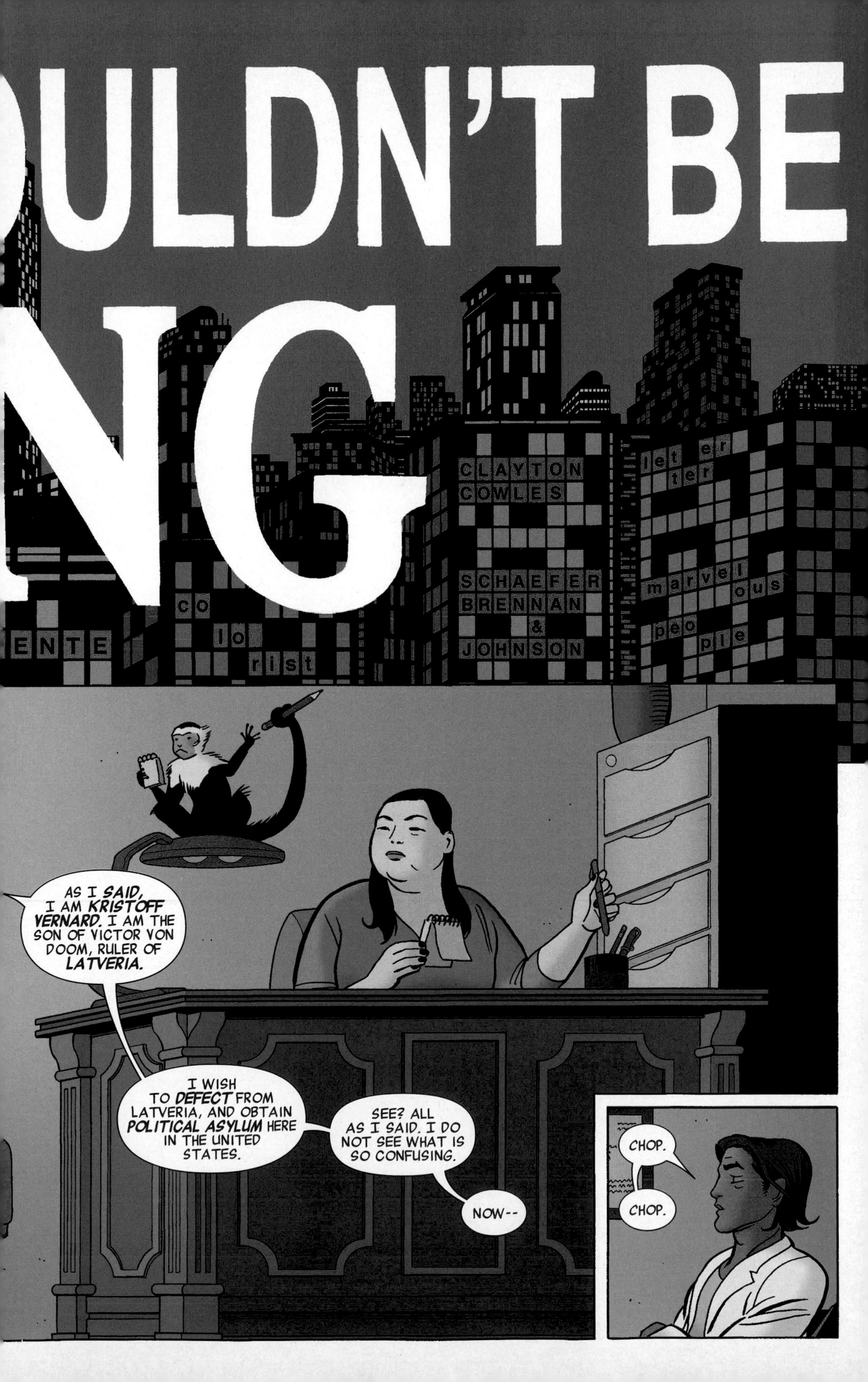
OULDN'T BE
NG
CLAYTON COWLES
let ter er
SCHAEFER BRENNAN & JOHNSON
marvel ous
peo ple
ENTE
co lo rist
AS I SAID, I AM KRISTOFF VERNARD. I AM THE SON OF VICTOR VON DOOM, RULER OF LATVERIA.
I WISH TO DEFECT FROM LATVERIA, AND OBTAIN POLITICAL ASYLUM HERE IN THE UNITED STATES.
SEE? ALL AS I SAID. I DO NOT SEE WHAT IS SO CONFUSING.
NOW--
CHOP.
CHOP.

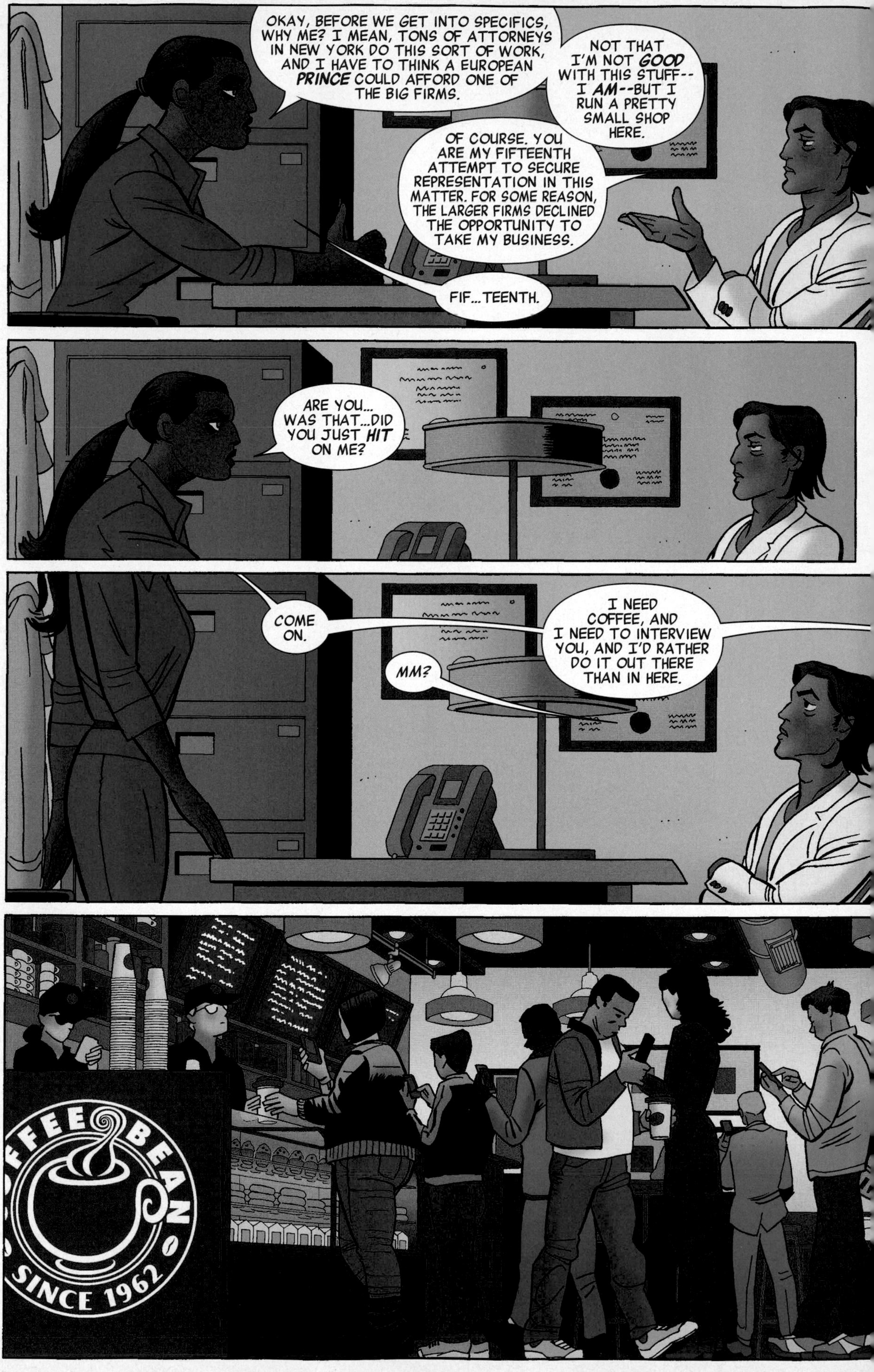
OKAY, BEFORE WE GET INTO SPECIFICS, WHY ME? I MEAN, TONS OF ATTORNEYS IN NEW YORK DO THIS SORT OF WORK, AND I HAVE TO THINK A EUROPEAN PRINCE COULD AFFORD ONE OF THE BIG FIRMS.
NOT THAT I'M NOT GOOD WITH THIS STUFF-- I AM--BUT I RUN A PRETTY SMALL SHOP HERE.
OF COURSE. YOU ARE MY FIFTEENTH ATTEMPT TO SECURE REPRESENTATION IN THIS MATTER. FOR SOME REASON, THE LARGER FIRMS DECLINED THE OPPORTUNITY TO TAKE MY BUSINESS.
FIF...TEENTH.
ARE YOU... WAS THAT...DID YOU JUST HIT ON ME?
COME ON.
I NEED COFFEE, AND I NEED TO INTERVIEW YOU, AND I'D RATHER DO IT OUT THERE THAN IN HERE.
MM?
COFFEE BEAN
SINCE 1962

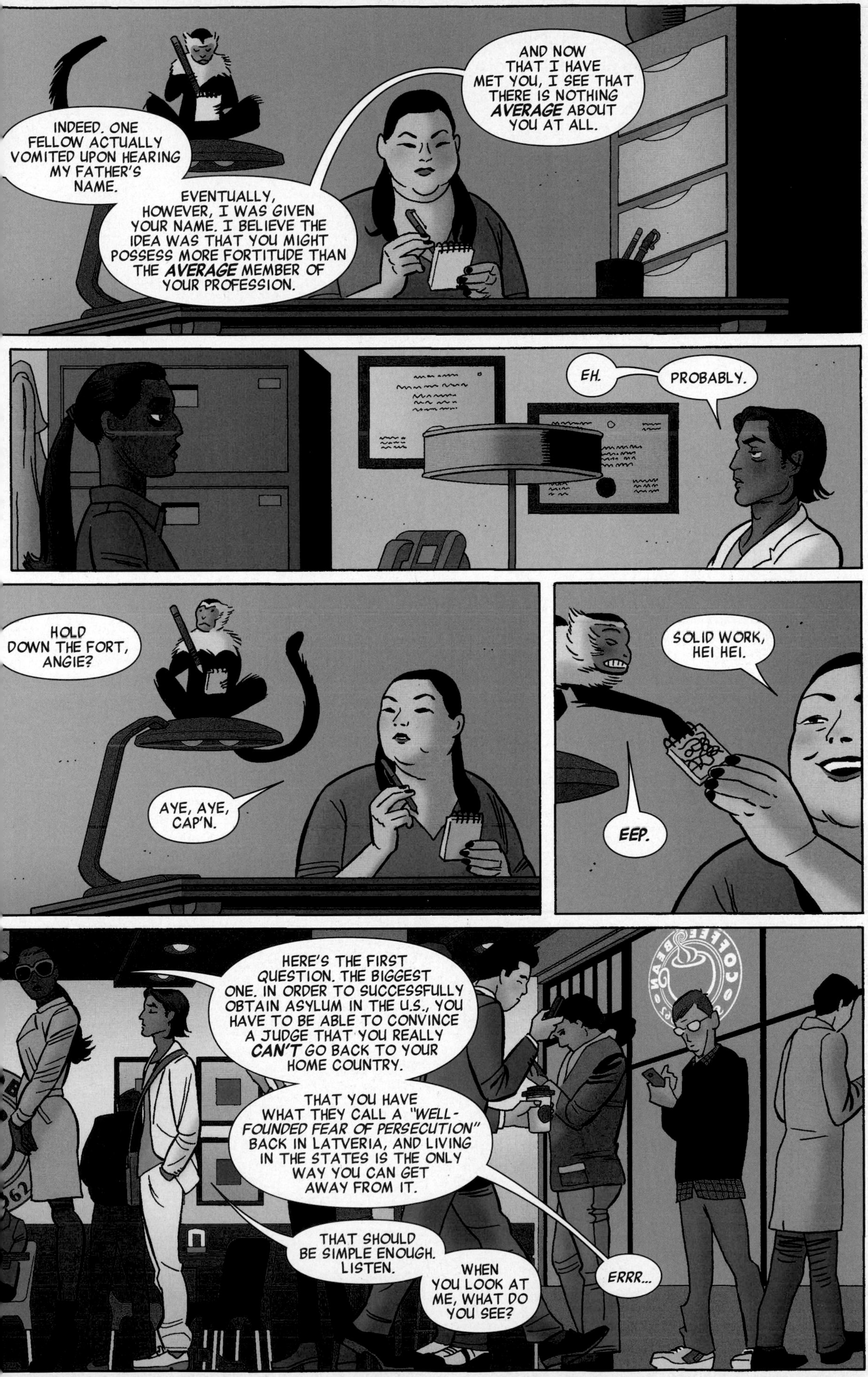
INDEED. ONE FELLOW ACTUALLY VOMITED UPON HEARING MY FATHER'S NAME.
EVENTUALLY, HOWEVER, I WAS GIVEN YOUR NAME. I BELIEVE THE IDEA WAS THAT YOU MIGHT POSSESS MORE FORTITUDE THAN THE AVERAGE MEMBER OF YOUR PROFESSION.
AND NOW THAT I HAVE MET YOU, I SEE THAT THERE IS NOTHING AVERAGE ABOUT YOU AT ALL.
EH.
PROBABLY.
HOLD DOWN THE FORT, ANGIE?
AYE, AYE, CAP'N.
SOLID WORK, HEI HEI.
EEP.
HERE'S THE FIRST QUESTION. THE BIGGEST ONE. IN ORDER TO SUCCESSFULLY OBTAIN ASYLUM IN THE U.S., YOU HAVE TO BE ABLE TO CONVINCE A JUDGE THAT YOU REALLY CAN'T GO BACK TO YOUR HOME COUNTRY.
THAT YOU HAVE WHAT THEY CALL A "WELL-FOUNDED FEAR OF PERSECUTION" BACK IN LATVERIA, AND LIVING IN THE STATES IS THE ONLY WAY YOU CAN GET AWAY FROM IT.
ERRR...
THAT SHOULD BE SIMPLE ENOUGH. LISTEN.
WHEN YOU LOOK AT ME, WHAT DO YOU SEE?

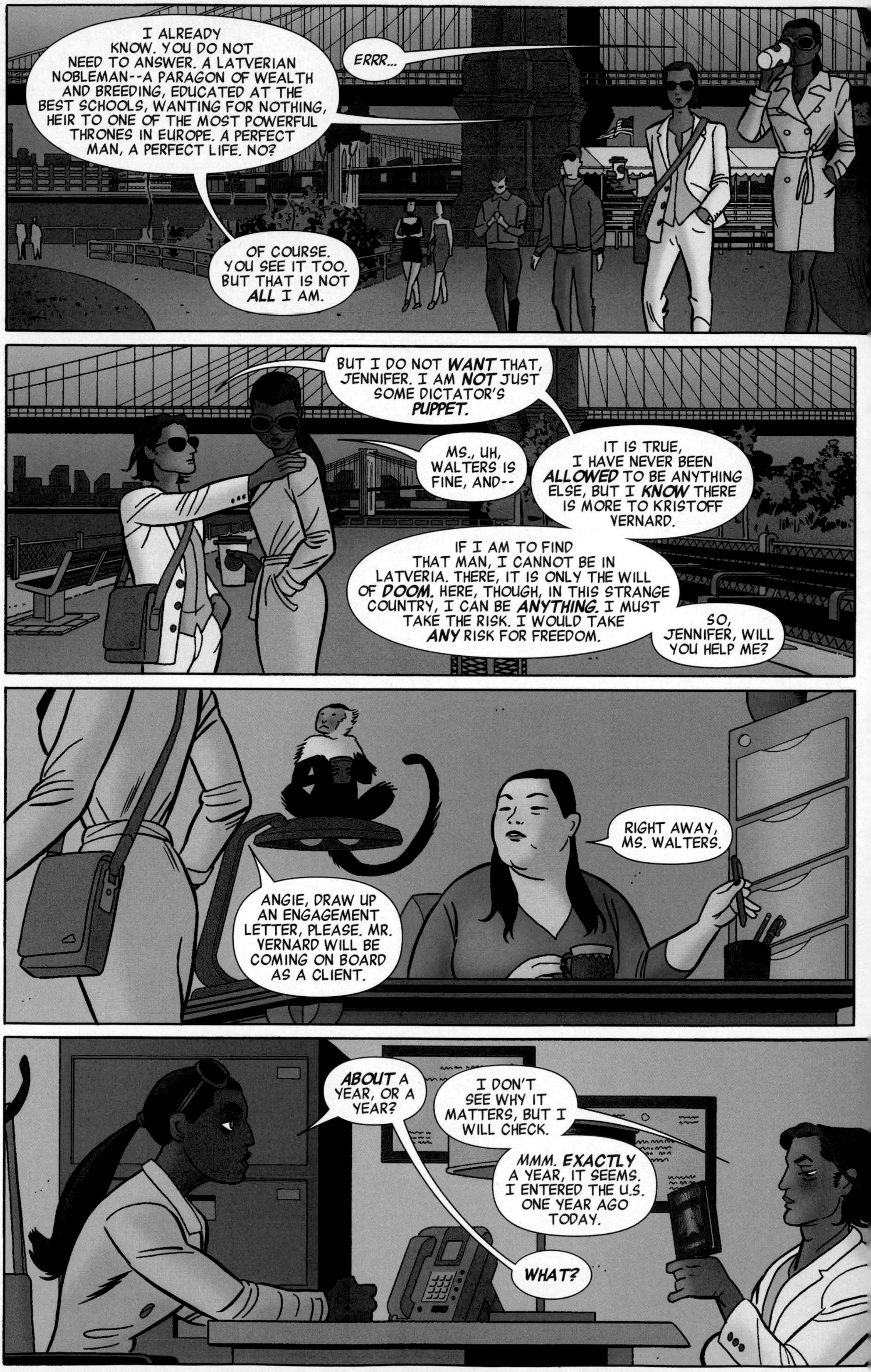
I ALREADY KNOW. YOU DO NOT NEED TO ANSWER. A LATVERIAN NOBLEMAN--A PARAGON OF WEALTH AND BREEDING, EDUCATED AT THE BEST SCHOOLS, WANTING FOR NOTHING, HEIR TO ONE OF THE MOST POWERFUL THRONES IN EUROPE. A PERFECT MAN, A PERFECT LIFE. NO?
ERRR...
OF COURSE. YOU SEE IT TOO. BUT THAT IS NOT ALL I AM.
BUT I DO NOT WANT THAT, JENNIFER. I AM NOT JUST SOME DICTATOR'S PUPPET.
MS., UH, WALTERS IS FINE, AND--
IT IS TRUE, I HAVE NEVER BEEN ALLOWED TO BE ANYTHING ELSE, BUT I KNOW THERE IS MORE TO KRISTOFF VERNARD.
IF I AM TO FIND THAT MAN, I CANNOT BE IN LATVERIA. THERE, IT IS ONLY THE WILL OF DOOM. HERE, THOUGH, IN THIS STRANGE COUNTRY, I CAN BE ANYTHING. I MUST TAKE THE RISK. I WOULD TAKE ANY RISK FOR FREEDOM.
SO, JENNIFER, WILL YOU HELP ME?
ANGIE, DRAW UP AN ENGAGEMENT LETTER, PLEASE. MR. VERNARD WILL BE COMING ON BOARD AS A CLIENT.
RIGHT AWAY, MS. WALTERS.
ABOUT A YEAR, OR A YEAR?
I DON'T SEE WHY IT MATTERS, BUT I WILL CHECK.
MMM. EXACTLY A YEAR, IT SEEMS. I ENTERED THE U.S. ONE YEAR AGO TODAY.
WHAT?

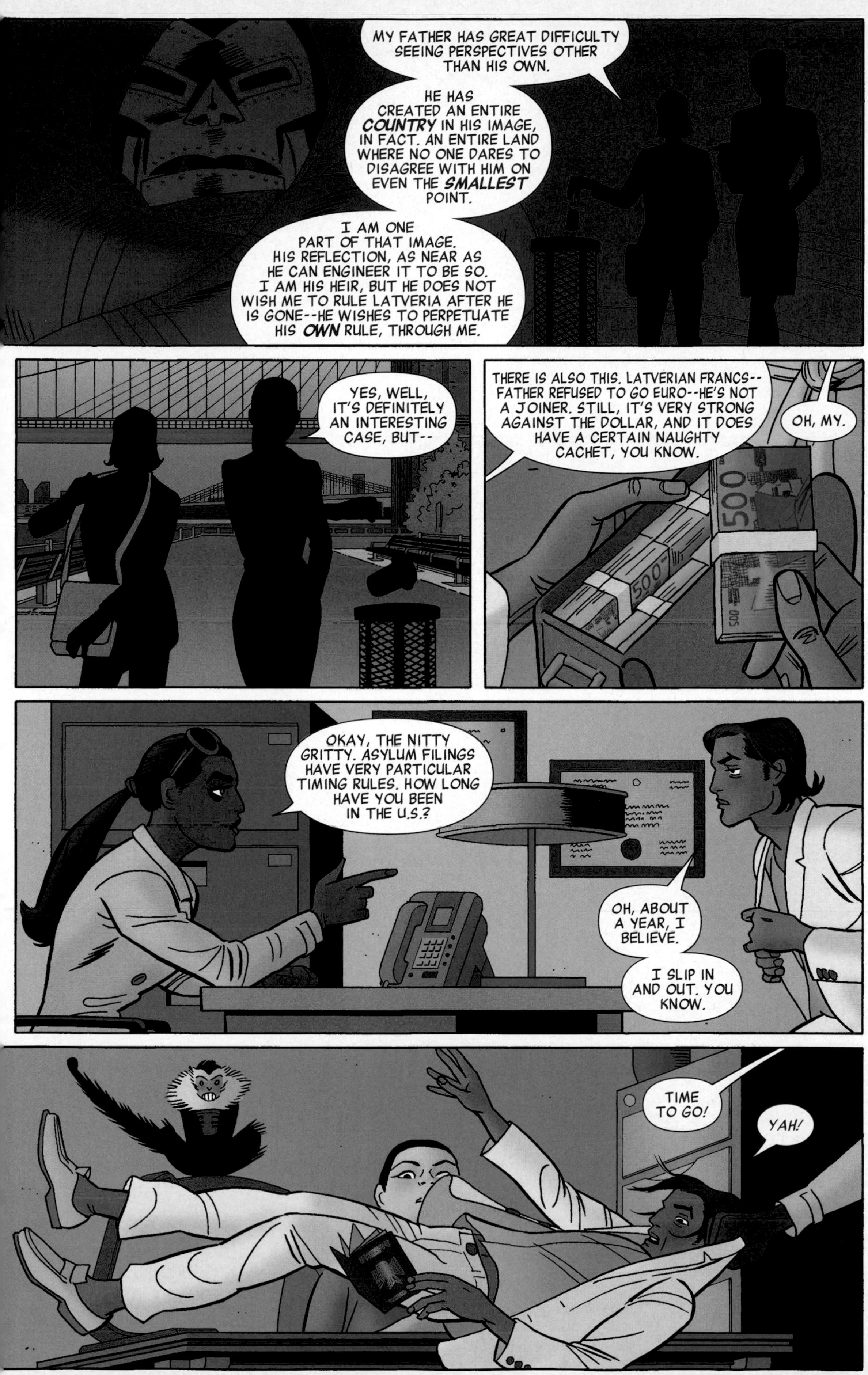
MY FATHER HAS GREAT DIFFICULTY SEEING PERSPECTIVES OTHER THAN HIS OWN.
HE HAS CREATED AN ENTIRE COUNTRY IN HIS IMAGE, IN FACT. AN ENTIRE LAND WHERE NO ONE DARES TO DISAGREE WITH HIM ON EVEN THE SMALLEST POINT.
I AM ONE PART OF THAT IMAGE. HIS REFLECTION, AS NEAR AS HE CAN ENGINEER IT TO BE SO. I AM HIS HEIR, BUT HE DOES NOT WISH ME TO RULE LATVERIA AFTER HE IS GONE--HE WISHES TO PERPETUATE HIS OWN RULE, THROUGH ME.
YES, WELL, IT'S DEFINITELY AN INTERESTING CASE, BUT--
THERE IS ALSO THIS. LATVERIAN FRANCS--FATHER REFUSED TO GO EURO--HE'S NOT A JOINER. STILL, IT'S VERY STRONG AGAINST THE DOLLAR, AND IT DOES HAVE A CERTAIN NAUGHTY CACHET, YOU KNOW.
OH, MY.
500
OKAY, THE NITTY GRITTY. ASYLUM FILINGS HAVE VERY PARTICULAR TIMING RULES. HOW LONG HAVE YOU BEEN IN THE U.S.?
OH, ABOUT A YEAR, I BELIEVE.
I SLIP IN AND OUT. YOU KNOW.
TIME TO GO!
YAH!

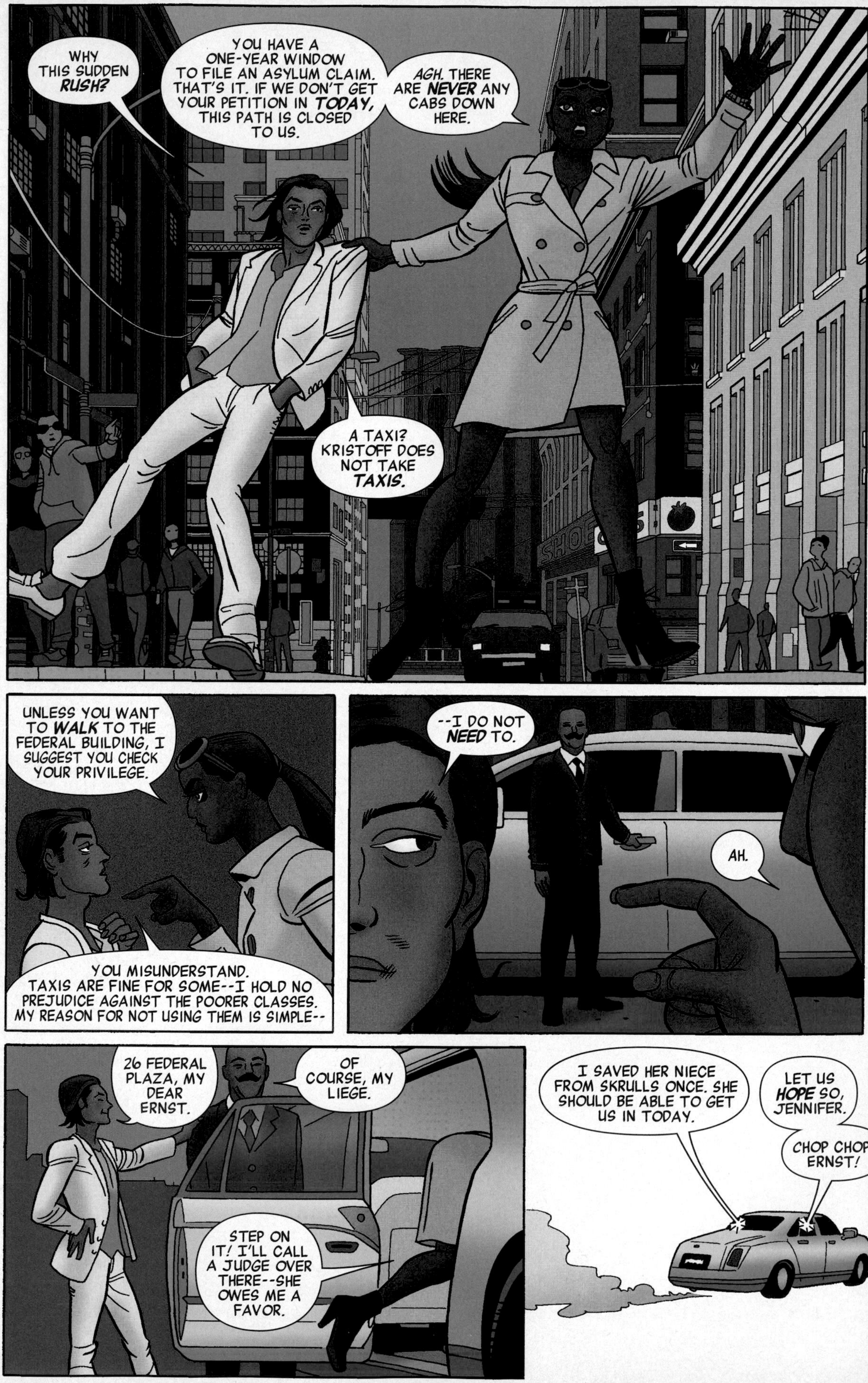
WHY THIS SUDDEN RUSH?
YOU HAVE A ONE-YEAR WINDOW TO FILE AN ASYLUM CLAIM. THAT'S IT. IF WE DON'T GET YOUR PETITION IN TODAY, THIS PATH IS CLOSED TO US.
AGH. THERE ARE NEVER ANY CABS DOWN HERE.
A TAXI? KRISTOFF DOES NOT TAKE TAXIS.
SHOES
UNLESS YOU WANT TO WALK TO THE FEDERAL BUILDING, I SUGGEST YOU CHECK YOUR PRIVILEGE.
YOU MISUNDERSTAND. TAXIS ARE FINE FOR SOME--I HOLD NO PREJUDICE AGAINST THE POORER CLASSES. MY REASON FOR NOT USING THEM IS SIMPLE--
--I DO NOT NEED TO.
AH.
26 FEDERAL PLAZA, MY DEAR ERNST.
OF COURSE, MY LIEGE.
STEP ON IT! I'LL CALL A JUDGE OVER THERE--SHE OWES ME A FAVOR.
I SAVED HER NIECE FROM SKRULLS ONCE. SHE SHOULD BE ABLE TO GET US IN TODAY.
LET US HOPE SO, JENNIFER.
CHOP CHOP, ERNST!

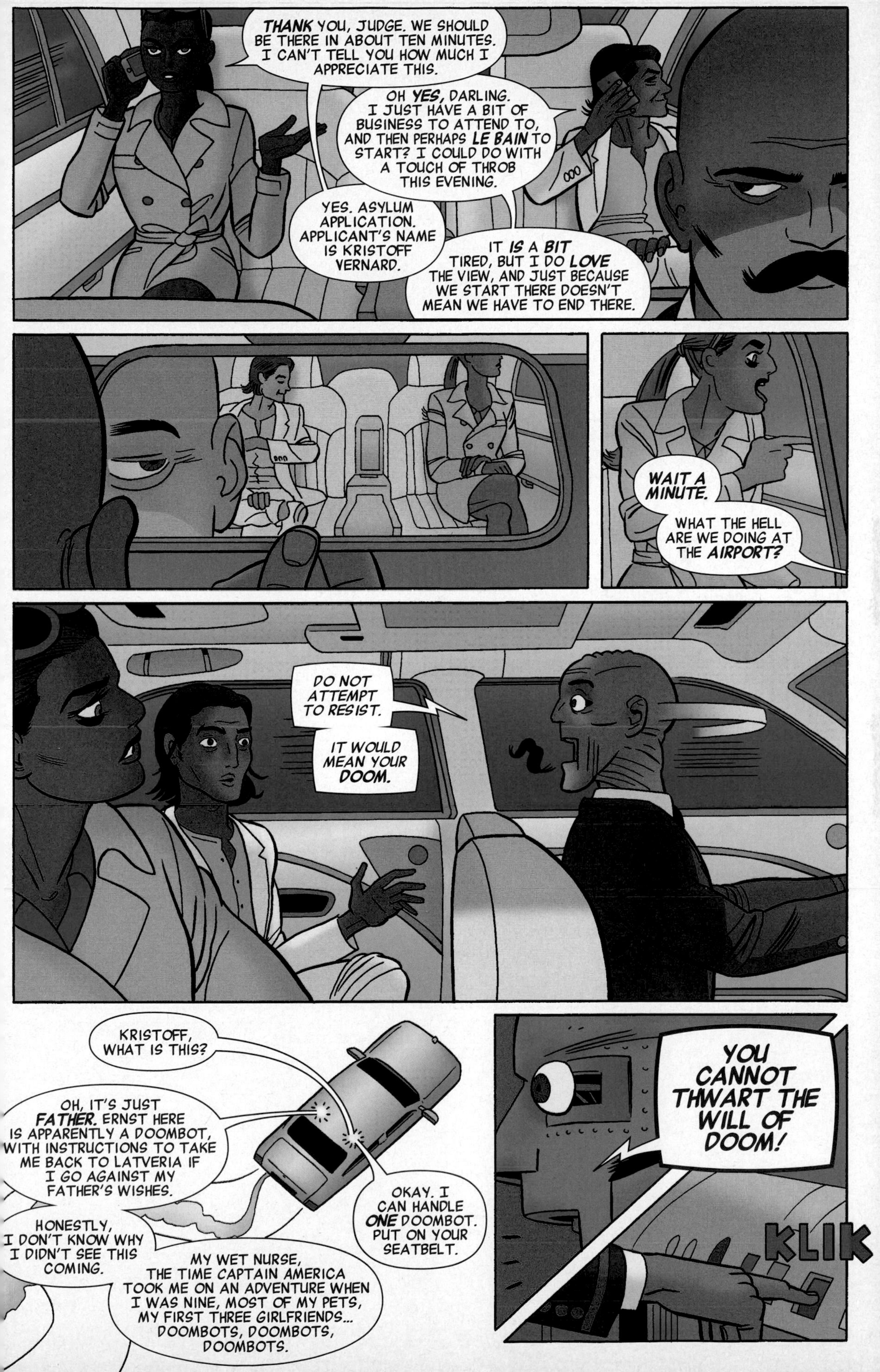
THANK YOU, JUDGE. WE SHOULD BE THERE IN ABOUT TEN MINUTES. I CAN'T TELL YOU HOW MUCH I APPRECIATE THIS.
OH YES, DARLING. I JUST HAVE A BIT OF BUSINESS TO ATTEND TO, AND THEN PERHAPS LE BAIN TO START? I COULD DO WITH A TOUCH OF THROB THIS EVENING.
YES. ASYLUM APPLICATION. APPLICANT'S NAME IS KRISTOFF VERNARD.
IT IS A BIT TIRED, BUT I DO LOVE THE VIEW, AND JUST BECAUSE WE START THERE DOESN'T MEAN WE HAVE TO END THERE.
WAIT A MINUTE.
WHAT THE HELL ARE WE DOING AT THE AIRPORT?
DO NOT ATTEMPT TO RESIST.
IT WOULD MEAN YOUR DOOM.
KRISTOFF, WHAT IS THIS?
OH, IT'S JUST FATHER. ERNST HERE IS APPARENTLY A DOOMBOT, WITH INSTRUCTIONS TO TAKE ME BACK TO LATVERIA IF I GO AGAINST MY FATHER'S WISHES.
HONESTLY, I DON'T KNOW WHY I DIDN'T SEE THIS COMING.
MY WET NURSE, THE TIME CAPTAIN AMERICA TOOK ME ON AN ADVENTURE WHEN I WAS NINE, MOST OF MY PETS, MY FIRST THREE GIRLFRIENDS... DOOMBOTS, DOOMBOTS, DOOMBOTS.
OKAY. I CAN HANDLE ONE DOOMBOT. PUT ON YOUR SEATBELT.
YOU CANNOT THWART THE WILL OF DOOM!
KLIK

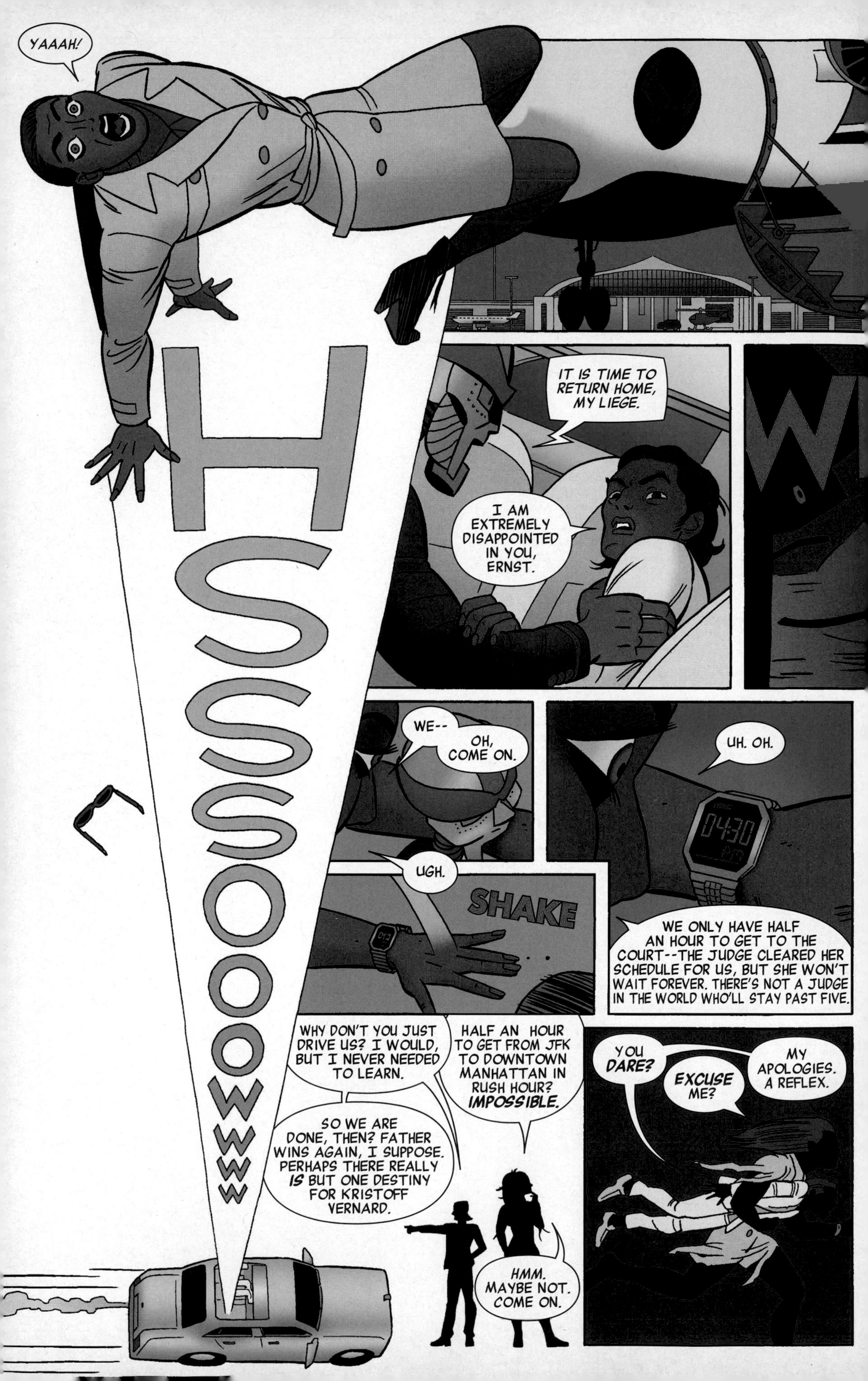
YAAAH!
HSSSSOOOOWWWWW
IT IS TIME TO RETURN HOME, MY LIEGE.
I AM EXTREMELY DISAPPOINTED IN YOU, ERNST.
WE--
OH, COME ON.
UGH.
SHAKE
UH. OH.
WE ONLY HAVE HALF AN HOUR TO GET TO THE COURT--THE JUDGE CLEARED HER SCHEDULE FOR US, BUT SHE WON'T WAIT FOREVER. THERE'S NOT A JUDGE IN THE WORLD WHO'LL STAY PAST FIVE.
YOU DARE?
EXCUSE ME?
MY APOLOGIES. A REFLEX.
WHY DON'T YOU JUST DRIVE US? I WOULD, BUT I NEVER NEEDED TO LEARN.
HALF AN HOUR TO GET FROM JFK TO DOWNTOWN MANHATTAN IN RUSH HOUR? IMPOSSIBLE.
SO WE ARE DONE, THEN? FATHER WINS AGAIN, I SUPPOSE. PERHAPS THERE REALLY IS BUT ONE DESTINY FOR KRISTOFF VERNARD.
HMM. MAYBE NOT. COME ON.

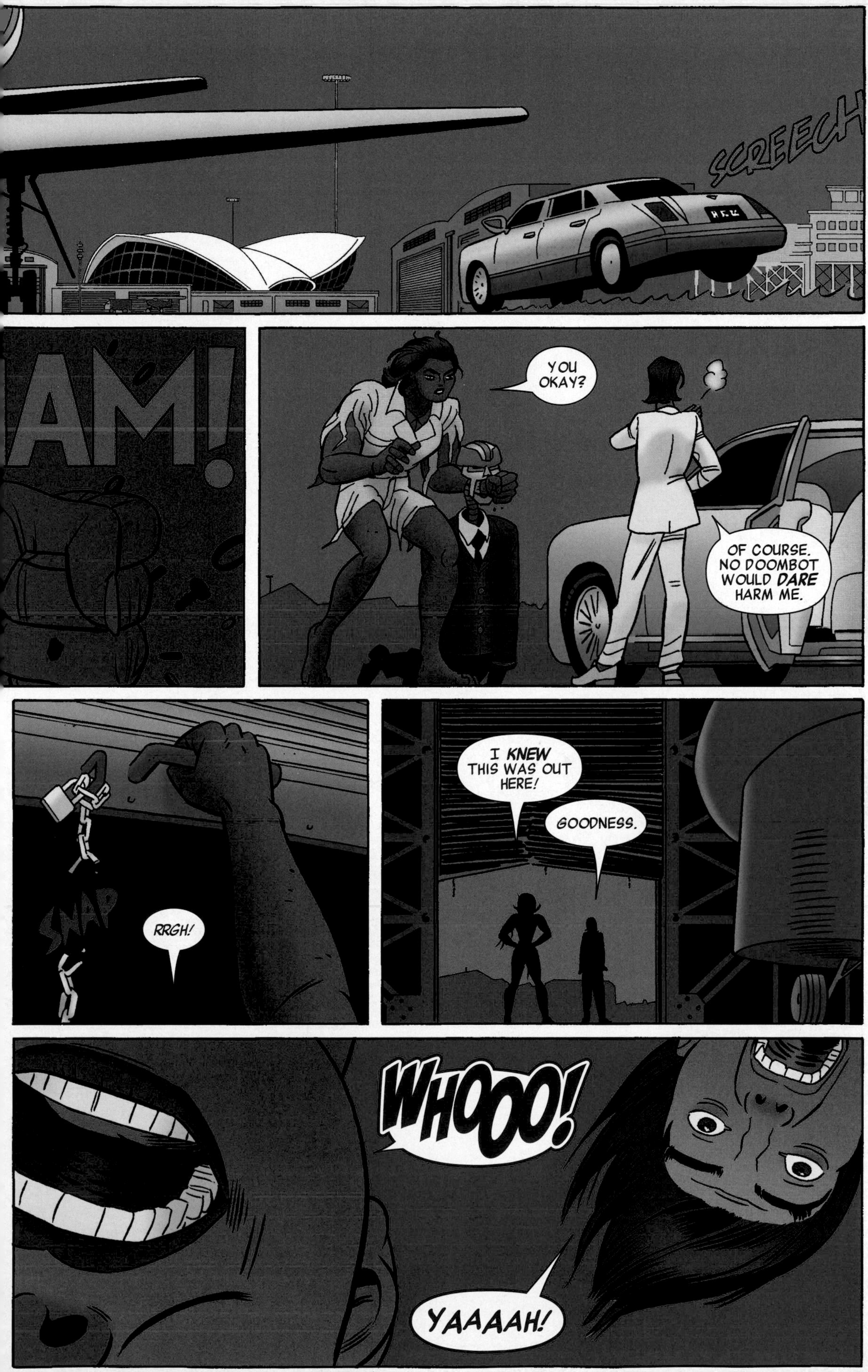
SCREECH
AM!
YOU OKAY?
OF COURSE. NO DOOMBOT WOULD DARE HARM ME.
SNAP
RRGH!
I KNEW THIS WAS OUT HERE!
GOODNESS.
WHOOO!
YAAAAH!

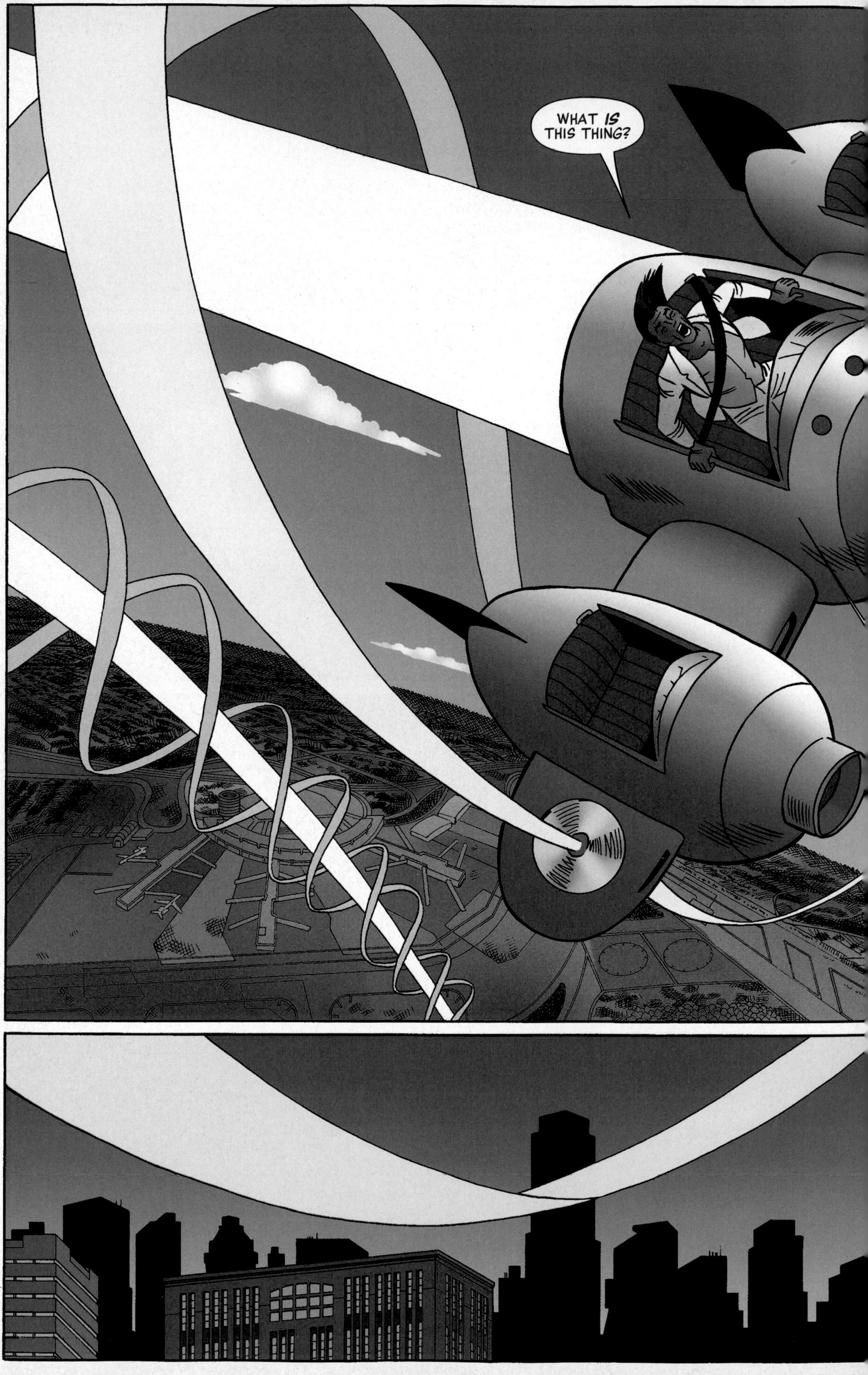
WHAT IS THIS THING?

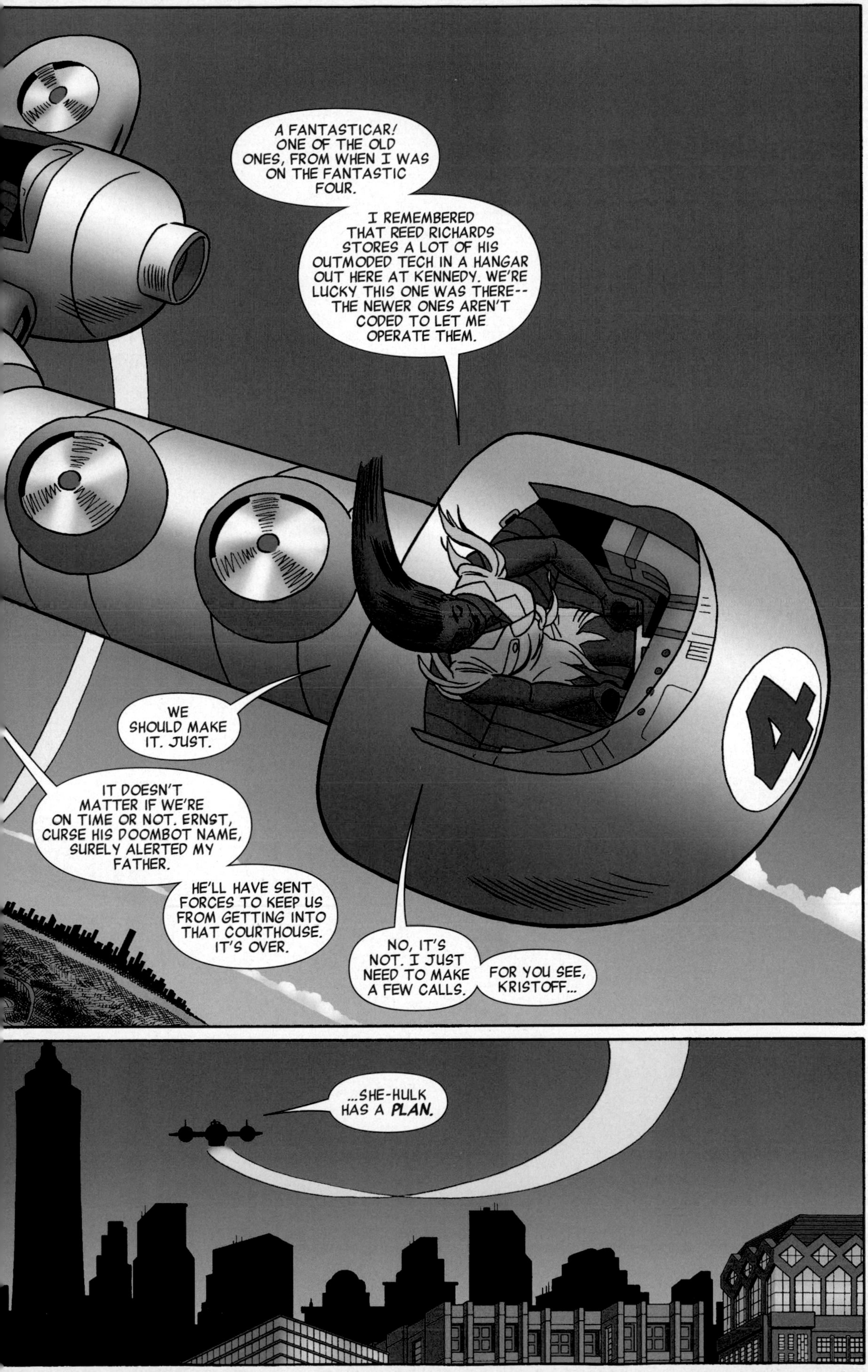
A FANTASTICAR! ONE OF THE OLD ONES, FROM WHEN I WAS ON THE FANTASTIC FOUR.
I REMEMBERED THAT REED RICHARDS STORES A LOT OF HIS OUTMODED TECH IN A HANGAR OUT HERE AT KENNEDY. WE'RE LUCKY THIS ONE WAS THERE-- THE NEWER ONES AREN'T CODED TO LET ME OPERATE THEM.
WE SHOULD MAKE IT. JUST.
IT DOESN'T MATTER IF WE'RE ON TIME OR NOT. ERNST, CURSE HIS DOOMBOT NAME, SURELY ALERTED MY FATHER.
HE'LL HAVE SENT FORCES TO KEEP US FROM GETTING INTO THAT COURTHOUSE. IT'S OVER.
NO, IT'S NOT. I JUST NEED TO MAKE A FEW CALLS.
FOR YOU SEE, KRISTOFF...
...SHE-HULK HAS A *PLAN.*

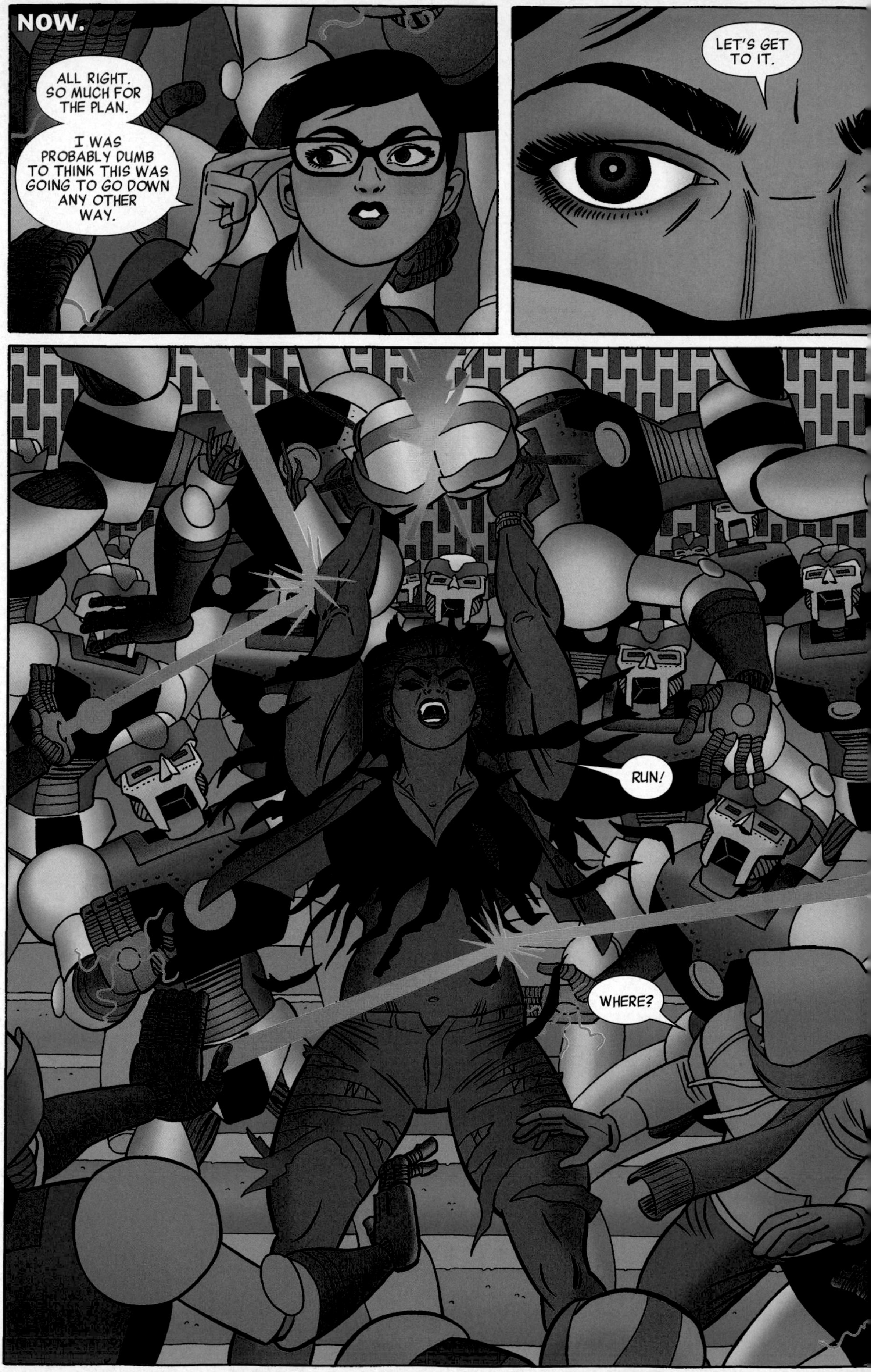
NOW.
ALL RIGHT. SO MUCH FOR THE PLAN.
I WAS PROBABLY DUMB TO THINK THIS WAS GOING TO GO DOWN ANY OTHER WAY.
LET'S GET TO IT.
RUN!
WHERE?

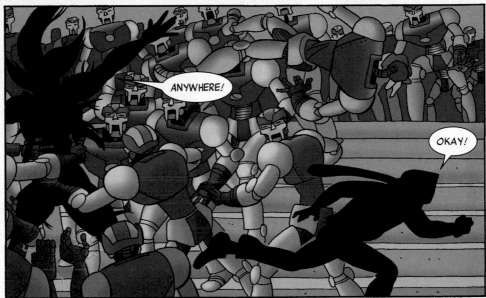

ANYWHERE!

OKAY!

AGH!

ENOUGH RUNNING, KRISTOFF.

SHHHP

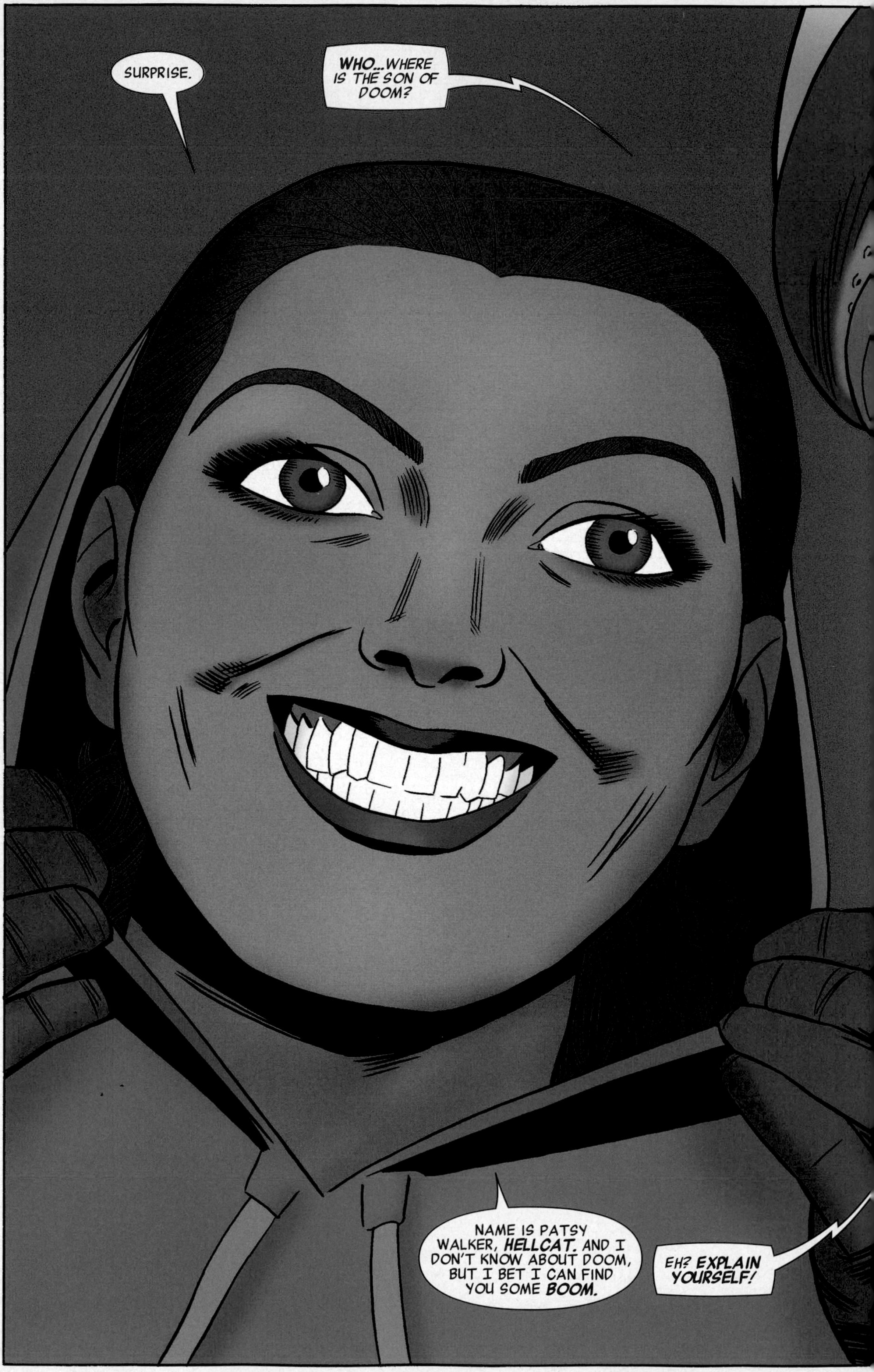
SURPRISE.
WHO...WHERE IS THE SON OF DOOM?
NAME IS PATSY WALKER, HELLCAT. AND I DON'T KNOW ABOUT DOOM, BUT I BET I CAN FIND YOU SOME BOOM.
EH? EXPLAIN YOURSELF!

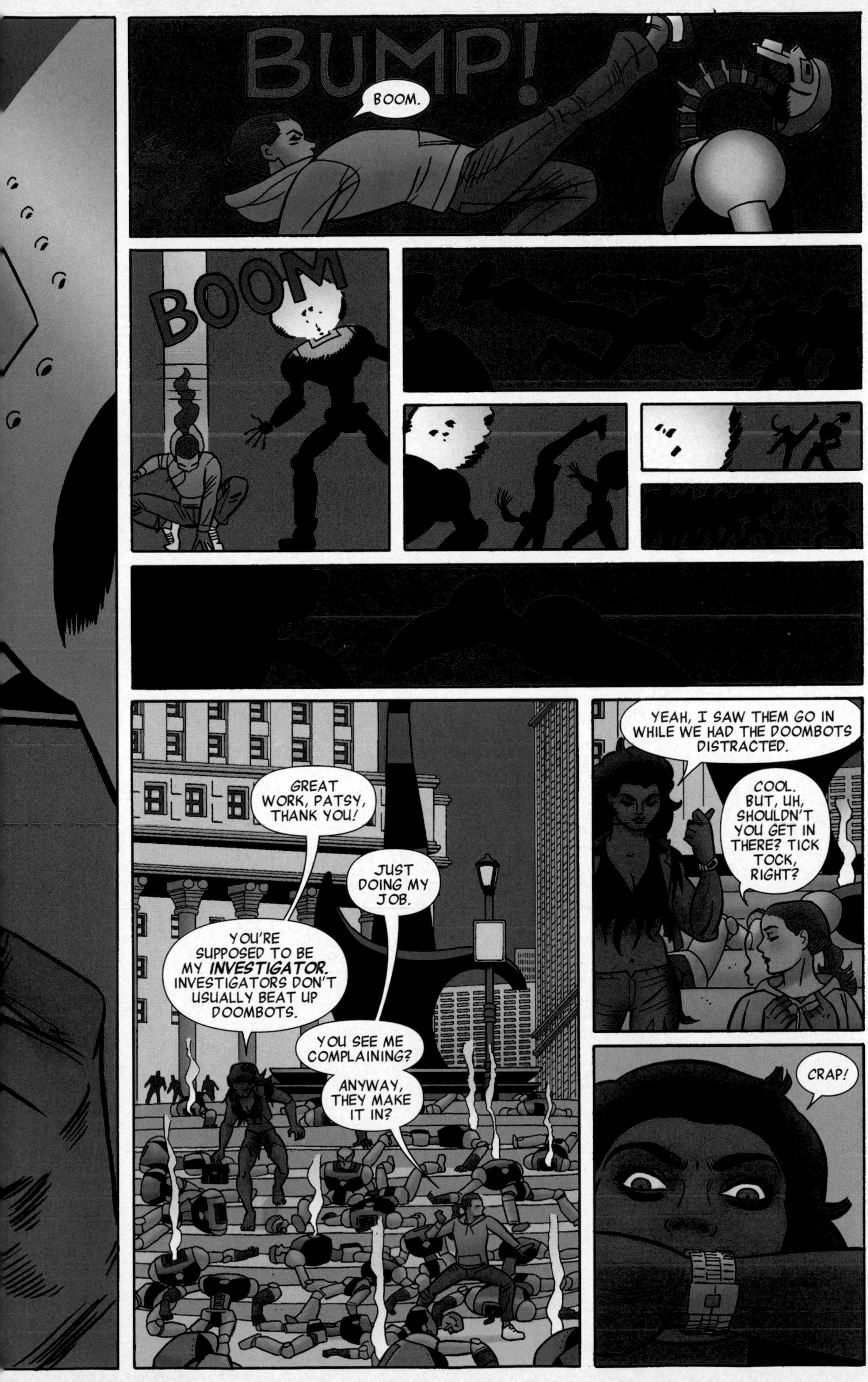
BUMP!
BOOM.
BOOM
GREAT WORK, PATSY, THANK YOU!
JUST DOING MY JOB.
YOU'RE SUPPOSED TO BE MY INVESTIGATOR. INVESTIGATORS DON'T USUALLY BEAT UP DOOMBOTS.
YOU SEE ME COMPLAINING?
ANYWAY, THEY MAKE IT IN?
YEAH, I SAW THEM GO IN WHILE WE HAD THE DOOMBOTS DISTRACTED.
COOL. BUT, UH, SHOULDN'T YOU GET IN THERE? TICK TOCK, RIGHT?
CRAP!

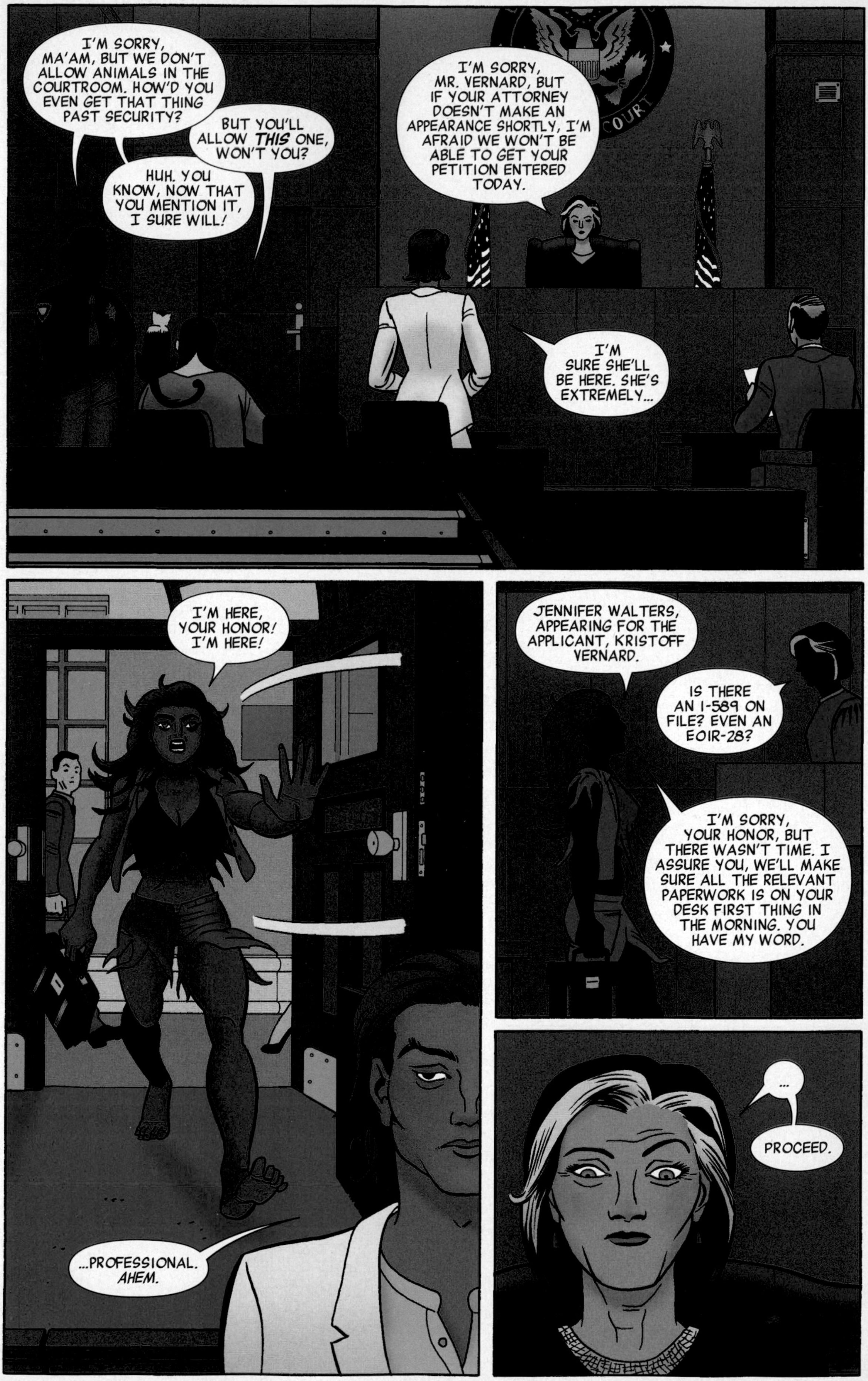
I'M SORRY, MA'AM, BUT WE DON'T ALLOW ANIMALS IN THE COURTROOM. HOW'D YOU EVEN GET THAT THING PAST SECURITY?
BUT YOU'LL ALLOW *THIS* ONE, WON'T YOU?
HUH. YOU KNOW, NOW THAT YOU MENTION IT, I SURE WILL!
I'M SORRY, MR. VERNARD, BUT IF YOUR ATTORNEY DOESN'T MAKE AN APPEARANCE SHORTLY, I'M AFRAID WE WON'T BE ABLE TO GET YOUR PETITION ENTERED TODAY.
I'M SURE SHE'LL BE HERE. SHE'S EXTREMELY...
I'M HERE, YOUR HONOR! I'M HERE!
...PROFESSIONAL. *AHEM.*
JENNIFER WALTERS, APPEARING FOR THE APPLICANT, KRISTOFF VERNARD.
IS THERE AN I-589 ON FILE? EVEN AN EOIR-28?
I'M SORRY, YOUR HONOR, BUT THERE WASN'T TIME. I ASSURE YOU, WE'LL MAKE SURE ALL THE RELEVANT PAPERWORK IS ON YOUR DESK FIRST THING IN THE MORNING. YOU HAVE MY WORD.
...
PROCEED.

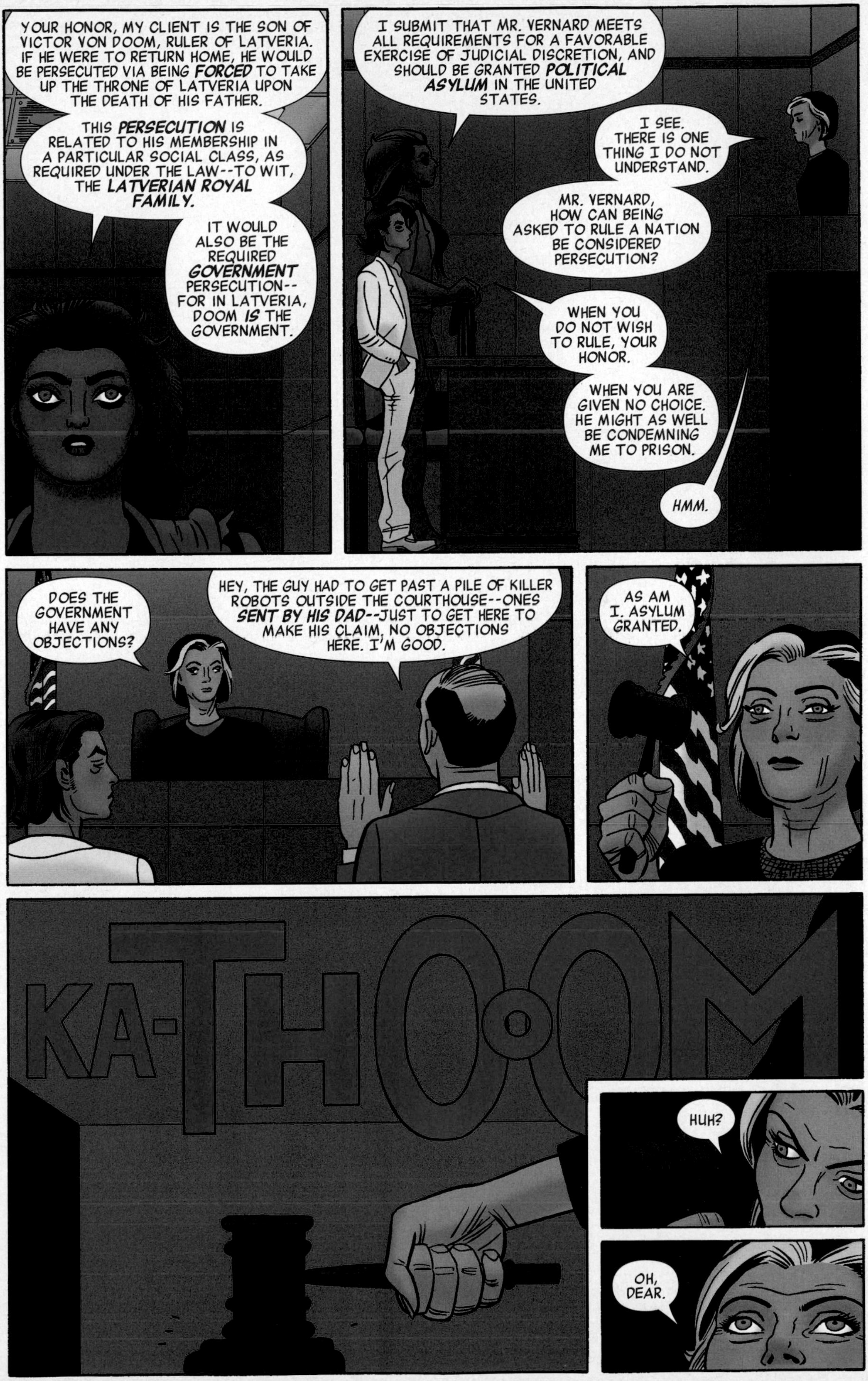
YOUR HONOR, MY CLIENT IS THE SON OF VICTOR VON DOOM, RULER OF LATVERIA. IF HE WERE TO RETURN HOME, HE WOULD BE PERSECUTED VIA BEING FORCED TO TAKE UP THE THRONE OF LATVERIA UPON THE DEATH OF HIS FATHER.
THIS PERSECUTION IS RELATED TO HIS MEMBERSHIP IN A PARTICULAR SOCIAL CLASS, AS REQUIRED UNDER THE LAW--TO WIT, THE LATVERIAN ROYAL FAMILY.
IT WOULD ALSO BE THE REQUIRED GOVERNMENT PERSECUTION-- FOR IN LATVERIA, DOOM IS THE GOVERNMENT.
I SUBMIT THAT MR. VERNARD MEETS ALL REQUIREMENTS FOR A FAVORABLE EXERCISE OF JUDICIAL DISCRETION, AND SHOULD BE GRANTED POLITICAL ASYLUM IN THE UNITED STATES.
I SEE. THERE IS ONE THING I DO NOT UNDERSTAND.
MR. VERNARD, HOW CAN BEING ASKED TO RULE A NATION BE CONSIDERED PERSECUTION?
WHEN YOU DO NOT WISH TO RULE, YOUR HONOR.
WHEN YOU ARE GIVEN NO CHOICE. HE MIGHT AS WELL BE CONDEMNING ME TO PRISON.
HMM.
DOES THE GOVERNMENT HAVE ANY OBJECTIONS?
HEY, THE GUY HAD TO GET PAST A PILE OF KILLER ROBOTS OUTSIDE THE COURTHOUSE--ONES SENT BY HIS DAD--JUST TO GET HERE TO MAKE HIS CLAIM, NO OBJECTIONS HERE. I'M GOOD.
AS AM I. ASYLUM GRANTED.
KA-THOOM
HUH?
OH, DEAR.

ENOUGH OF THIS FARCE!

OH. HELLO, FATHER.

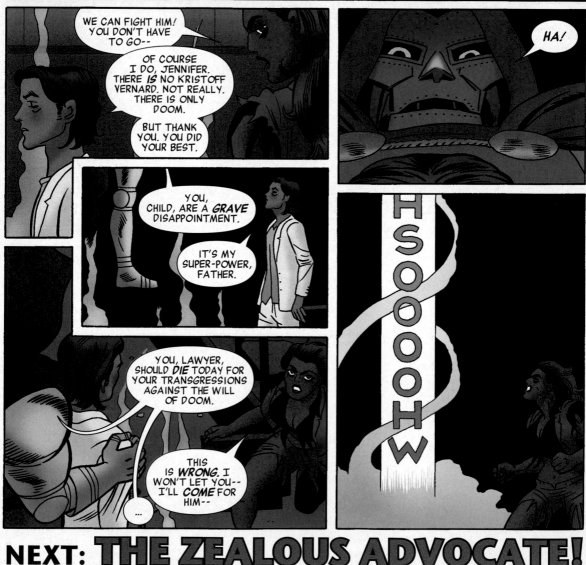

WE CAN FIGHT HIM! YOU DON'T HAVE TO GO--

OF COURSE I DO, JENNIFER. THERE *IS* NO KRISTOFF VERNARD. NOT REALLY. THERE IS ONLY DOOM.

BUT THANK YOU. YOU DID YOUR BEST.

HA!

YOU, CHILD, ARE A *GRAVE* DISAPPOINTMENT.

IT'S MY SUPER-POWER, FATHER.

WHOOOSH

YOU, LAWYER, SHOULD *DIE* TODAY FOR YOUR TRANSGRESSIONS AGAINST THE WILL OF DOOM.

THIS IS *WRONG*. I WON'T LET YOU-- I'LL *COME* FOR HIM--

...

NEXT: **THE ZEALOUS ADVOCATE!**

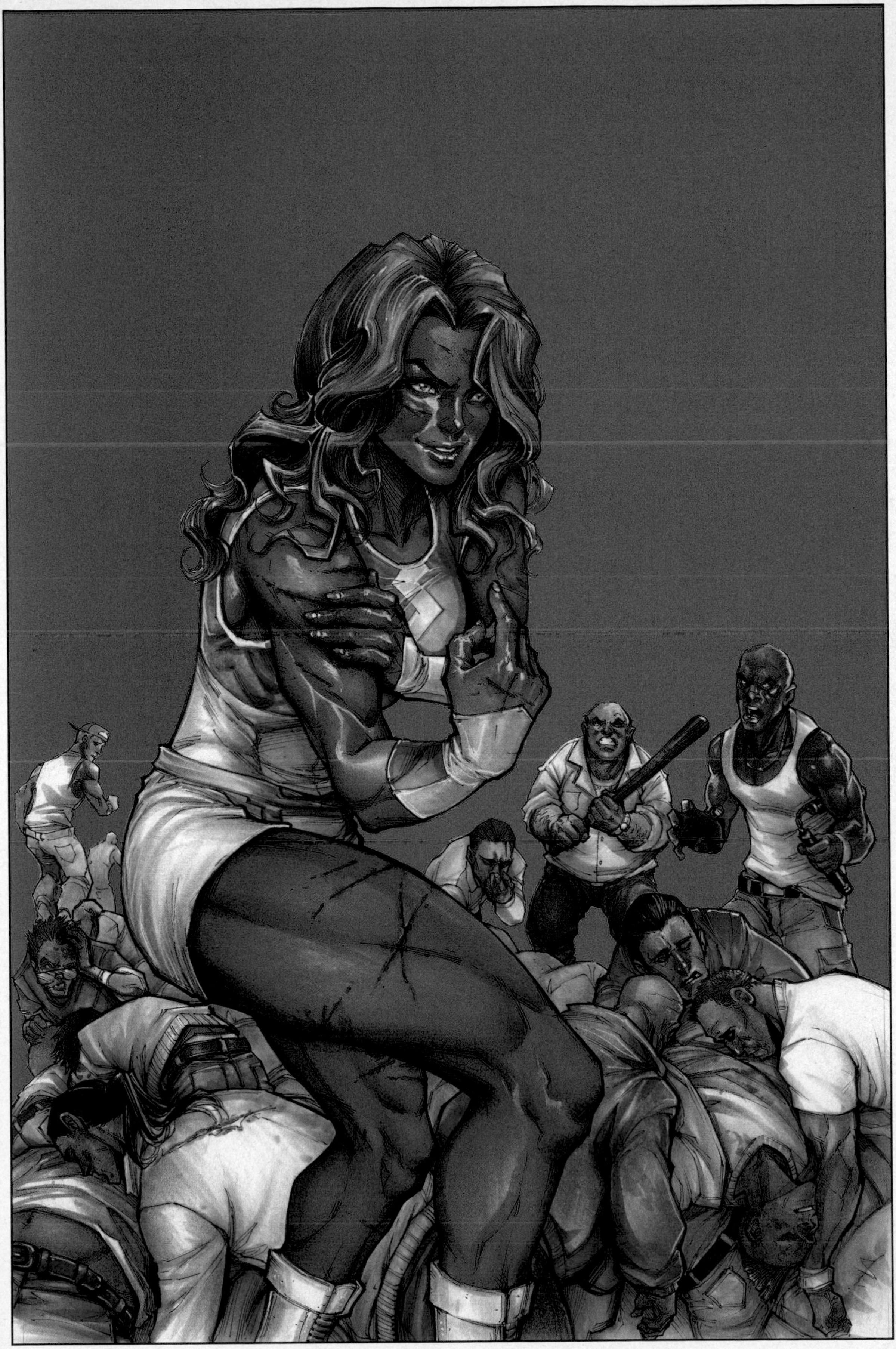

SHE-HULK #1 VARIANT BY SIYA OUM

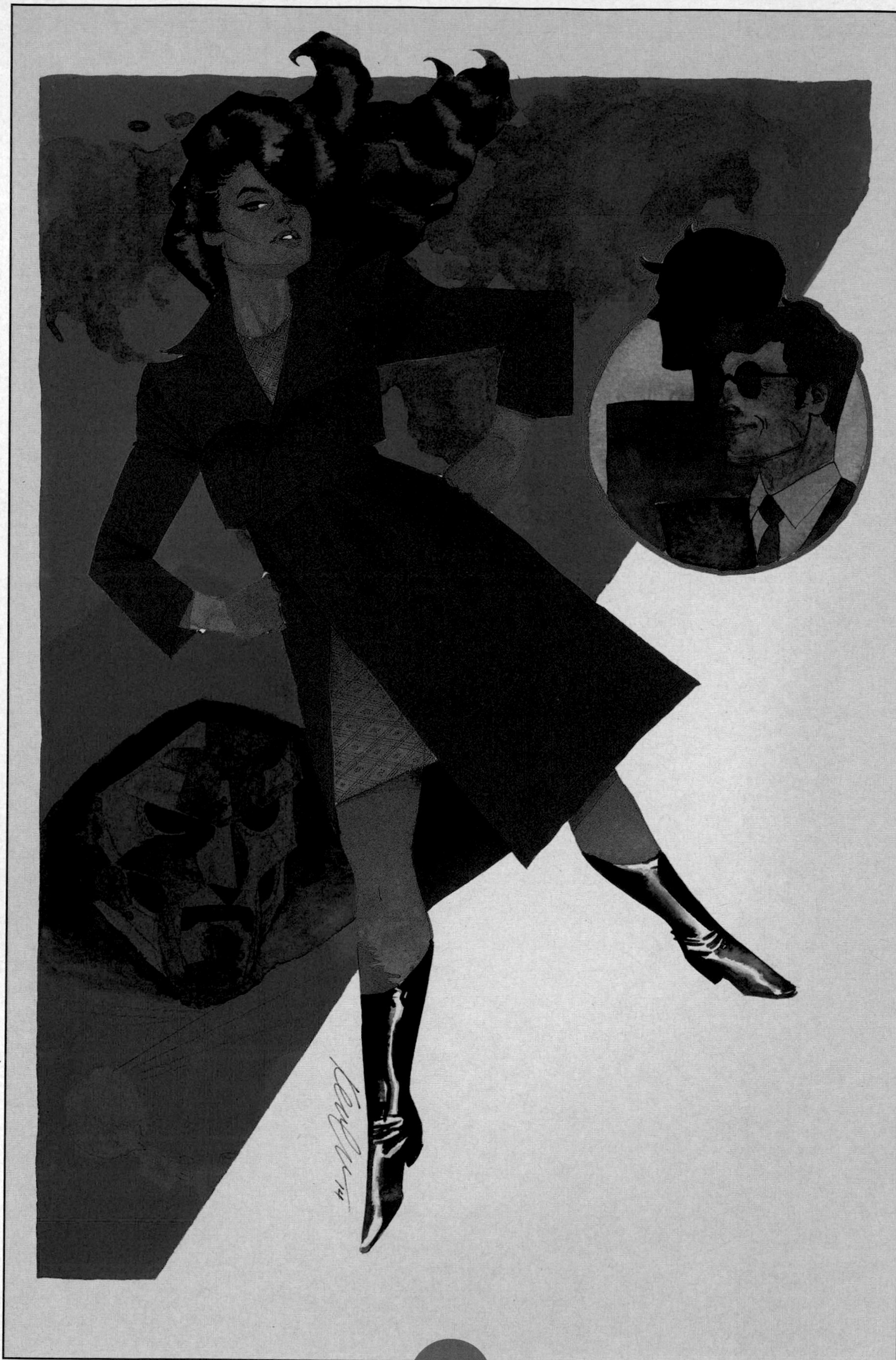

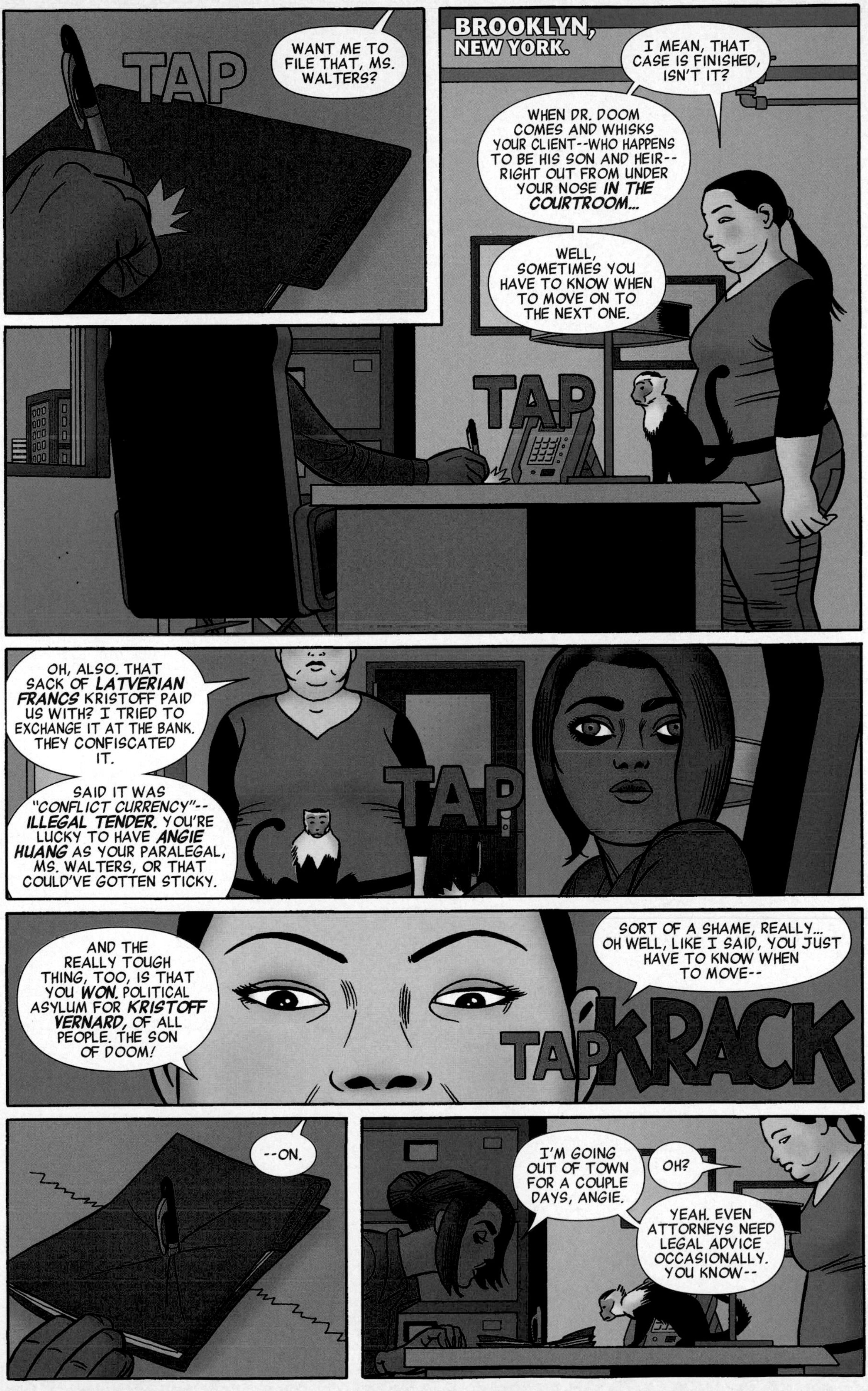
TAP
WANT ME TO FILE THAT, MS. WALTERS?
BROOKLYN, NEW YORK.
I MEAN, THAT CASE IS FINISHED, ISN'T IT?
WHEN DR. DOOM COMES AND WHISKS YOUR CLIENT--WHO HAPPENS TO BE HIS SON AND HEIR--RIGHT OUT FROM UNDER YOUR NOSE IN THE COURTROOM...
WELL, SOMETIMES YOU HAVE TO KNOW WHEN TO MOVE ON TO THE NEXT ONE.
TAP
OH, ALSO. THAT SACK OF LATVERIAN FRANCS KRISTOFF PAID US WITH? I TRIED TO EXCHANGE IT AT THE BANK. THEY CONFISCATED IT.
SAID IT WAS "CONFLICT CURRENCY"--ILLEGAL TENDER. YOU'RE LUCKY TO HAVE ANGIE HUANG AS YOUR PARALEGAL, MS. WALTERS, OR THAT COULD'VE GOTTEN STICKY.
TAP
AND THE REALLY TOUGH THING, TOO, IS THAT YOU WON. POLITICAL ASYLUM FOR KRISTOFF VERNARD, OF ALL PEOPLE. THE SON OF DOOM!
SORT OF A SHAME, REALLY... OH WELL, LIKE I SAID, YOU JUST HAVE TO KNOW WHEN TO MOVE--
TAP
KRACK
--ON.
I'M GOING OUT OF TOWN FOR A COUPLE DAYS, ANGIE.
OH?
YEAH. EVEN ATTORNEYS NEED LEGAL ADVICE OCCASIONALLY. YOU KNOW--

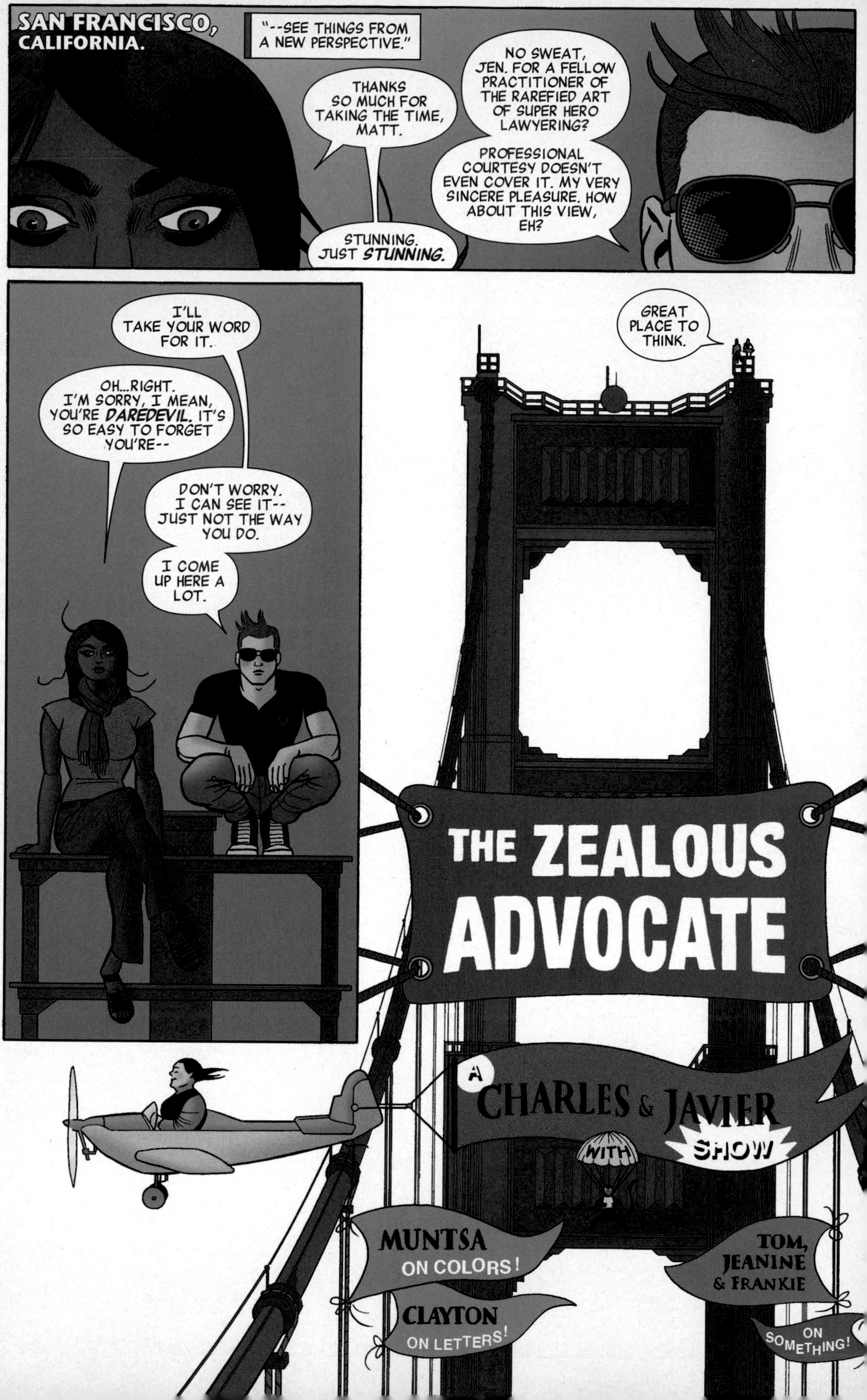
SAN FRANCISCO, CALIFORNIA.
"--SEE THINGS FROM A NEW PERSPECTIVE."
THANKS SO MUCH FOR TAKING THE TIME, MATT.
NO SWEAT, JEN. FOR A FELLOW PRACTITIONER OF THE RAREFIED ART OF SUPER HERO LAWYERING?
PROFESSIONAL COURTESY DOESN'T EVEN COVER IT. MY VERY SINCERE PLEASURE. HOW ABOUT THIS VIEW, EH?
STUNNING. JUST STUNNING.
I'LL TAKE YOUR WORD FOR IT.
OH...RIGHT. I'M SORRY, I MEAN, YOU'RE DAREDEVIL. IT'S SO EASY TO FORGET YOU'RE--
DON'T WORRY. I CAN SEE IT--JUST NOT THE WAY YOU DO.
I COME UP HERE A LOT.
GREAT PLACE TO THINK.
THE ZEALOUS ADVOCATE
A CHARLES & JAVIER SHOW
WITH
MUNTSA ON COLORS!
CLAYTON ON LETTERS!
TOM, JEANINE & FRANKIE ON SOMETHING!

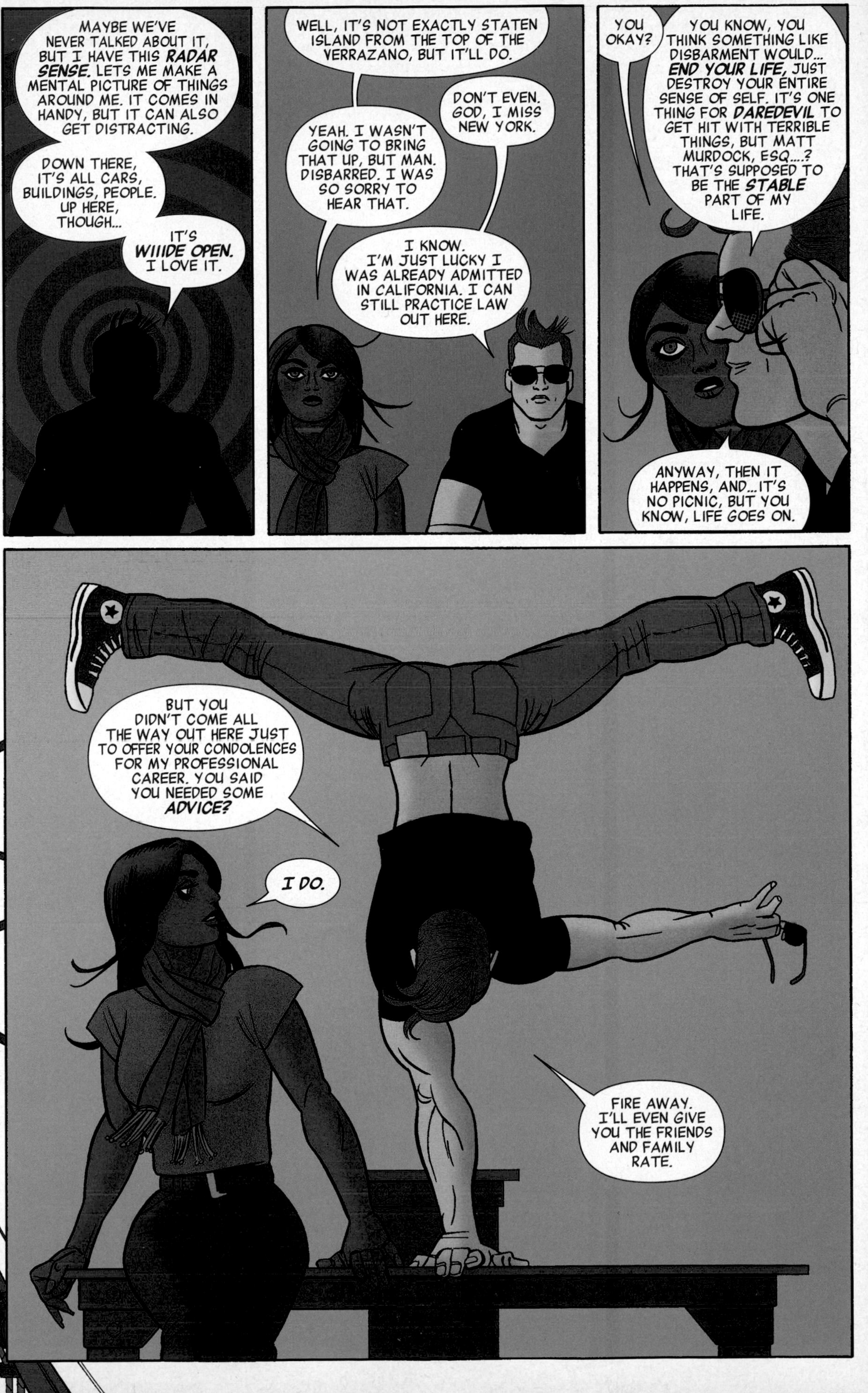
MAYBE WE'VE NEVER TALKED ABOUT IT, BUT I HAVE THIS RADAR SENSE. LETS ME MAKE A MENTAL PICTURE OF THINGS AROUND ME. IT COMES IN HANDY, BUT IT CAN ALSO GET DISTRACTING.
DOWN THERE, IT'S ALL CARS, BUILDINGS, PEOPLE. UP HERE, THOUGH...
IT'S WIIIDE OPEN. I LOVE IT.
WELL, IT'S NOT EXACTLY STATEN ISLAND FROM THE TOP OF THE VERRAZANO, BUT IT'LL DO.
DON'T EVEN. GOD, I MISS NEW YORK.
YEAH. I WASN'T GOING TO BRING THAT UP, BUT MAN. DISBARRED. I WAS SO SORRY TO HEAR THAT.
I KNOW. I'M JUST LUCKY I WAS ALREADY ADMITTED IN CALIFORNIA. I CAN STILL PRACTICE LAW OUT HERE.
YOU OKAY?
YOU KNOW, YOU THINK SOMETHING LIKE DISBARMENT WOULD... END YOUR LIFE, JUST DESTROY YOUR ENTIRE SENSE OF SELF. IT'S ONE THING FOR DAREDEVIL TO GET HIT WITH TERRIBLE THINGS, BUT MATT MURDOCK, ESQ....? THAT'S SUPPOSED TO BE THE STABLE PART OF MY LIFE.
ANYWAY, THEN IT HAPPENS, AND...IT'S NO PICNIC, BUT YOU KNOW, LIFE GOES ON.
BUT YOU DIDN'T COME ALL THE WAY OUT HERE JUST TO OFFER YOUR CONDOLENCES FOR MY PROFESSIONAL CAREER. YOU SAID YOU NEEDED SOME ADVICE?
I DO.
FIRE AWAY. I'LL EVEN GIVE YOU THE FRIENDS AND FAMILY RATE.

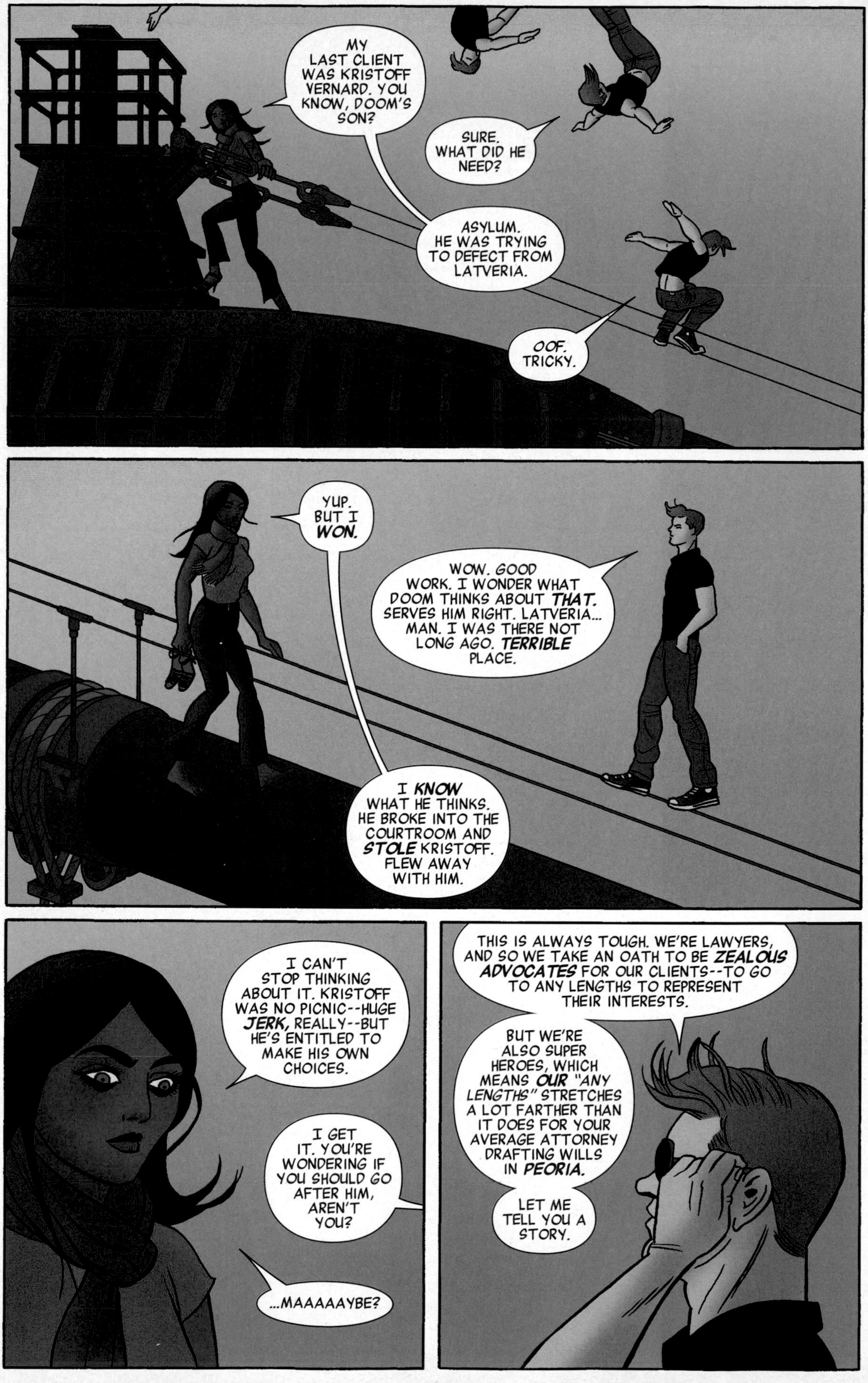

MY LAST CLIENT WAS KRISTOFF VERNARD. YOU KNOW, DOOM'S SON?
SURE. WHAT DID HE NEED?
ASYLUM. HE WAS TRYING TO DEFECT FROM LATVERIA.
OOF. TRICKY.
YUP. BUT I WON.
WOW. GOOD WORK. I WONDER WHAT DOOM THINKS ABOUT THAT. SERVES HIM RIGHT. LATVERIA... MAN. I WAS THERE NOT LONG AGO. TERRIBLE PLACE.
I KNOW WHAT HE THINKS. HE BROKE INTO THE COURTROOM AND STOLE KRISTOFF. FLEW AWAY WITH HIM.
I CAN'T STOP THINKING ABOUT IT. KRISTOFF WAS NO PICNIC--HUGE JERK, REALLY--BUT HE'S ENTITLED TO MAKE HIS OWN CHOICES.
I GET IT. YOU'RE WONDERING IF YOU SHOULD GO AFTER HIM, AREN'T YOU?
...MAAAAAYBE?
THIS IS ALWAYS TOUGH. WE'RE LAWYERS, AND SO WE TAKE AN OATH TO BE ZEALOUS ADVOCATES FOR OUR CLIENTS--TO GO TO ANY LENGTHS TO REPRESENT THEIR INTERESTS.
BUT WE'RE ALSO SUPER HEROES, WHICH MEANS OUR "ANY LENGTHS" STRETCHES A LOT FARTHER THAN IT DOES FOR YOUR AVERAGE ATTORNEY DRAFTING WILLS IN PEORIA.
LET ME TELL YOU A STORY.

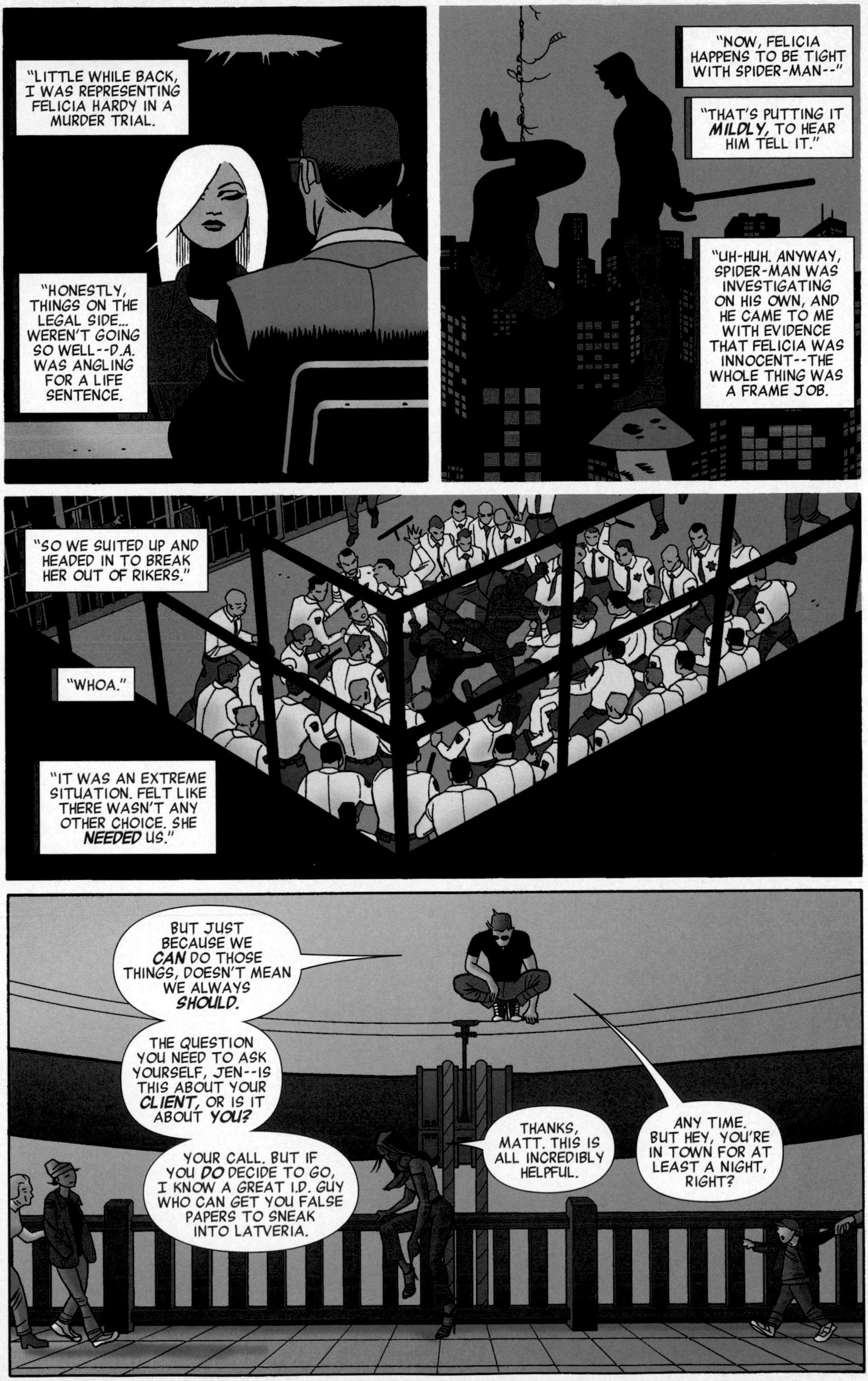

"LITTLE WHILE BACK, I WAS REPRESENTING FELICIA HARDY IN A MURDER TRIAL.
"HONESTLY, THINGS ON THE LEGAL SIDE... WEREN'T GOING SO WELL--D.A. WAS ANGLING FOR A LIFE SENTENCE.
"NOW, FELICIA HAPPENS TO BE TIGHT WITH SPIDER-MAN--"
"THAT'S PUTTING IT MILDLY, TO HEAR HIM TELL IT."
"UH-HUH. ANYWAY, SPIDER-MAN WAS INVESTIGATING ON HIS OWN, AND HE CAME TO ME WITH EVIDENCE THAT FELICIA WAS INNOCENT--THE WHOLE THING WAS A FRAME JOB.
"SO WE SUITED UP AND HEADED IN TO BREAK HER OUT OF RIKERS."
"WHOA."
"IT WAS AN EXTREME SITUATION. FELT LIKE THERE WASN'T ANY OTHER CHOICE. SHE NEEDED US."
BUT JUST BECAUSE WE CAN DO THOSE THINGS, DOESN'T MEAN WE ALWAYS SHOULD.
THE QUESTION YOU NEED TO ASK YOURSELF, JEN--IS THIS ABOUT YOUR CLIENT, OR IS IT ABOUT YOU?
YOUR CALL. BUT IF YOU DO DECIDE TO GO, I KNOW A GREAT I.D. GUY WHO CAN GET YOU FALSE PAPERS TO SNEAK INTO LATVERIA.
THANKS, MATT. THIS IS ALL INCREDIBLY HELPFUL.
ANY TIME. BUT HEY, YOU'RE IN TOWN FOR AT LEAST A NIGHT, RIGHT?

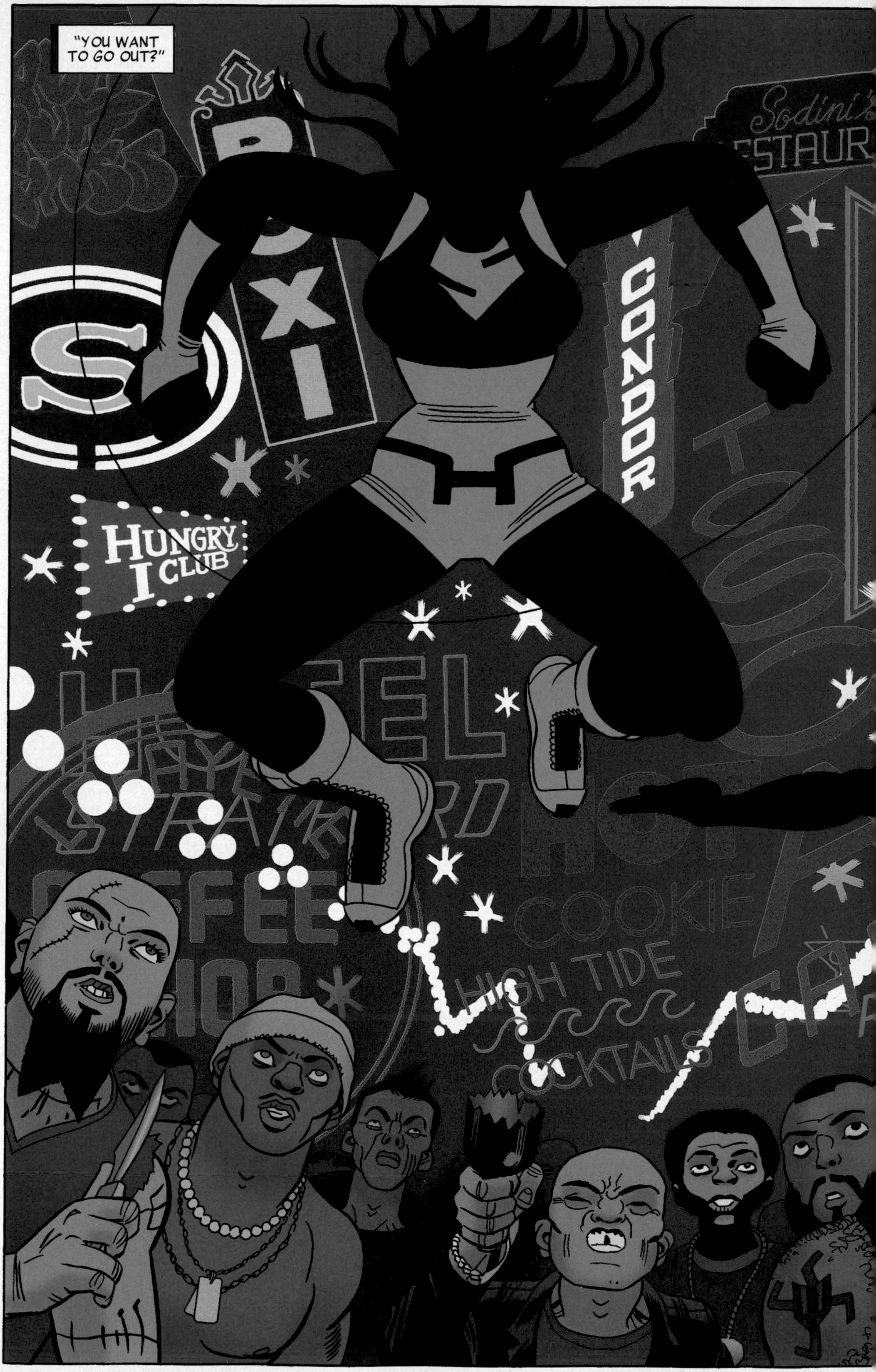
"YOU WANT TO GO OUT?"
CONDOR
HUNGRY I CLUB
COOKIE
HIGH TIDE
COCKTAILS

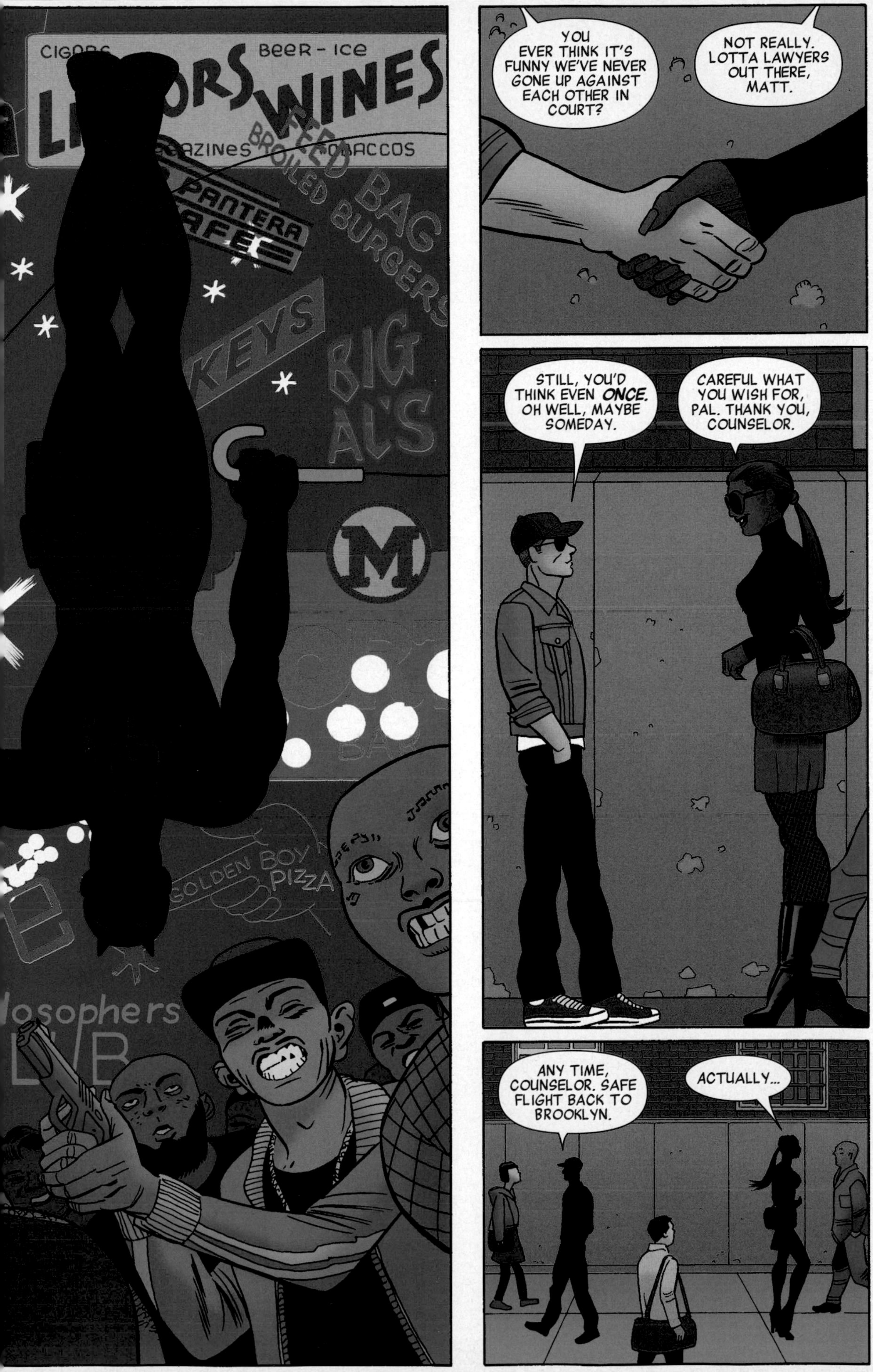
BEER - ICE
WINES
FEED BAG
BROILED BURGERS
PANTERA
KEYS
BIG AL'S
GOLDEN BOY PIZZA
YOU EVER THINK IT'S FUNNY WE'VE NEVER GONE UP AGAINST EACH OTHER IN COURT?
NOT REALLY. LOTTA LAWYERS OUT THERE, MATT.
STILL, YOU'D THINK EVEN ONCE. OH WELL, MAYBE SOMEDAY.
CAREFUL WHAT YOU WISH FOR, PAL. THANK YOU, COUNSELOR.
ANY TIME, COUNSELOR. SAFE FLIGHT BACK TO BROOKLYN.
ACTUALLY...

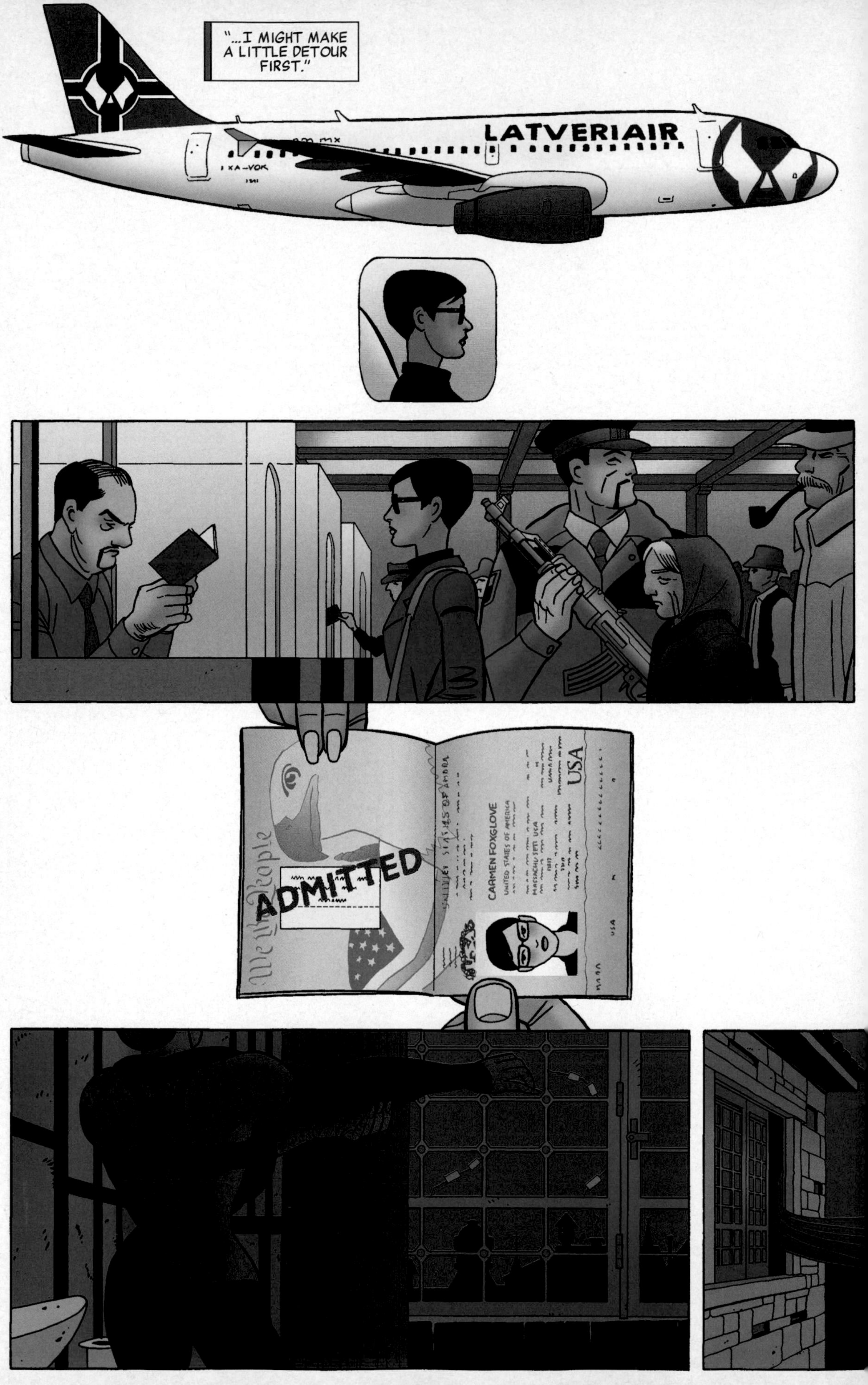
"...I MIGHT MAKE A LITTLE DETOUR FIRST."
LATVERIAIR
XA-VOK
ADMITTED
CARMEN FOXGLOVE
UNITED STATES OF AMERICA
USA

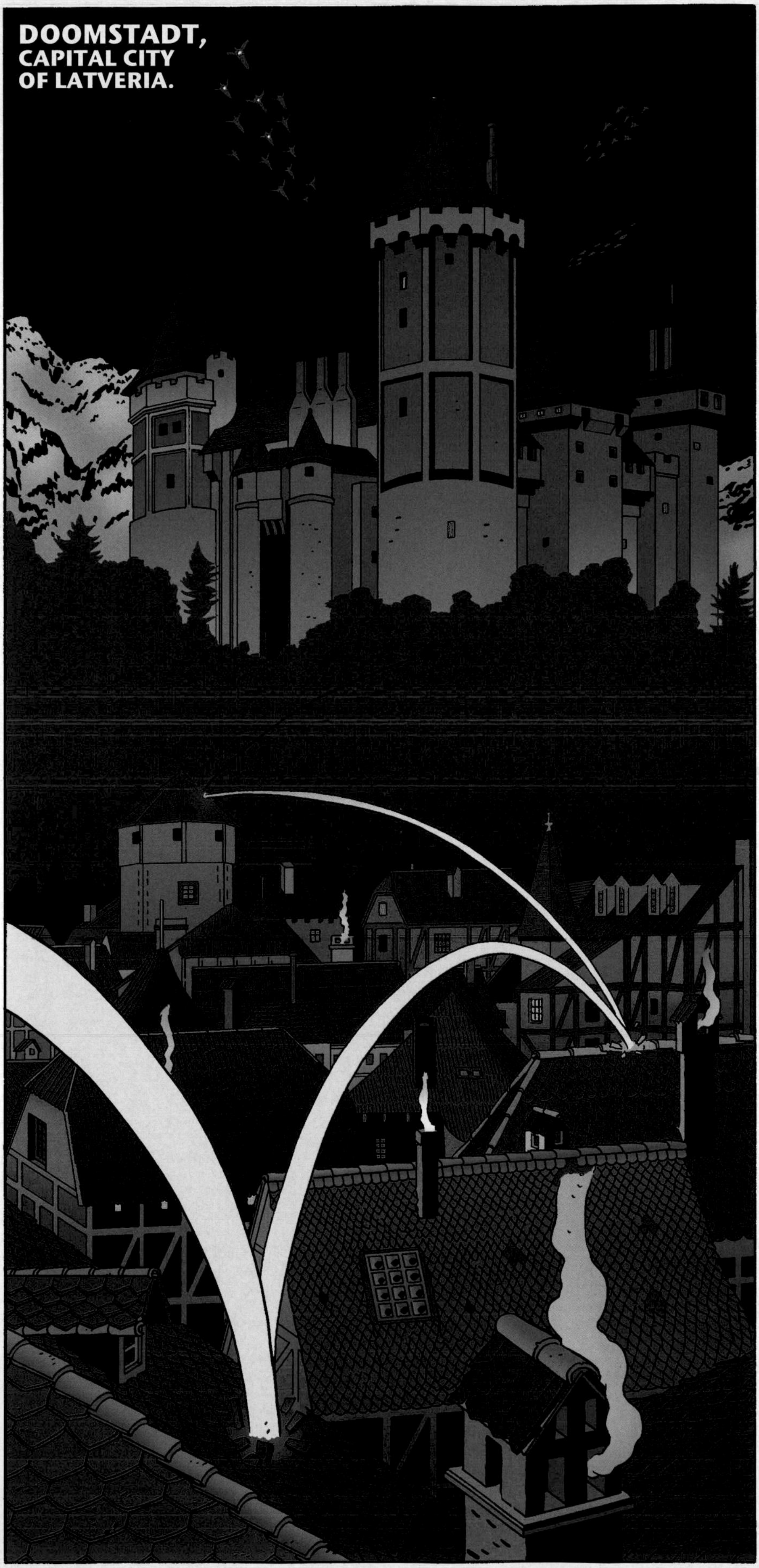
DOOMSTADT, CAPITAL CITY OF LATVERIA.

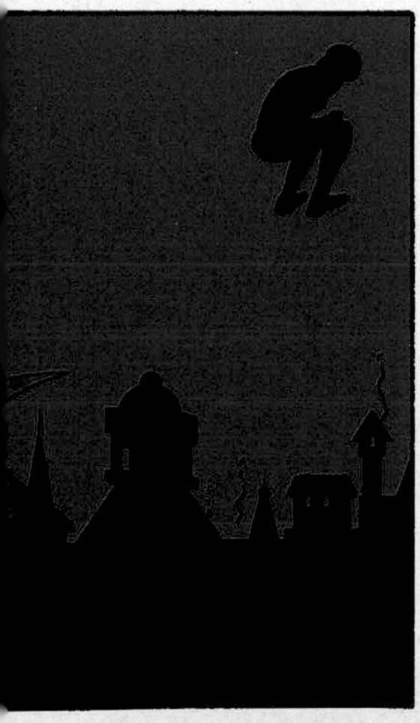

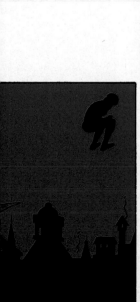

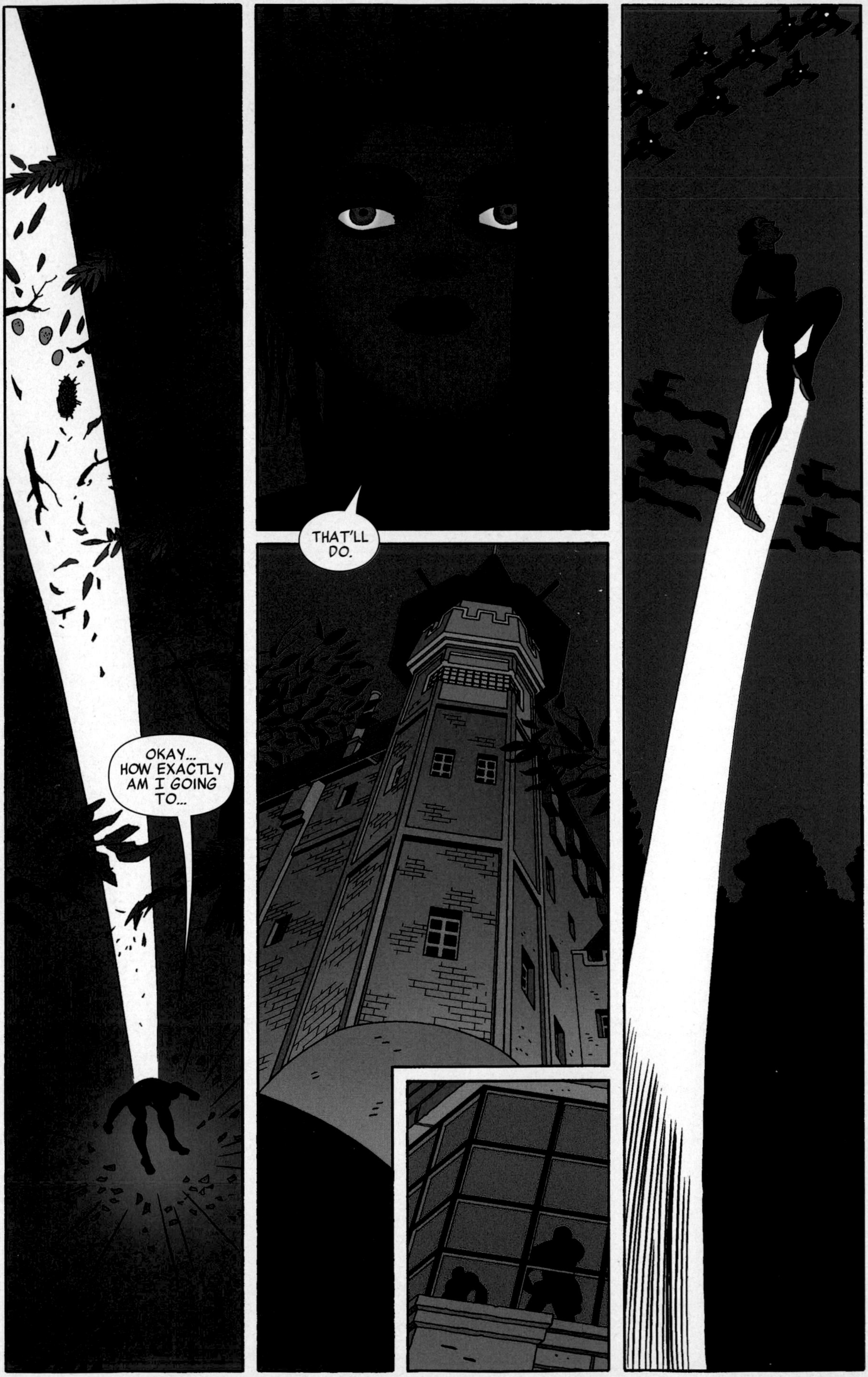
OKAY... HOW EXACTLY AM I GOING TO...
THAT'LL DO.

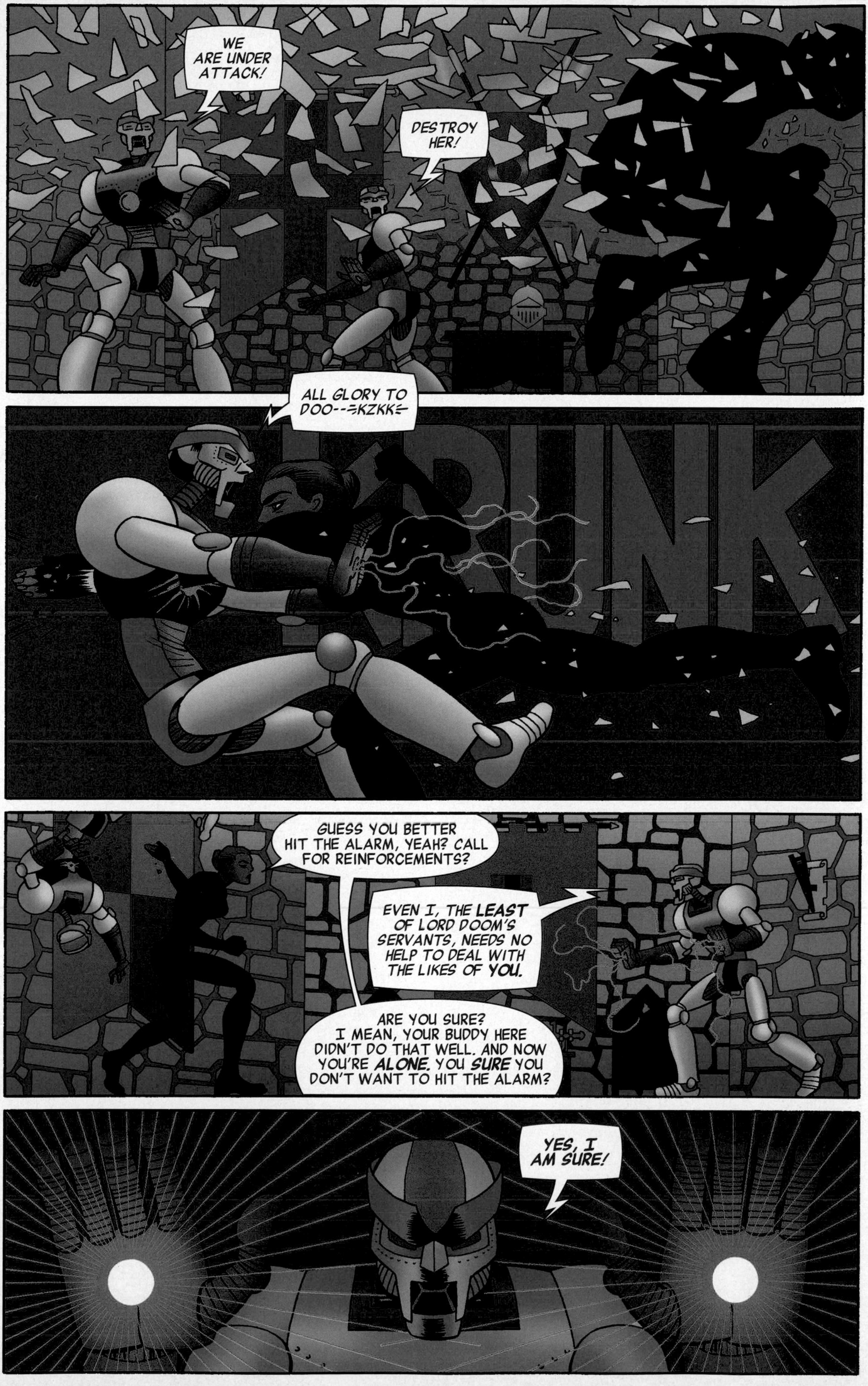
WE ARE UNDER ATTACK!
DESTROY HER!
ALL GLORY TO DOO--≡KZKK≡
KRUNK
GUESS YOU BETTER HIT THE ALARM, YEAH? CALL FOR REINFORCEMENTS?
EVEN I, THE LEAST OF LORD DOOM'S SERVANTS, NEEDS NO HELP TO DEAL WITH THE LIKES OF YOU.
ARE YOU SURE? I MEAN, YOUR BUDDY HERE DIDN'T DO THAT WELL. AND NOW YOU'RE ALONE. YOU SURE YOU DON'T WANT TO HIT THE ALARM?
YES, I AM SURE!

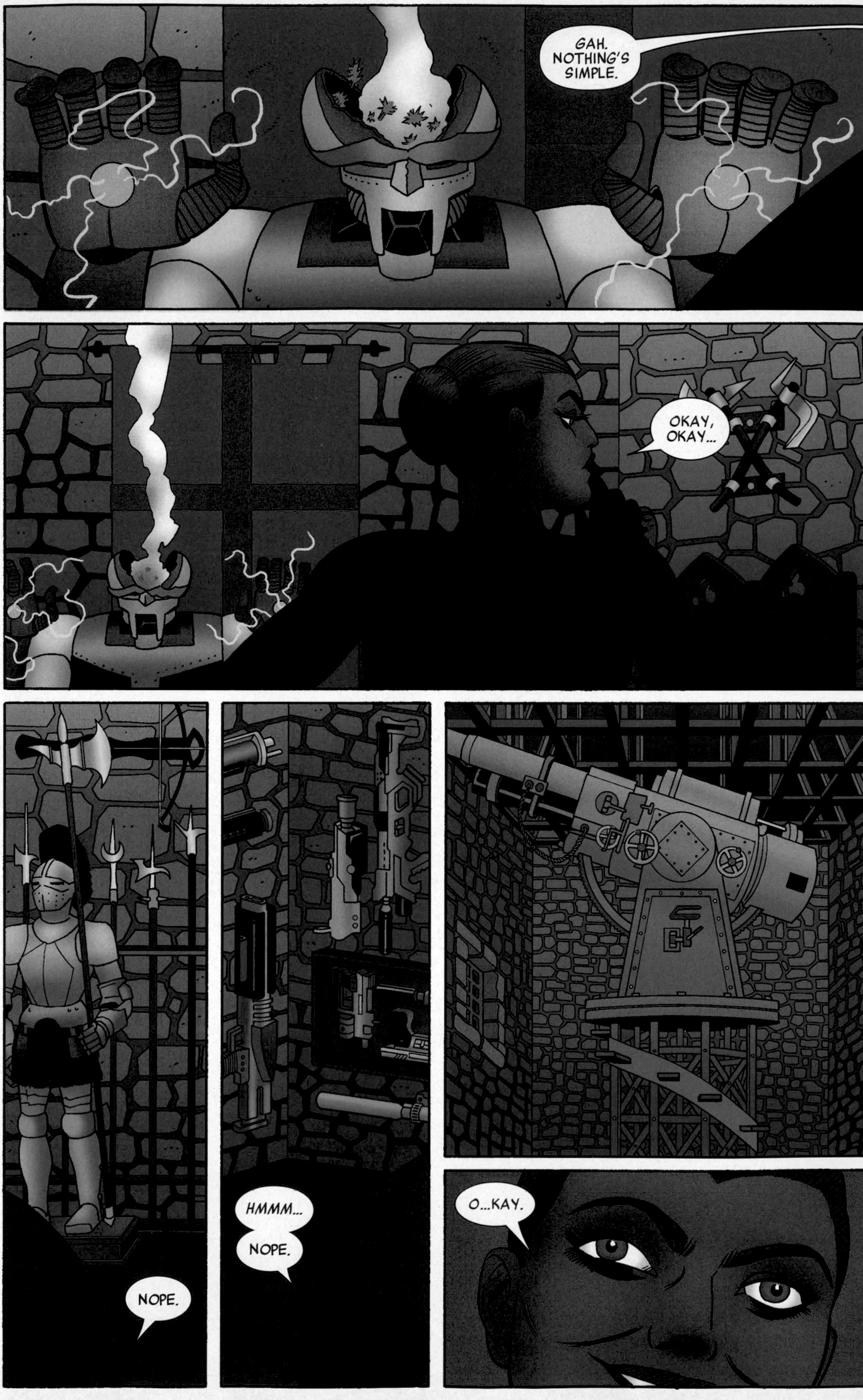
GAH. NOTHING'S SIMPLE.
OKAY, OKAY...
NOPE.
HMMM...
NOPE.
O...KAY.

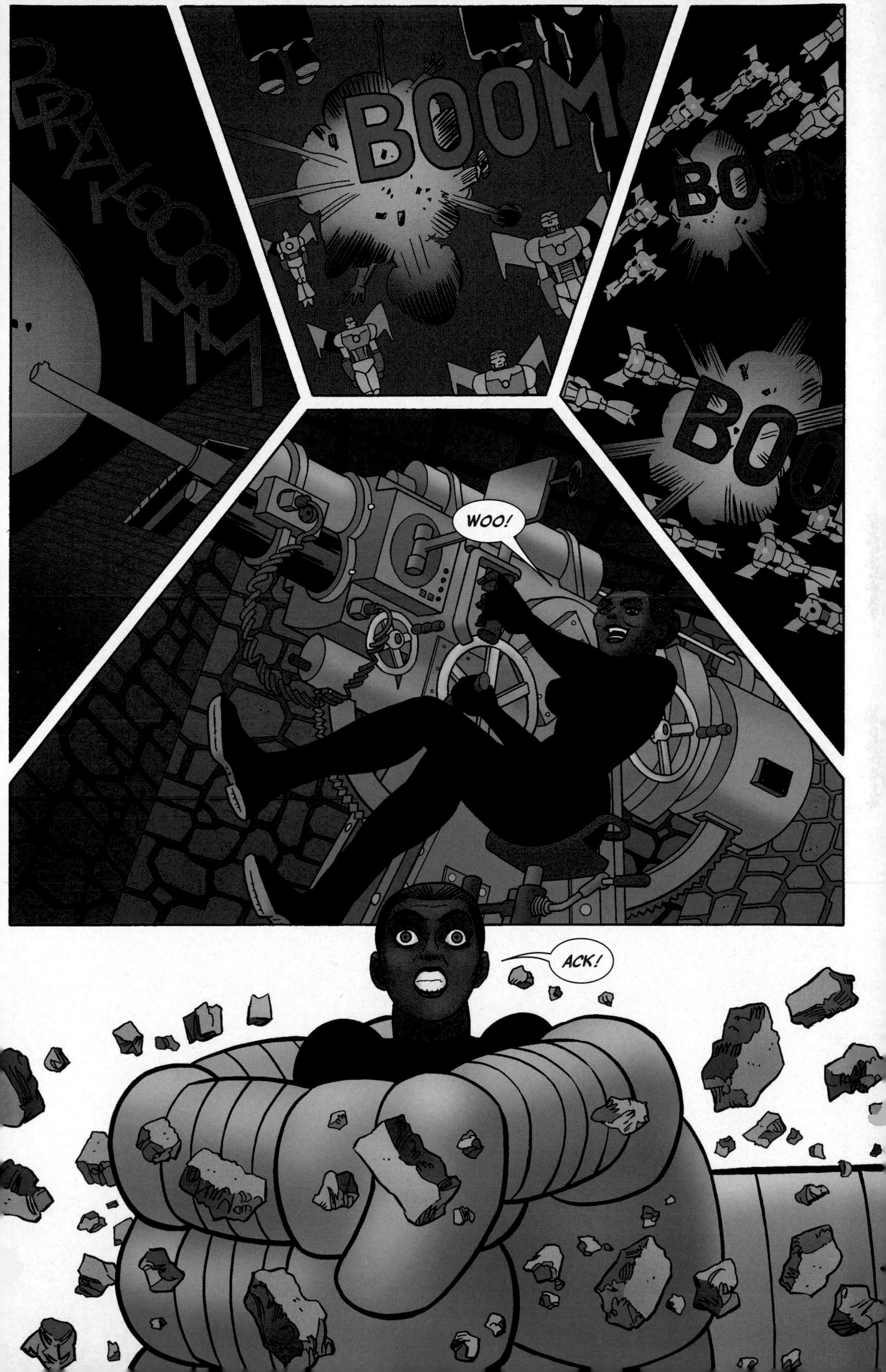
DDRAKOOOMMM
BOOM
BOOM
BOO
WOO!
ACK!

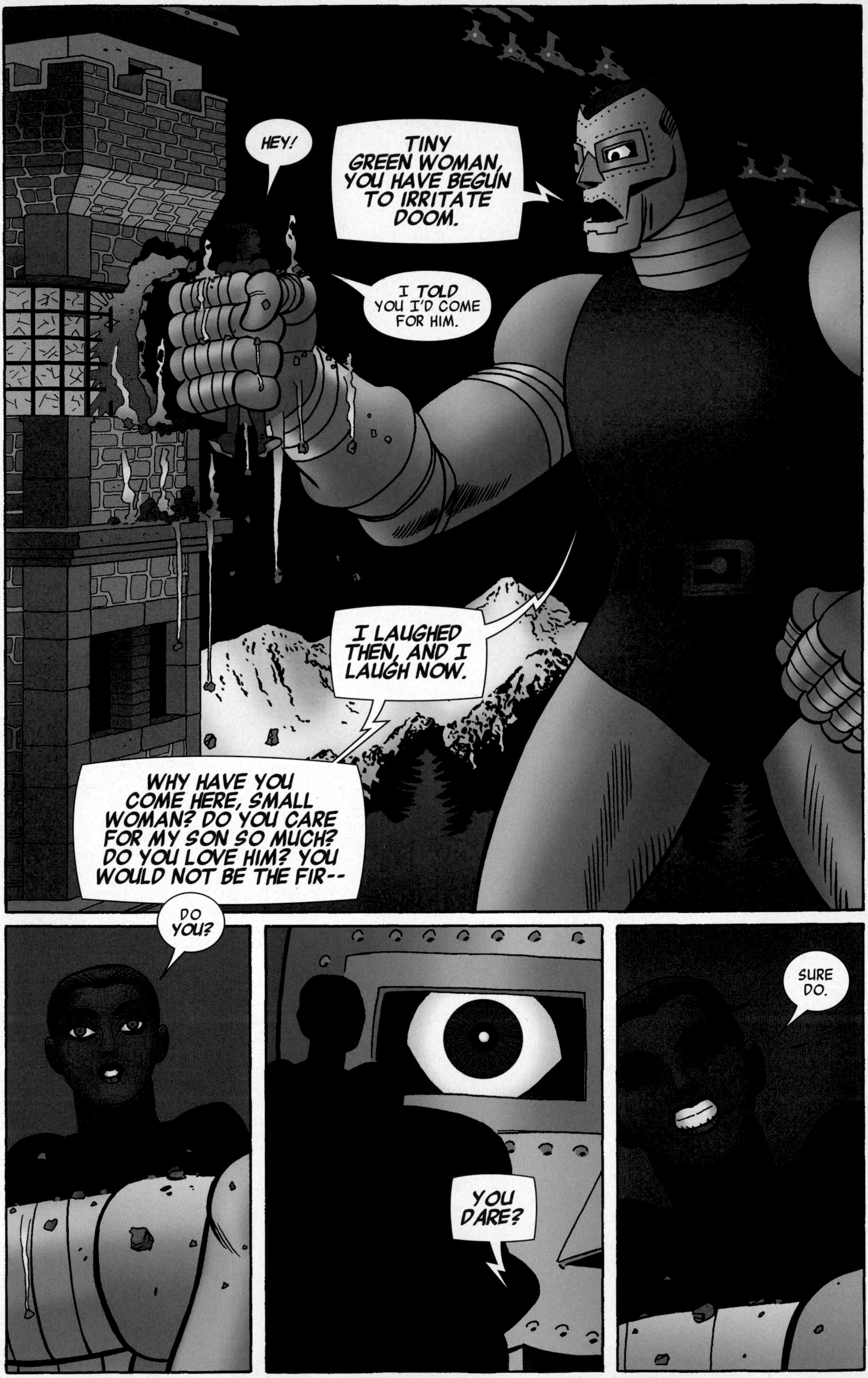

HEY!
TINY GREEN WOMAN, YOU HAVE BEGUN TO IRRITATE DOOM.
I TOLD YOU I'D COME FOR HIM.
I LAUGHED THEN, AND I LAUGH NOW.
WHY HAVE YOU COME HERE, SMALL WOMAN? DO YOU CARE FOR MY SON SO MUCH? DO YOU LOVE HIM? YOU WOULD NOT BE THE FIR--
DO YOU?
YOU DARE?
SURE DO.

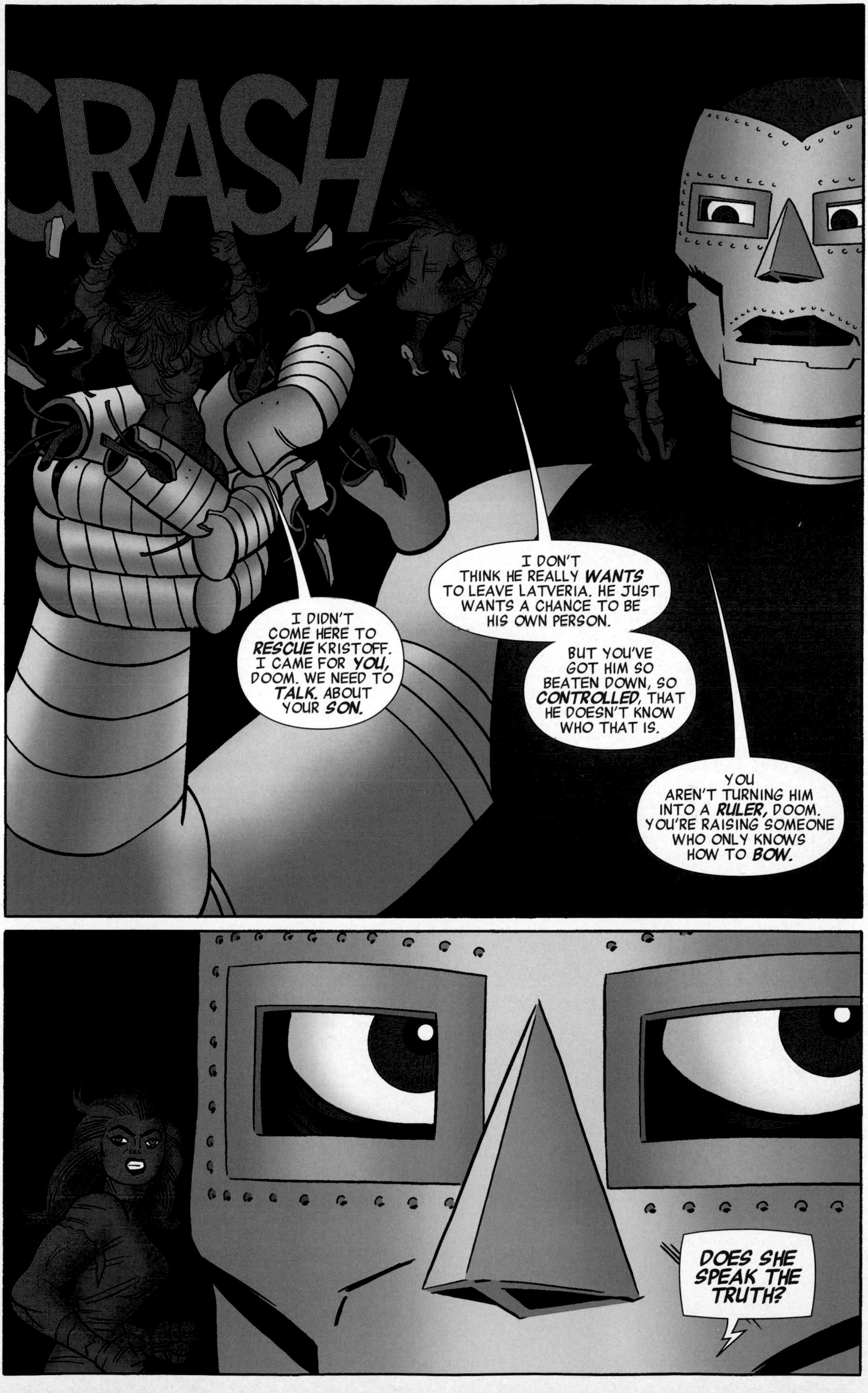
CRASH
I DIDN'T COME HERE TO RESCUE KRISTOFF. I CAME FOR YOU, DOOM. WE NEED TO TALK. ABOUT YOUR SON.
I DON'T THINK HE REALLY WANTS TO LEAVE LATVERIA. HE JUST WANTS A CHANCE TO BE HIS OWN PERSON.
BUT YOU'VE GOT HIM SO BEATEN DOWN, SO CONTROLLED, THAT HE DOESN'T KNOW WHO THAT IS.
YOU AREN'T TURNING HIM INTO A RULER, DOOM. YOU'RE RAISING SOMEONE WHO ONLY KNOWS HOW TO BOW.
DOES SHE SPEAK THE TRUTH?

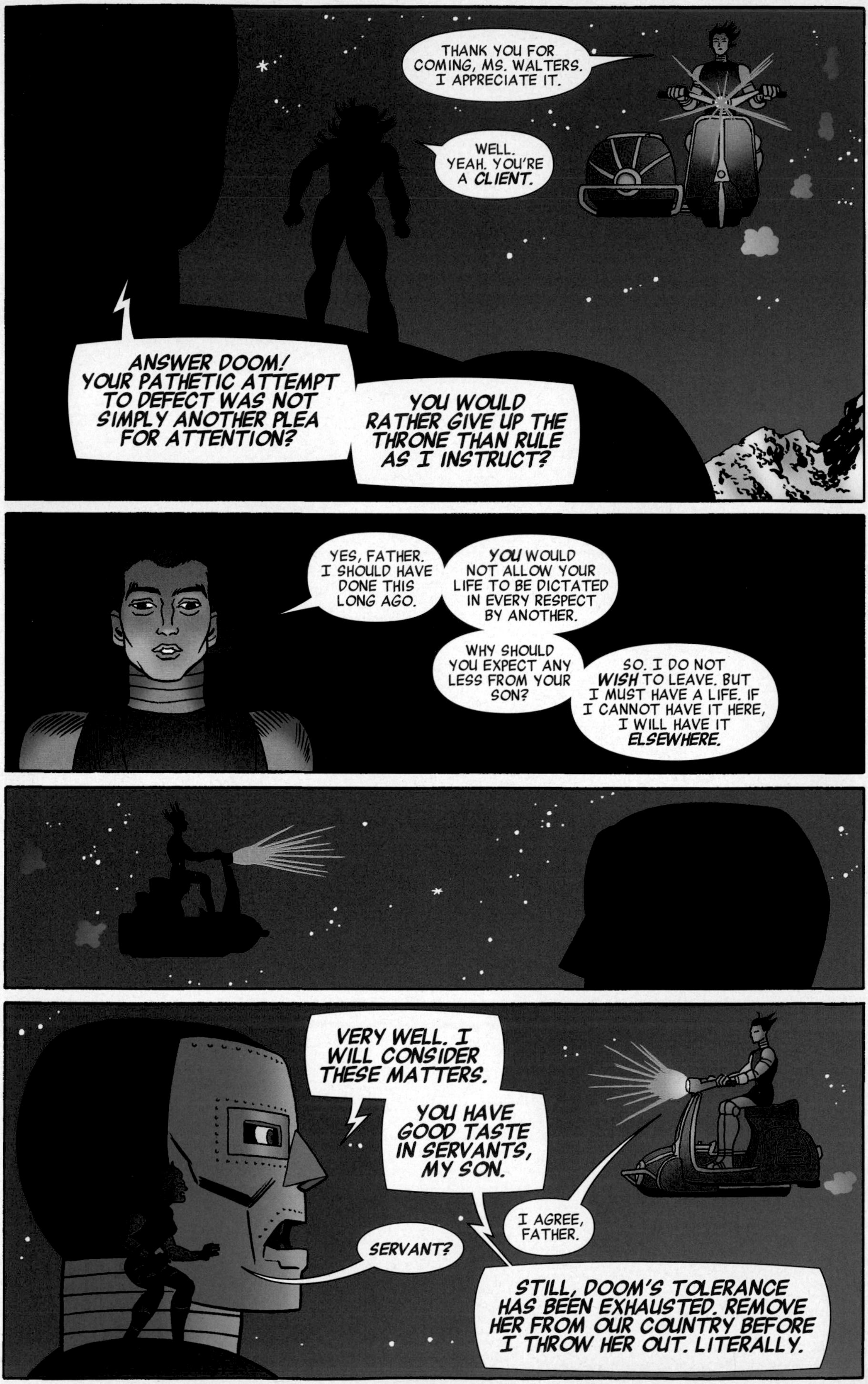
THANK YOU FOR COMING, MS. WALTERS. I APPRECIATE IT.
WELL. YEAH. YOU'RE A CLIENT.
ANSWER DOOM! YOUR PATHETIC ATTEMPT TO DEFECT WAS NOT SIMPLY ANOTHER PLEA FOR ATTENTION?
YOU WOULD RATHER GIVE UP THE THRONE THAN RULE AS I INSTRUCT?
YES, FATHER. I SHOULD HAVE DONE THIS LONG AGO.
YOU WOULD NOT ALLOW YOUR LIFE TO BE DICTATED IN EVERY RESPECT BY ANOTHER.
WHY SHOULD YOU EXPECT ANY LESS FROM YOUR SON?
SO. I DO NOT WISH TO LEAVE. BUT I MUST HAVE A LIFE. IF I CANNOT HAVE IT HERE, I WILL HAVE IT ELSEWHERE.
VERY WELL. I WILL CONSIDER THESE MATTERS.
YOU HAVE GOOD TASTE IN SERVANTS, MY SON.
I AGREE, FATHER.
SERVANT?
STILL, DOOM'S TOLERANCE HAS BEEN EXHAUSTED. REMOVE HER FROM OUR COUNTRY BEFORE I THROW HER OUT. LITERALLY.

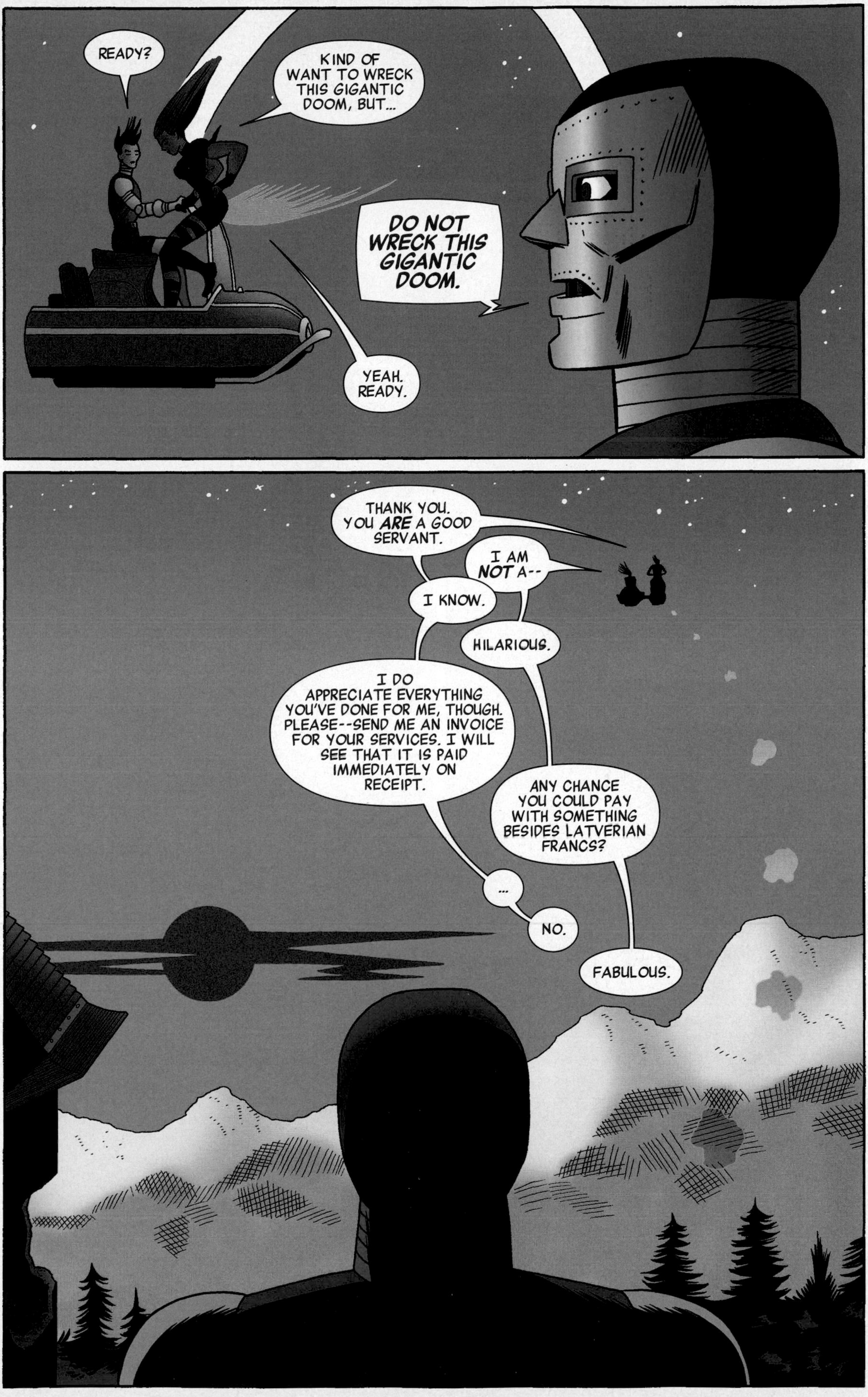
READY?
KIND OF WANT TO WRECK THIS GIGANTIC DOOM, BUT...
DO NOT WRECK THIS GIGANTIC DOOM.
YEAH. READY.
THANK YOU. YOU ARE A GOOD SERVANT.
I AM NOT A--
I KNOW.
HILARIOUS.
I DO APPRECIATE EVERYTHING YOU'VE DONE FOR ME, THOUGH. PLEASE--SEND ME AN INVOICE FOR YOUR SERVICES. I WILL SEE THAT IT IS PAID IMMEDIATELY ON RECEIPT.
ANY CHANCE YOU COULD PAY WITH SOMETHING BESIDES LATVERIAN FRANCS?
...
NO.
FABULOUS.

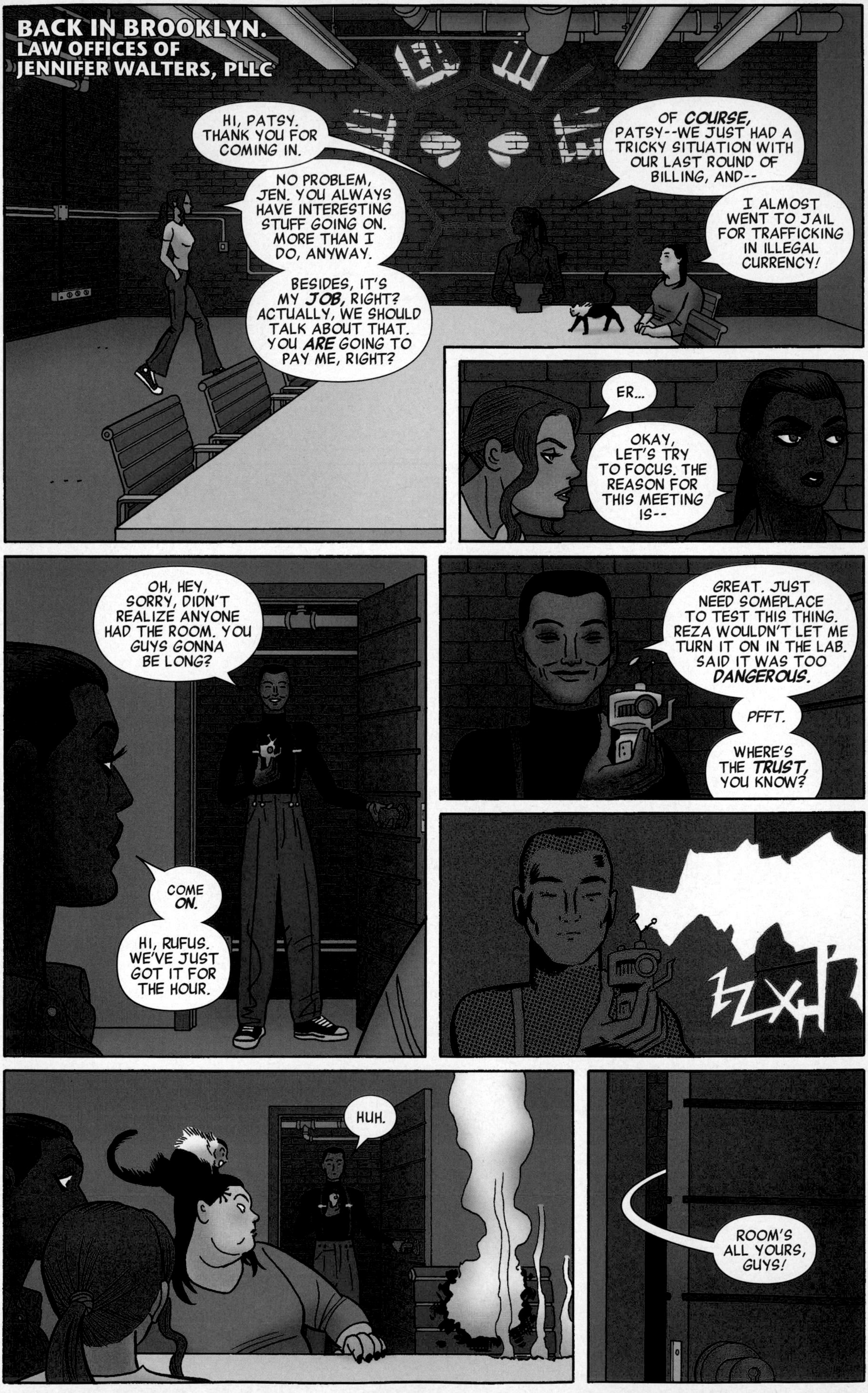
BACK IN BROOKLYN. LAW OFFICES OF JENNIFER WALTERS, PLLC
HI, PATSY. THANK YOU FOR COMING IN.
NO PROBLEM, JEN. YOU ALWAYS HAVE INTERESTING STUFF GOING ON. MORE THAN I DO, ANYWAY.
BESIDES, IT'S MY JOB, RIGHT? ACTUALLY, WE SHOULD TALK ABOUT THAT. YOU ARE GOING TO PAY ME, RIGHT?
OF COURSE, PATSY--WE JUST HAD A TRICKY SITUATION WITH OUR LAST ROUND OF BILLING, AND--
I ALMOST WENT TO JAIL FOR TRAFFICKING IN ILLEGAL CURRENCY!
ER...
OKAY, LET'S TRY TO FOCUS. THE REASON FOR THIS MEETING IS--
OH, HEY, SORRY, DIDN'T REALIZE ANYONE HAD THE ROOM. YOU GUYS GONNA BE LONG?
COME ON.
HI, RUFUS. WE'VE JUST GOT IT FOR THE HOUR.
GREAT. JUST NEED SOMEPLACE TO TEST THIS THING. REZA WOULDN'T LET ME TURN IT ON IN THE LAB. SAID IT WAS TOO DANGEROUS.
PFFT.
WHERE'S THE TRUST, YOU KNOW?
ZZXH!
HUH.
ROOM'S ALL YOURS, GUYS!

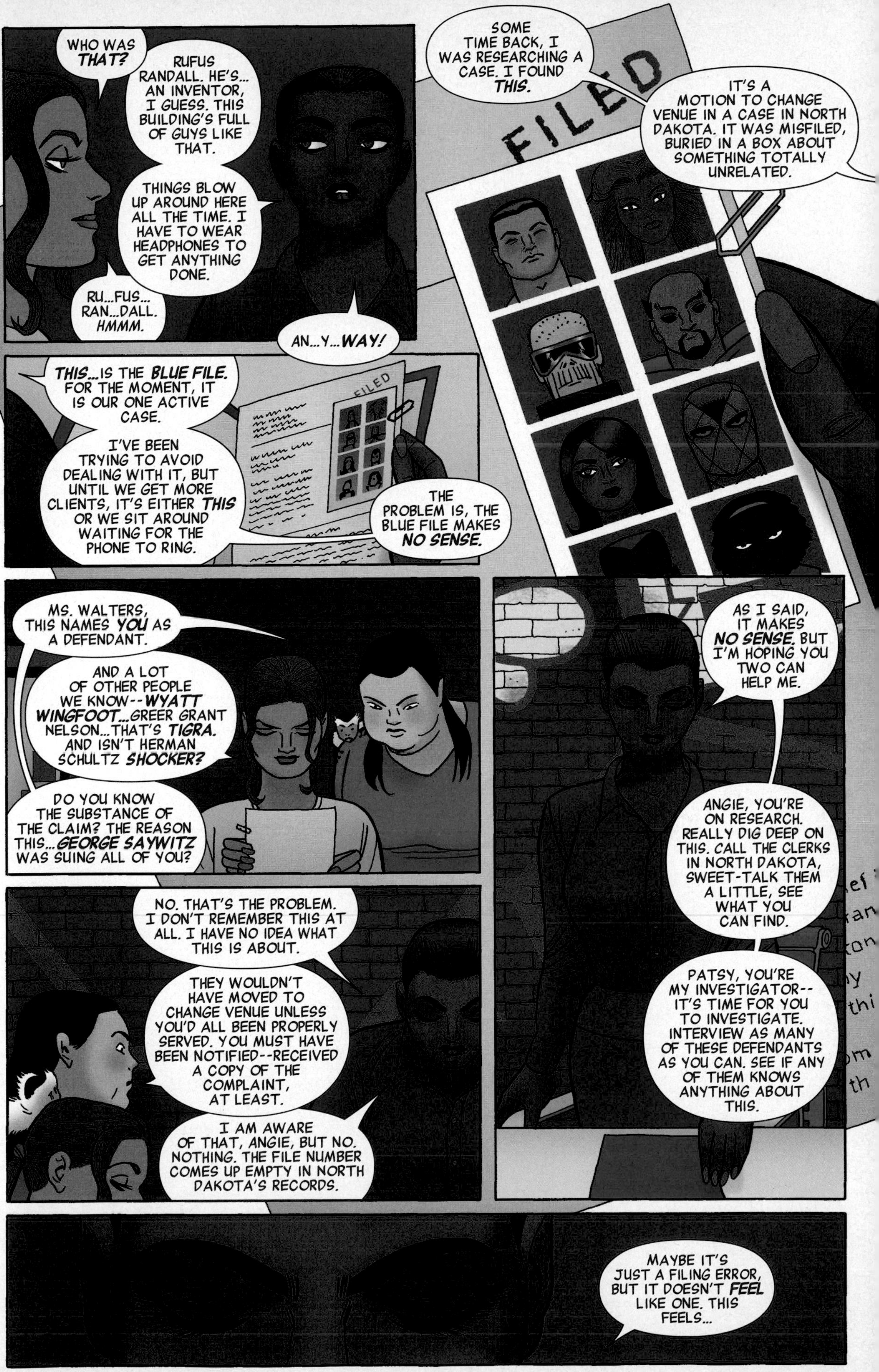
WHO WAS THAT?
RUFUS RANDALL. HE'S... AN INVENTOR, I GUESS. THIS BUILDING'S FULL OF GUYS LIKE THAT.
THINGS BLOW UP AROUND HERE ALL THE TIME. I HAVE TO WEAR HEADPHONES TO GET ANYTHING DONE.
RU...FUS... RAN...DALL. HMMM.
AN...Y...WAY!
SOME TIME BACK, I WAS RESEARCHING A CASE. I FOUND THIS.
FILED
IT'S A MOTION TO CHANGE VENUE IN A CASE IN NORTH DAKOTA. IT WAS MISFILED, BURIED IN A BOX ABOUT SOMETHING TOTALLY UNRELATED.
THIS...IS THE BLUE FILE. FOR THE MOMENT, IT IS OUR ONE ACTIVE CASE.
I'VE BEEN TRYING TO AVOID DEALING WITH IT, BUT UNTIL WE GET MORE CLIENTS, IT'S EITHER THIS OR WE SIT AROUND WAITING FOR THE PHONE TO RING.
THE PROBLEM IS, THE BLUE FILE MAKES NO SENSE.
MS. WALTERS, THIS NAMES YOU AS A DEFENDANT.
AND A LOT OF OTHER PEOPLE WE KNOW--WYATT WINGFOOT...GREER GRANT NELSON...THAT'S TIGRA. AND ISN'T HERMAN SCHULTZ SHOCKER?
DO YOU KNOW THE SUBSTANCE OF THE CLAIM? THE REASON THIS...GEORGE SAYWITZ WAS SUING ALL OF YOU?
AS I SAID, IT MAKES NO SENSE. BUT I'M HOPING YOU TWO CAN HELP ME.
NO. THAT'S THE PROBLEM. I DON'T REMEMBER THIS AT ALL. I HAVE NO IDEA WHAT THIS IS ABOUT.
THEY WOULDN'T HAVE MOVED TO CHANGE VENUE UNLESS YOU'D ALL BEEN PROPERLY SERVED. YOU MUST HAVE BEEN NOTIFIED--RECEIVED A COPY OF THE COMPLAINT, AT LEAST.
I AM AWARE OF THAT, ANGIE, BUT NO. NOTHING. THE FILE NUMBER COMES UP EMPTY IN NORTH DAKOTA'S RECORDS.
ANGIE, YOU'RE ON RESEARCH. REALLY DIG DEEP ON THIS. CALL THE CLERKS IN NORTH DAKOTA, SWEET-TALK THEM A LITTLE, SEE WHAT YOU CAN FIND.
PATSY, YOU'RE MY INVESTIGATOR--IT'S TIME FOR YOU TO INVESTIGATE. INTERVIEW AS MANY OF THESE DEFENDANTS AS YOU CAN. SEE IF ANY OF THEM KNOWS ANYTHING ABOUT THIS.
MAYBE IT'S JUST A FILING ERROR, BUT IT DOESN'T FEEL LIKE ONE. THIS FEELS...

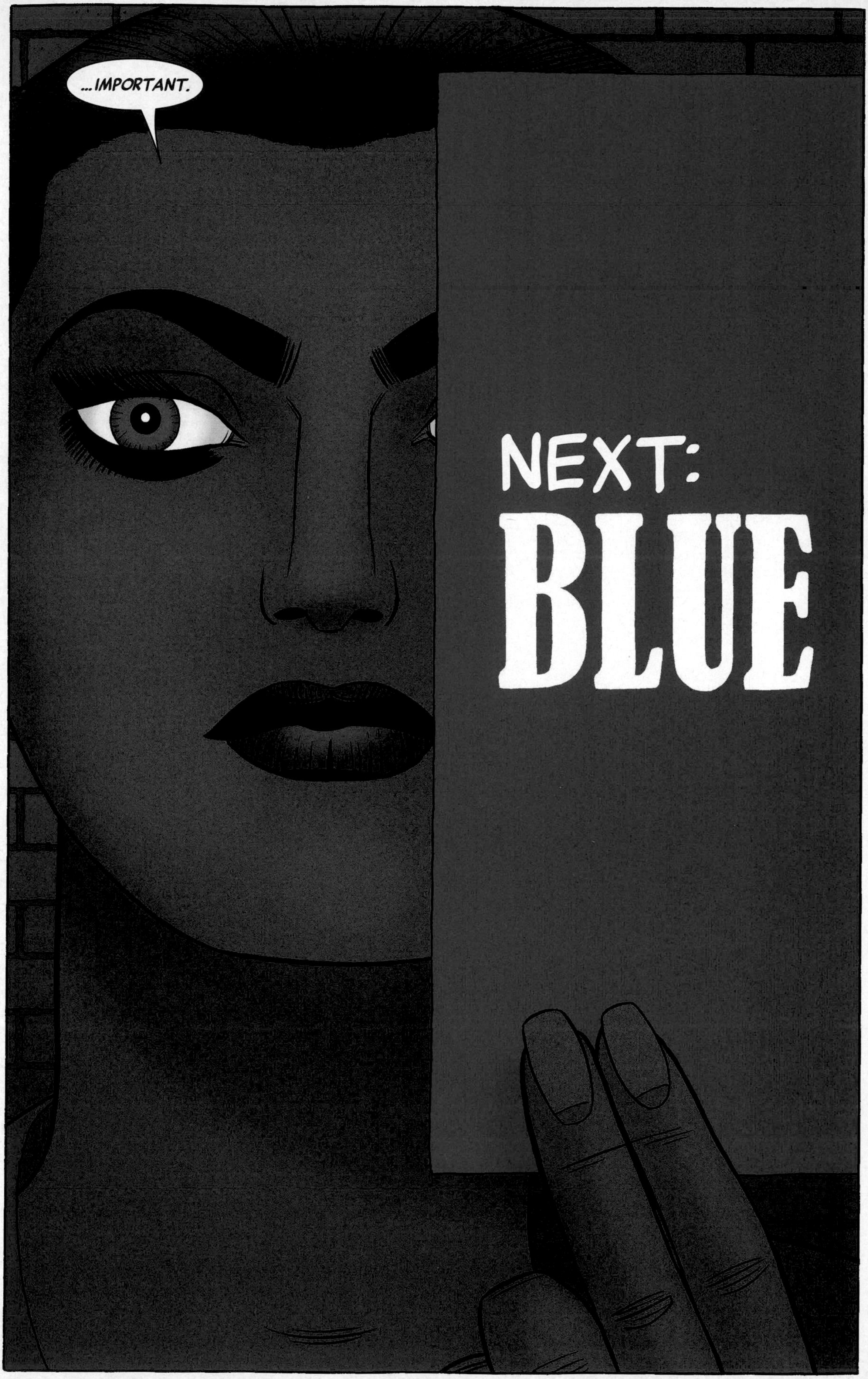
...IMPORTANT.
NEXT:
BLUE

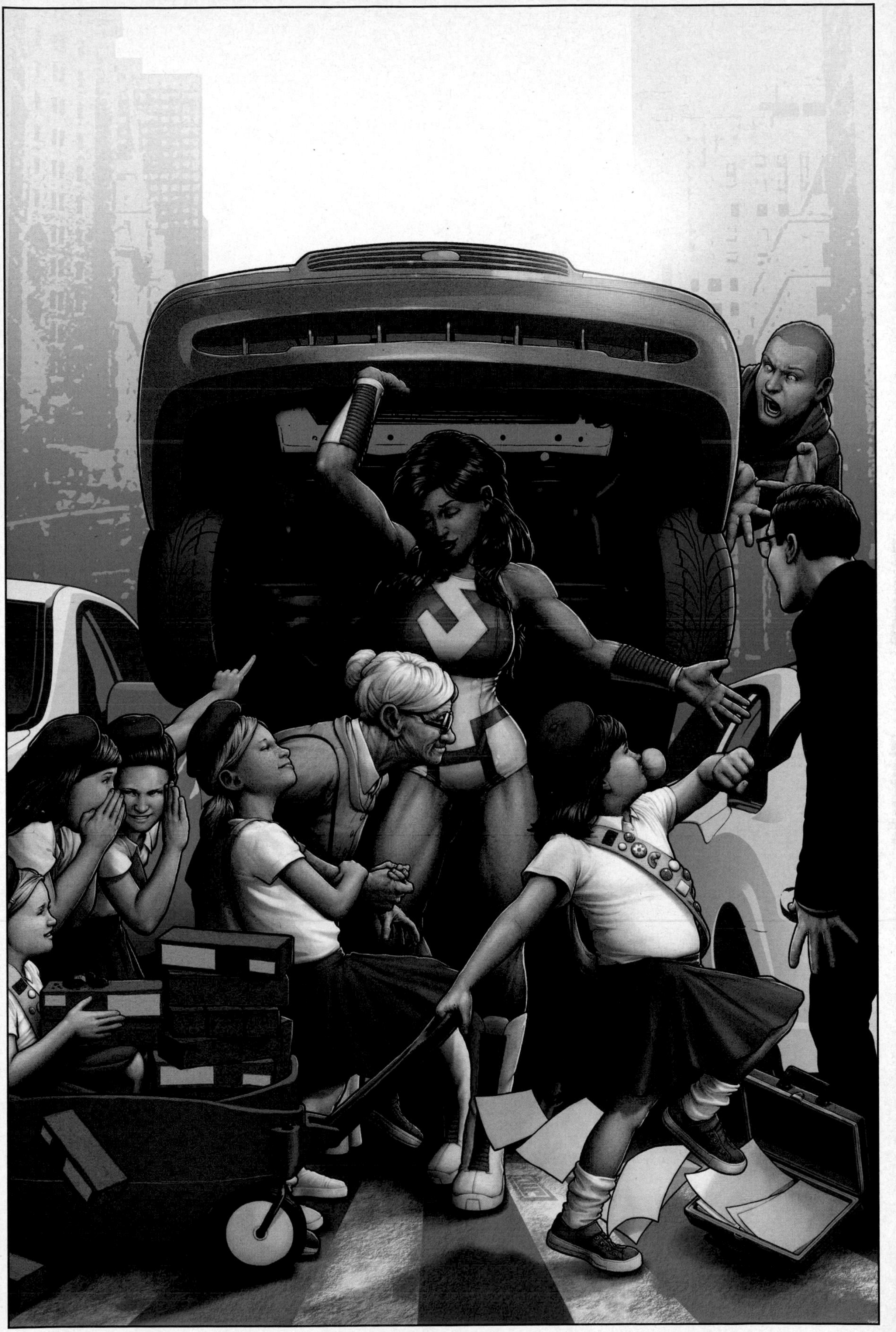

SHE-HULK #1 VARIANT BY JOHN TYLER CHRISTOPHER

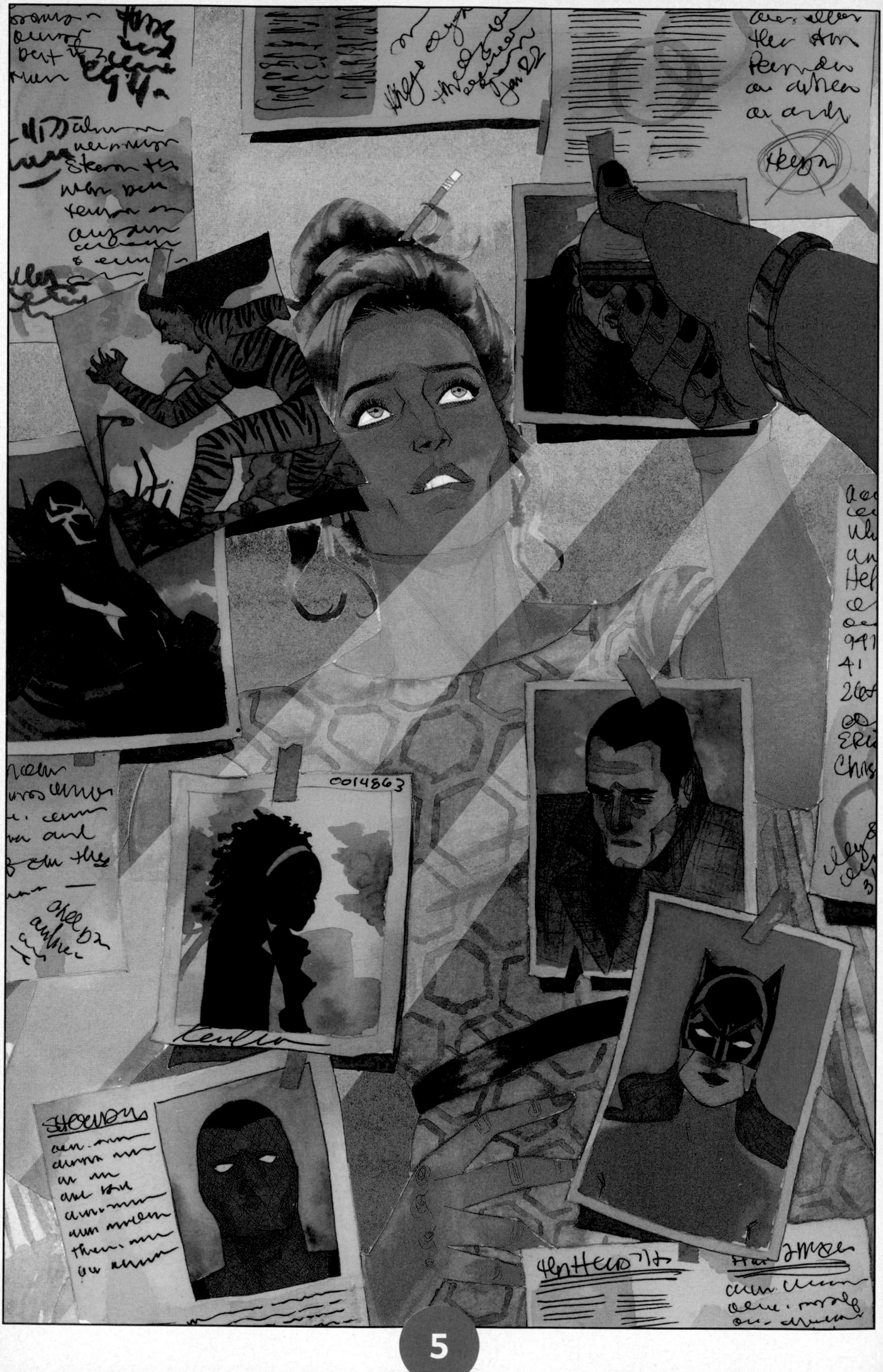
0014863

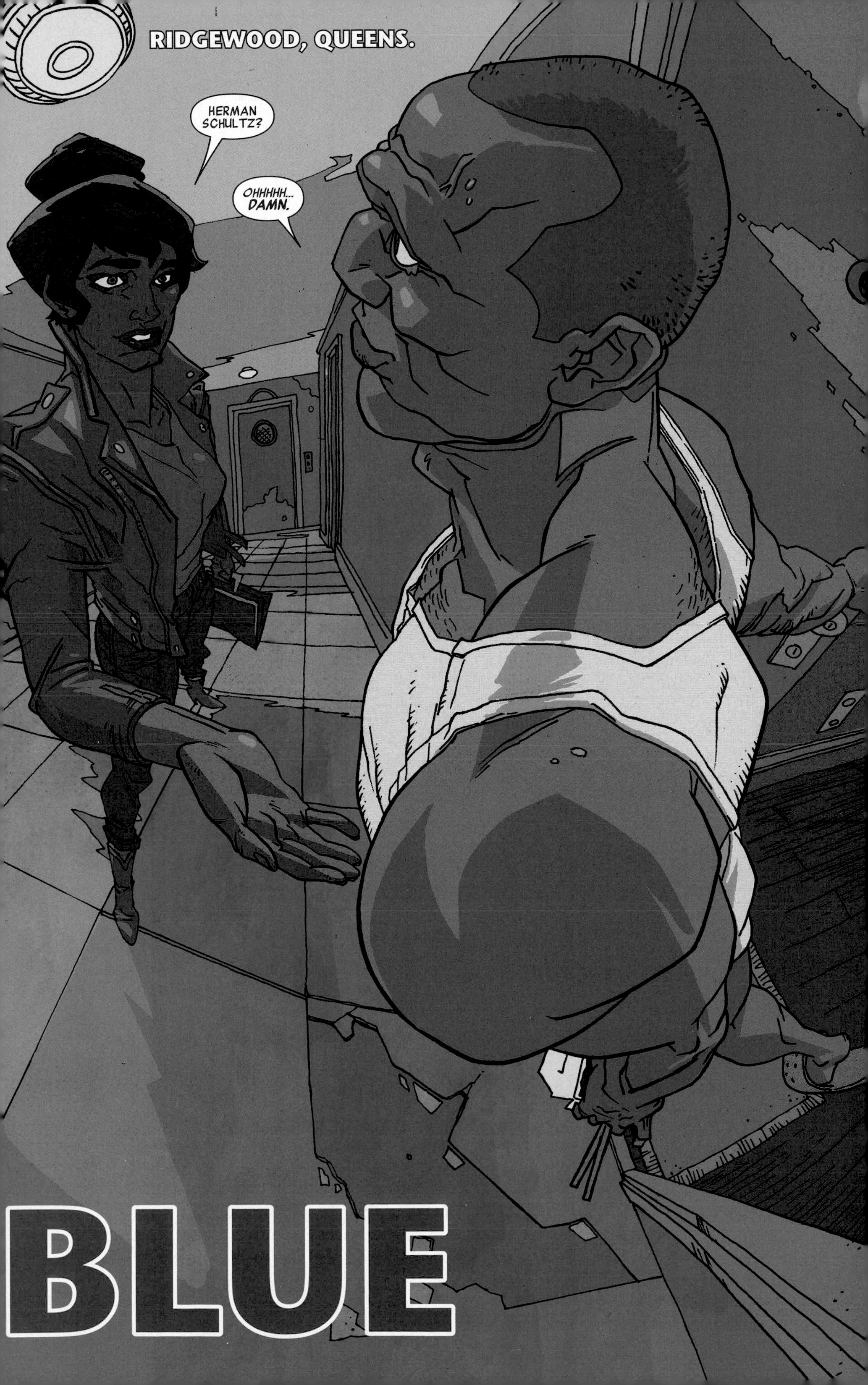
RIDGEWOOD, QUEENS.
HERMAN SCHULTZ?
OHHHHH... DAMN.
BLUE

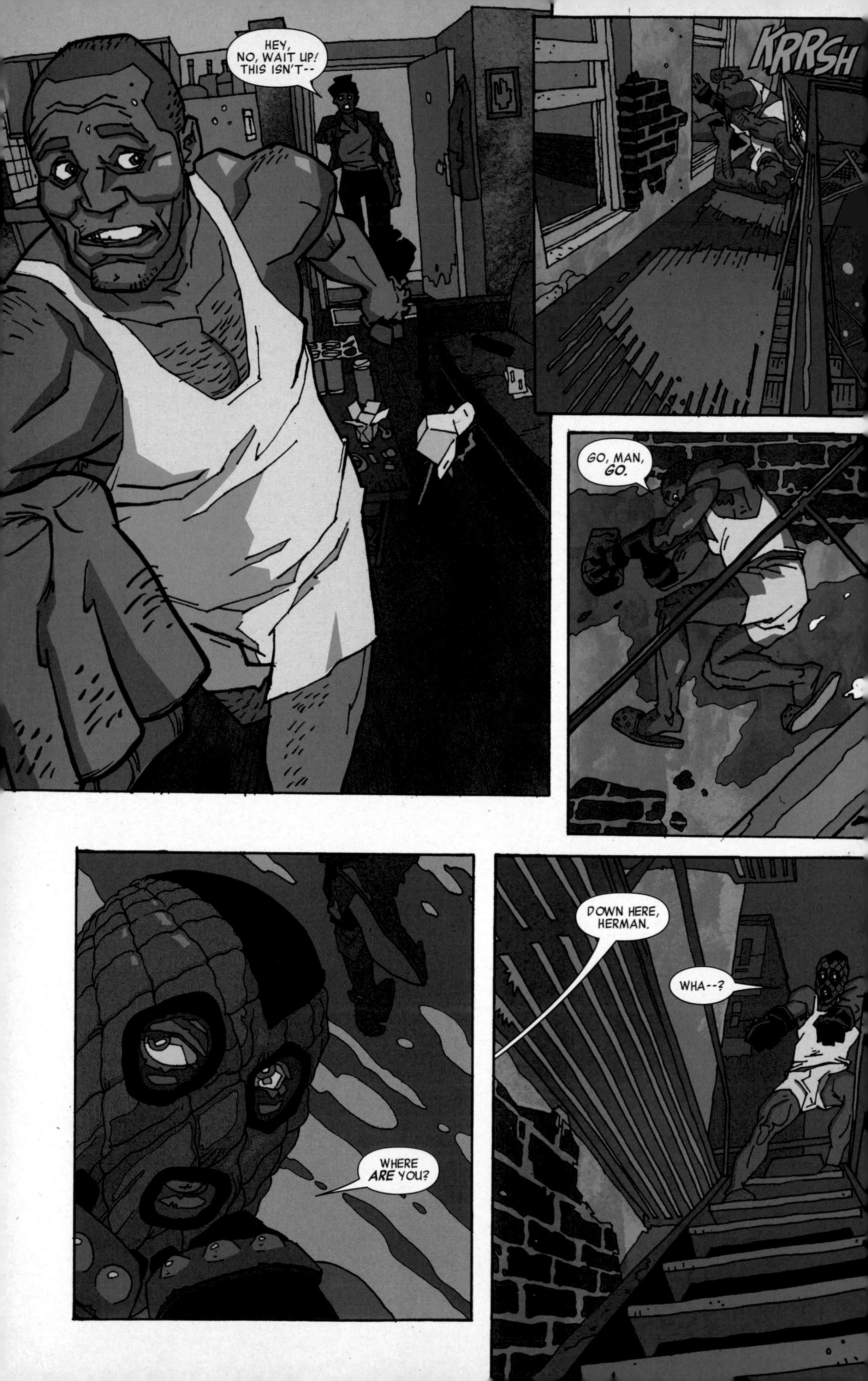
HEY, NO, WAIT UP! THIS ISN'T--
KRRSH
GO, MAN, GO.
WHERE ARE YOU?
DOWN HERE, HERMAN.
WHA--?

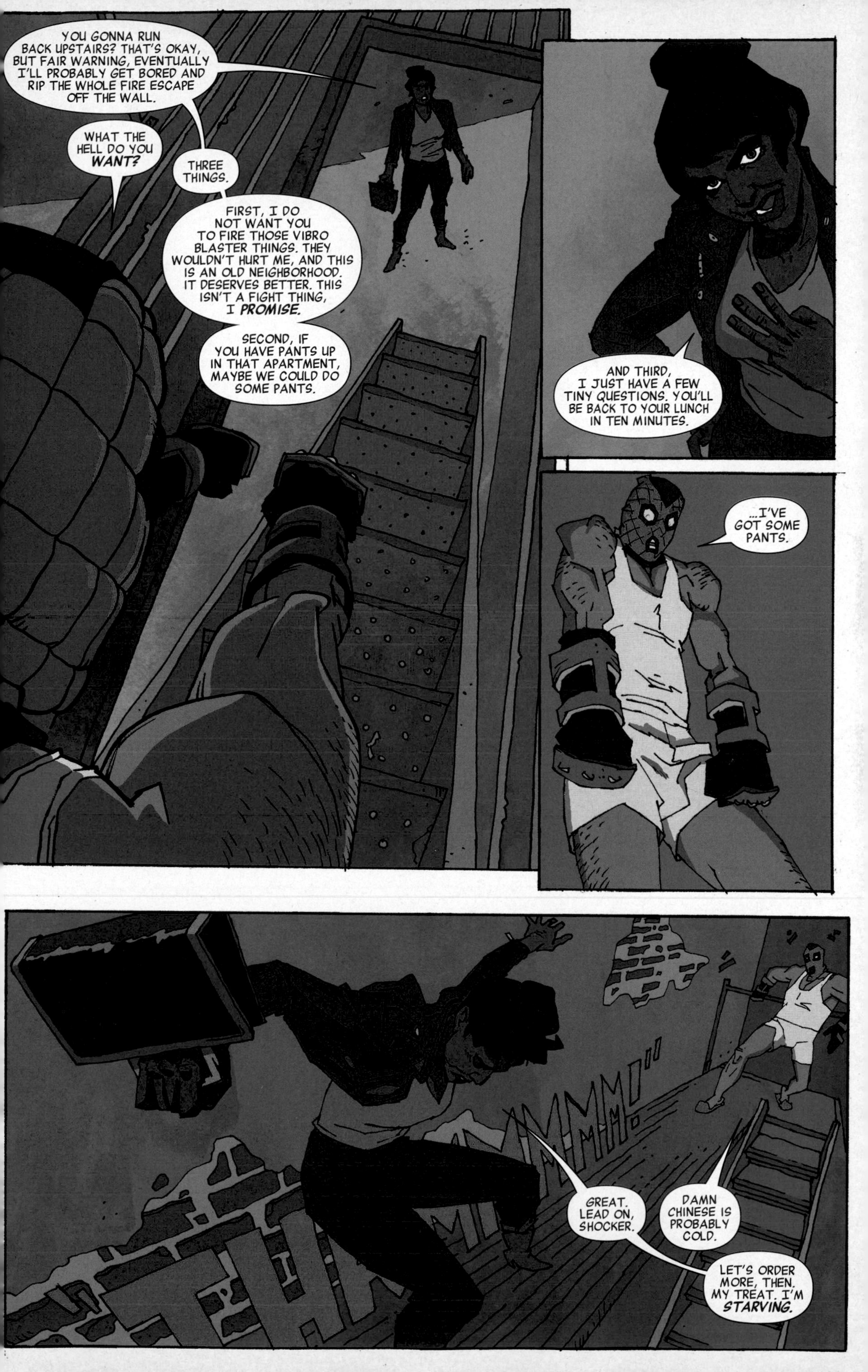
YOU GONNA RUN BACK UPSTAIRS? THAT'S OKAY, BUT FAIR WARNING, EVENTUALLY I'LL PROBABLY GET BORED AND RIP THE WHOLE FIRE ESCAPE OFF THE WALL.
WHAT THE HELL DO YOU **WANT?**
THREE THINGS.
FIRST, I DO NOT WANT YOU TO FIRE THOSE VIBRO BLASTER THINGS. THEY WOULDN'T HURT ME, AND THIS IS AN OLD NEIGHBORHOOD. IT DESERVES BETTER. THIS ISN'T A FIGHT THING, I **PROMISE.**
SECOND, IF YOU HAVE PANTS UP IN THAT APARTMENT, MAYBE WE COULD DO SOME PANTS.
AND THIRD, I JUST HAVE A FEW TINY QUESTIONS. YOU'LL BE BACK TO YOUR LUNCH IN TEN MINUTES.
...I'VE GOT SOME PANTS.
GREAT. LEAD ON, SHOCKER.
DAMN CHINESE IS PROBABLY COLD.
LET'S ORDER MORE, THEN. MY TREAT. I'M **STARVING.**

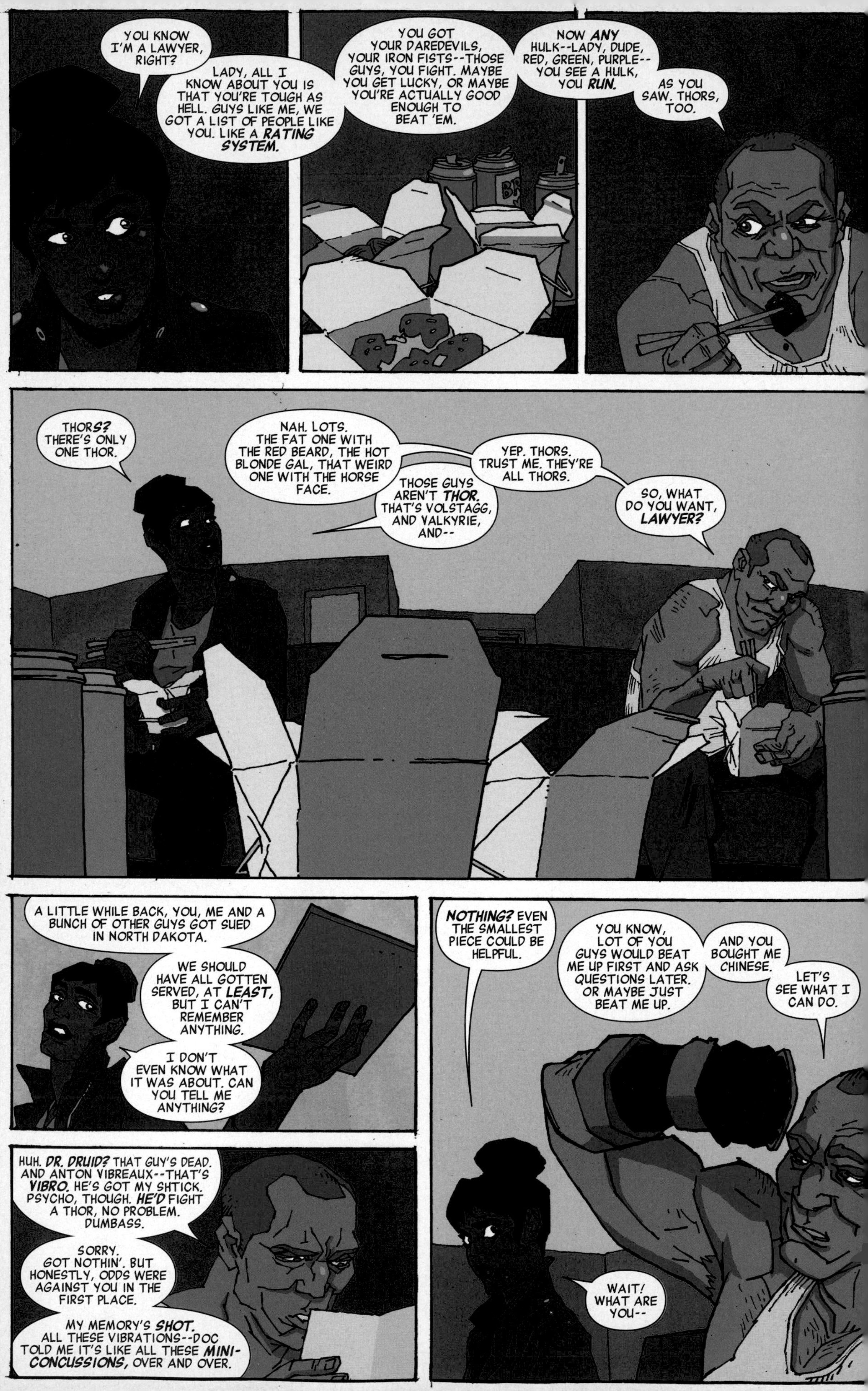
YOU KNOW I'M A LAWYER, RIGHT?
LADY, ALL I KNOW ABOUT YOU IS THAT YOU'RE TOUGH AS HELL. GUYS LIKE ME, WE GOT A LIST OF PEOPLE LIKE YOU. LIKE A RATING SYSTEM.
YOU GOT YOUR DAREDEVILS, YOUR IRON FISTS--THOSE GUYS, YOU FIGHT. MAYBE YOU GET LUCKY, OR MAYBE YOU'RE ACTUALLY GOOD ENOUGH TO BEAT 'EM.
NOW ANY HULK--LADY, DUDE, RED, GREEN, PURPLE--YOU SEE A HULK, YOU RUN.
AS YOU SAW. THORS, TOO.
THORS? THERE'S ONLY ONE THOR.
NAH. LOTS. THE FAT ONE WITH THE RED BEARD, THE HOT BLONDE GAL, THAT WEIRD ONE WITH THE HORSE FACE.
THOSE GUYS AREN'T THOR. THAT'S VOLSTAGG, AND VALKYRIE, AND--
YEP. THORS. TRUST ME. THEY'RE ALL THORS.
SO, WHAT DO YOU WANT, LAWYER?
A LITTLE WHILE BACK, YOU, ME AND A BUNCH OF OTHER GUYS GOT SUED IN NORTH DAKOTA.
WE SHOULD HAVE ALL GOTTEN SERVED, AT LEAST, BUT I CAN'T REMEMBER ANYTHING.
I DON'T EVEN KNOW WHAT IT WAS ABOUT. CAN YOU TELL ME ANYTHING?
HUH. DR. DRUID? THAT GUY'S DEAD. AND ANTON VIBREAUX--THAT'S VIBRO. HE'S GOT MY SHTICK. PSYCHO, THOUGH. HE'D FIGHT A THOR, NO PROBLEM. DUMBASS.
SORRY. GOT NOTHIN'. BUT HONESTLY, ODDS WERE AGAINST YOU IN THE FIRST PLACE.
MY MEMORY'S SHOT. ALL THESE VIBRATIONS--DOC TOLD ME IT'S LIKE ALL THESE MINI-CONCUSSIONS, OVER AND OVER.
NOTHING? EVEN THE SMALLEST PIECE COULD BE HELPFUL.
YOU KNOW, LOT OF YOU GUYS WOULD BEAT ME UP FIRST AND ASK QUESTIONS LATER. OR MAYBE JUST BEAT ME UP.
AND YOU BOUGHT ME CHINESE.
LET'S SEE WHAT I CAN DO.
WAIT! WHAT ARE YOU--

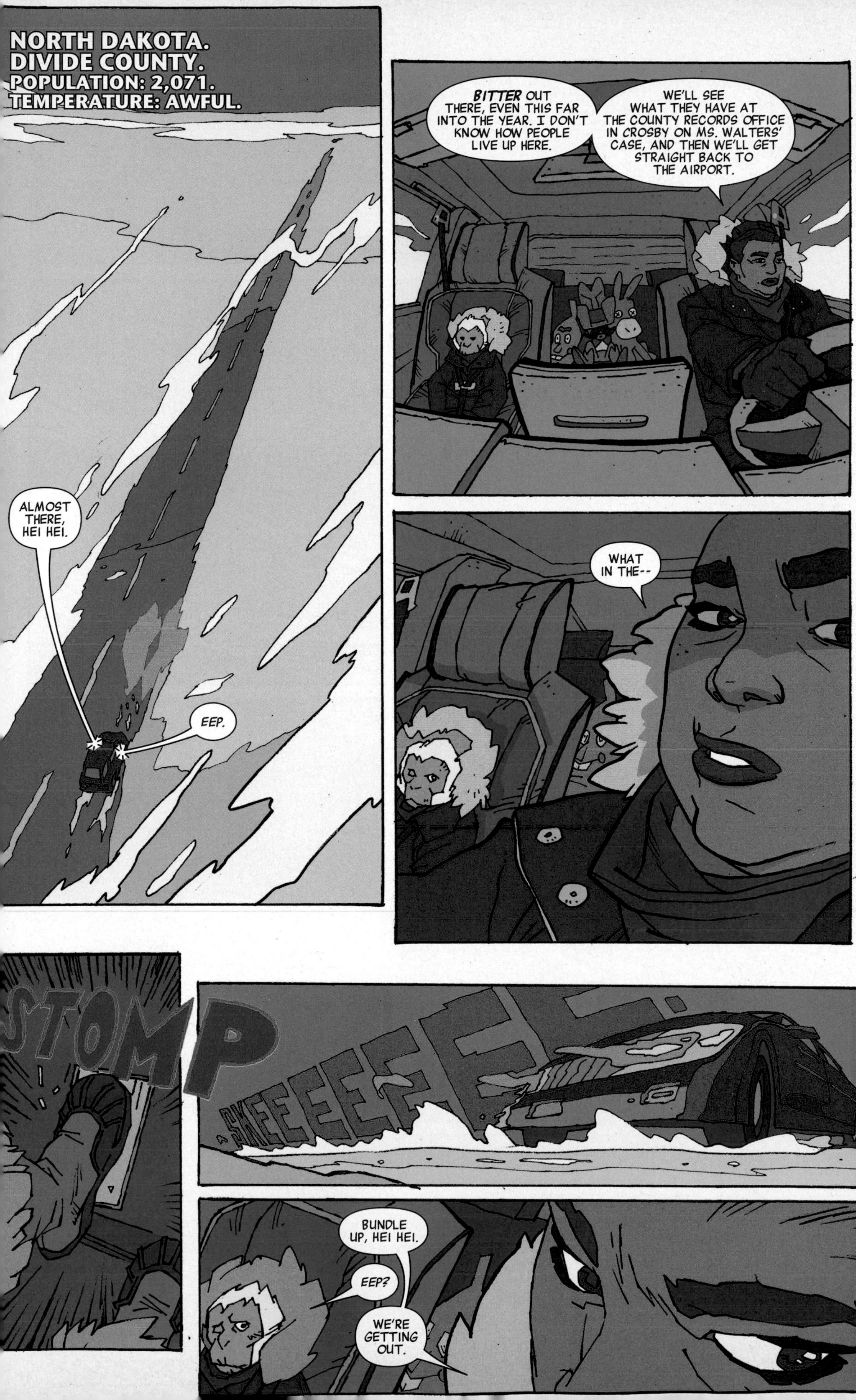
NORTH DAKOTA.
DIVIDE COUNTY.
POPULATION: 2,071.
TEMPERATURE: AWFUL.
ALMOST THERE, HEI HEI.
EEP.
BITTER OUT THERE, EVEN THIS FAR INTO THE YEAR. I DON'T KNOW HOW PEOPLE LIVE UP HERE.
WE'LL SEE WHAT THEY HAVE AT THE COUNTY RECORDS OFFICE IN CROSBY ON MS. WALTERS' CASE, AND THEN WE'LL GET STRAIGHT BACK TO THE AIRPORT.
WHAT IN THE--
STOMP
SKEEEEEEE
BUNDLE UP, HEI HEI.
EEP?
WE'RE GETTING OUT.

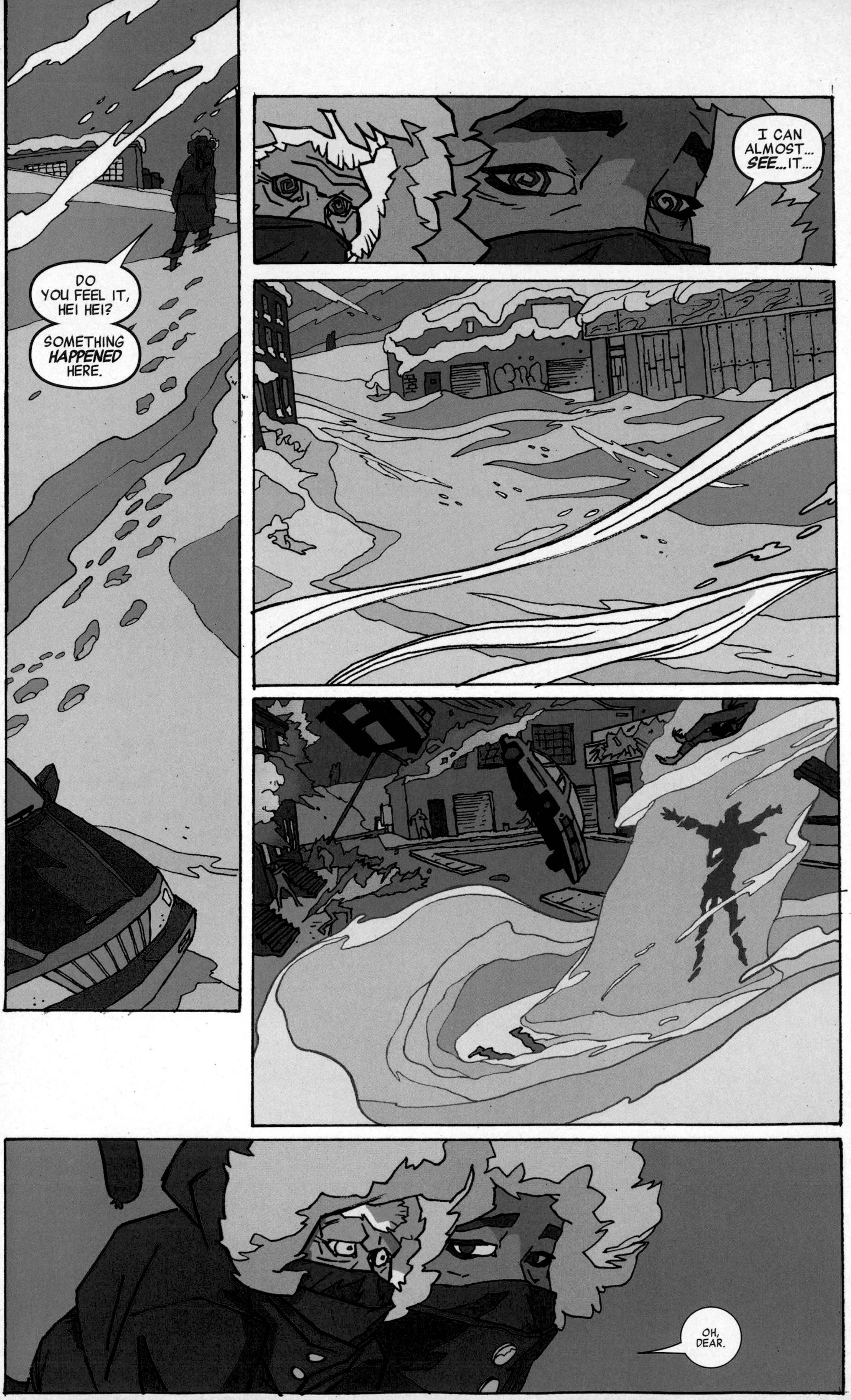
DO YOU FEEL IT, HEI HEI?
SOMETHING HAPPENED HERE.
I CAN ALMOST... SEE...IT...
OH, DEAR.

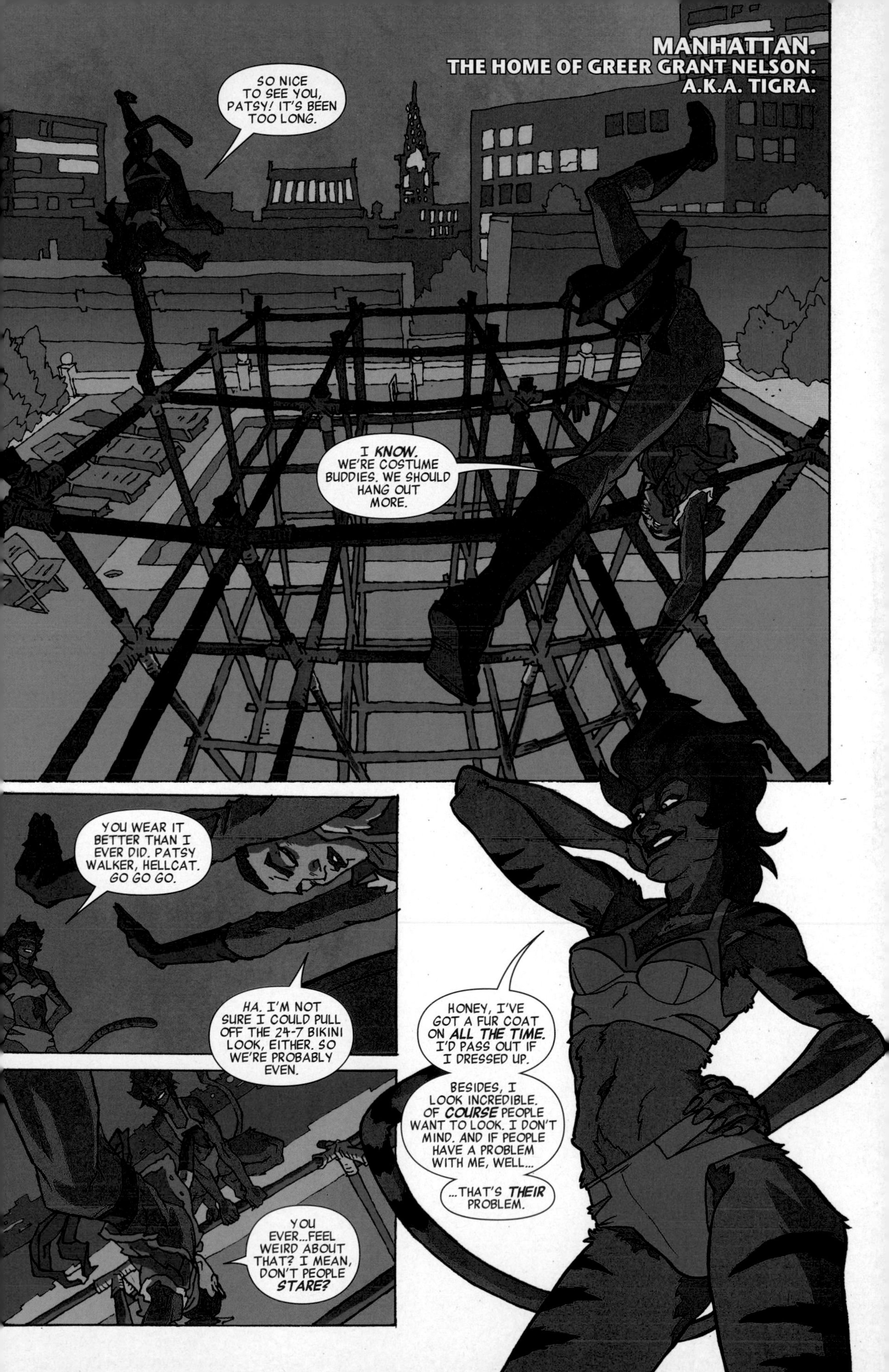
MANHATTAN.
THE HOME OF GREER GRANT NELSON.
A.K.A. TIGRA.
SO NICE TO SEE YOU, PATSY! IT'S BEEN TOO LONG.
I KNOW. WE'RE COSTUME BUDDIES. WE SHOULD HANG OUT MORE.
YOU WEAR IT BETTER THAN I EVER DID. PATSY WALKER, HELLCAT. GO GO GO.
HA. I'M NOT SURE I COULD PULL OFF THE 24-7 BIKINI LOOK, EITHER. SO WE'RE PROBABLY EVEN.
YOU EVER...FEEL WEIRD ABOUT THAT? I MEAN, DON'T PEOPLE STARE?
HONEY, I'VE GOT A FUR COAT ON ALL THE TIME. I'D PASS OUT IF I DRESSED UP.
BESIDES, I LOOK INCREDIBLE. OF COURSE PEOPLE WANT TO LOOK. I DON'T MIND. AND IF PEOPLE HAVE A PROBLEM WITH ME, WELL...
...THAT'S THEIR PROBLEM.

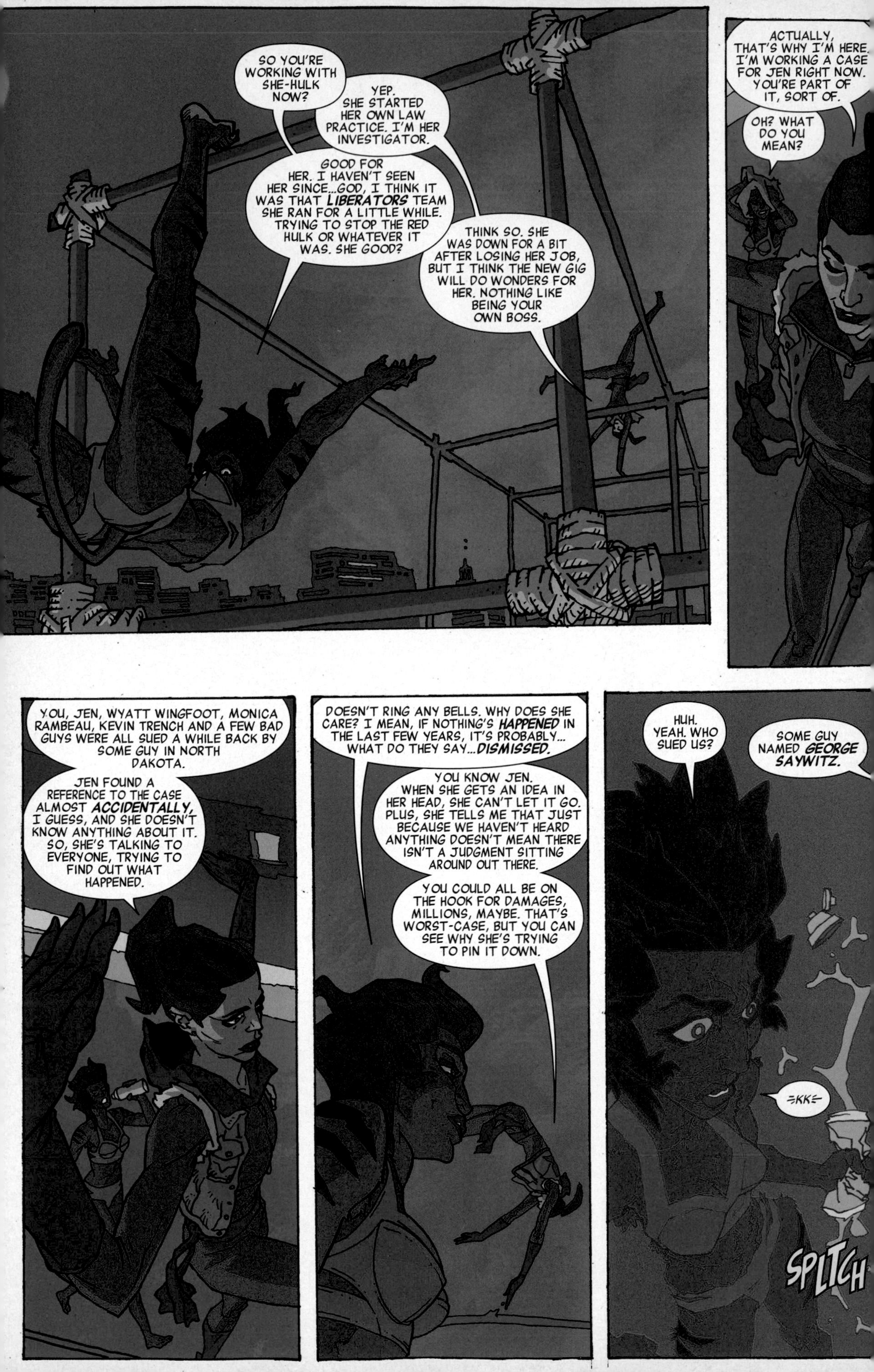
SO YOU'RE WORKING WITH SHE-HULK NOW?
YEP. SHE STARTED HER OWN LAW PRACTICE. I'M HER INVESTIGATOR.
GOOD FOR HER. I HAVEN'T SEEN HER SINCE...GOD, I THINK IT WAS THAT LIBERATORS TEAM SHE RAN FOR A LITTLE WHILE. TRYING TO STOP THE RED HULK OR WHATEVER IT WAS. SHE GOOD?
THINK SO. SHE WAS DOWN FOR A BIT AFTER LOSING HER JOB, BUT I THINK THE NEW GIG WILL DO WONDERS FOR HER. NOTHING LIKE BEING YOUR OWN BOSS.
ACTUALLY, THAT'S WHY I'M HERE. I'M WORKING A CASE FOR JEN RIGHT NOW. YOU'RE PART OF IT, SORT OF.
OH? WHAT DO YOU MEAN?
YOU, JEN, WYATT WINGFOOT, MONICA RAMBEAU, KEVIN TRENCH AND A FEW BAD GUYS WERE ALL SUED A WHILE BACK BY SOME GUY IN NORTH DAKOTA.
JEN FOUND A REFERENCE TO THE CASE ALMOST ACCIDENTALLY, I GUESS, AND SHE DOESN'T KNOW ANYTHING ABOUT IT. SO, SHE'S TALKING TO EVERYONE, TRYING TO FIND OUT WHAT HAPPENED.
DOESN'T RING ANY BELLS. WHY DOES SHE CARE? I MEAN, IF NOTHING'S HAPPENED IN THE LAST FEW YEARS, IT'S PROBABLY... WHAT DO THEY SAY...DISMISSED.
YOU KNOW JEN. WHEN SHE GETS AN IDEA IN HER HEAD, SHE CAN'T LET IT GO. PLUS, SHE TELLS ME THAT JUST BECAUSE WE HAVEN'T HEARD ANYTHING DOESN'T MEAN THERE ISN'T A JUDGMENT SITTING AROUND OUT THERE.
YOU COULD ALL BE ON THE HOOK FOR DAMAGES, MILLIONS, MAYBE. THAT'S WORST-CASE, BUT YOU CAN SEE WHY SHE'S TRYING TO PIN IT DOWN.
HUH. YEAH. WHO SUED US?
SOME GUY NAMED GEORGE SAYWITZ.
KK
SPLTCH

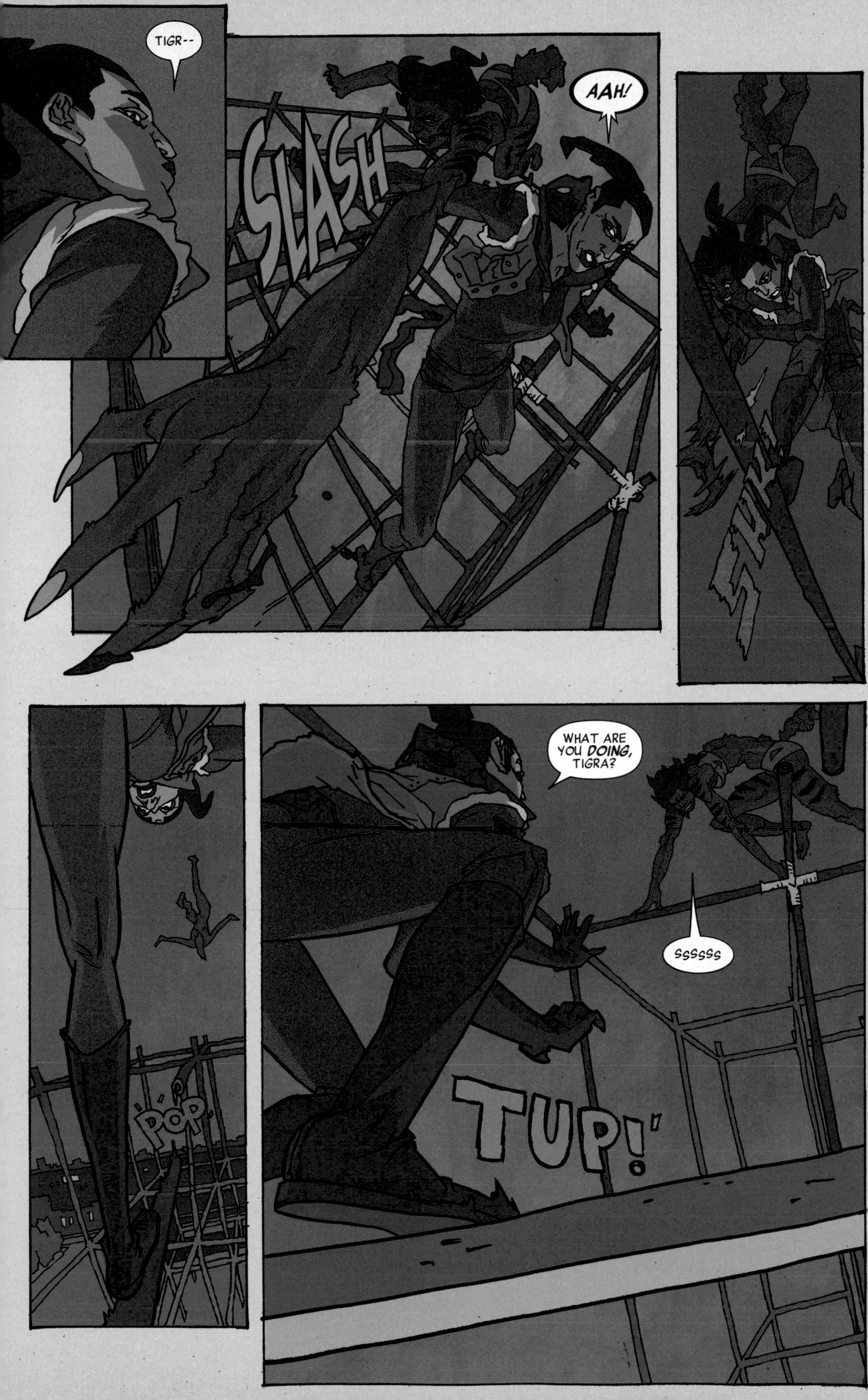
TIGR--
SLASH
AAH!
WHAT ARE YOU DOING, TIGRA?
SSSSSS
POP
TUP!

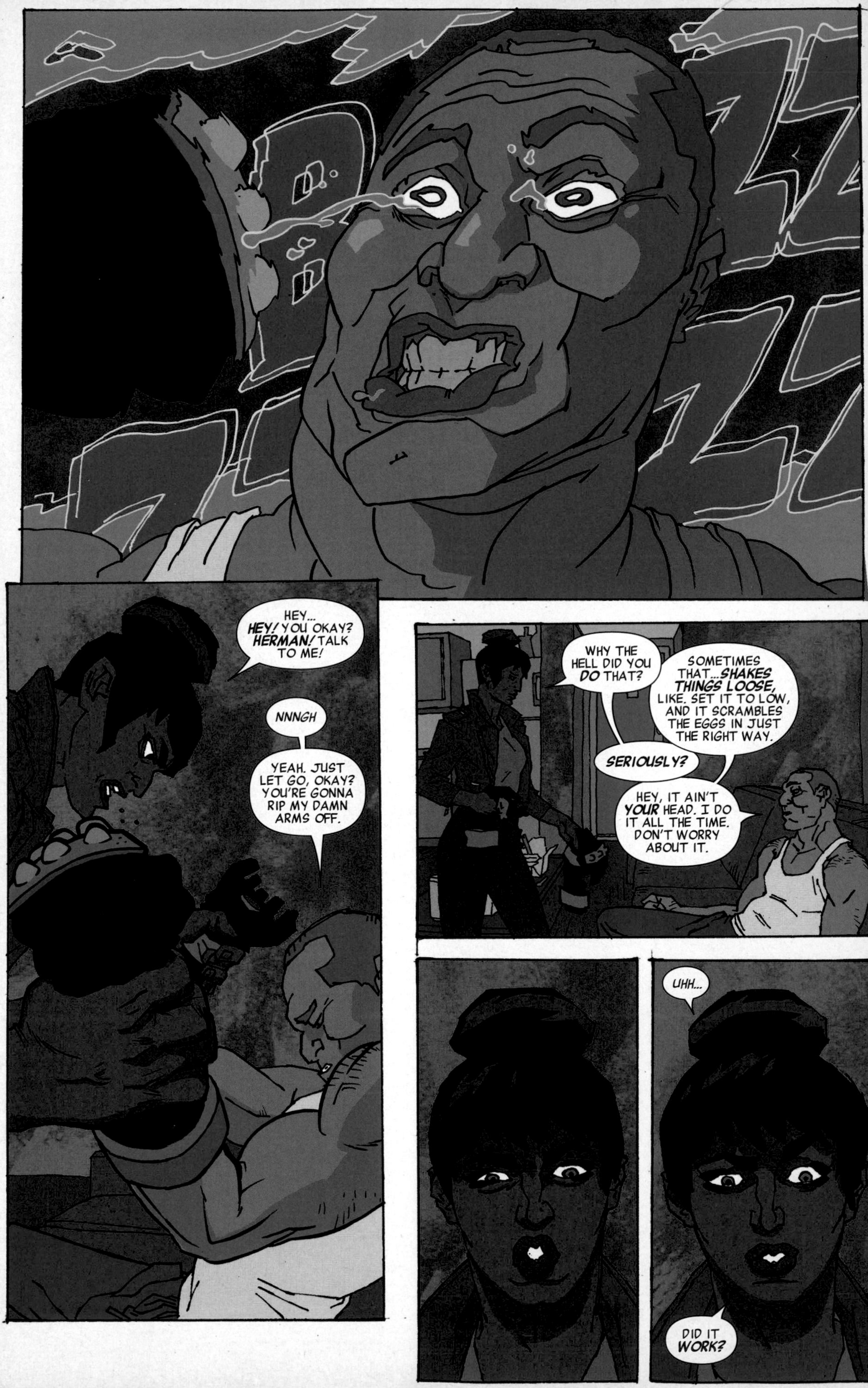
HEY... HEY! YOU OKAY? HERMAN! TALK TO ME!
NNNGH
YEAH. JUST LET GO, OKAY? YOU'RE GONNA RIP MY DAMN ARMS OFF.
WHY THE HELL DID YOU DO THAT?
SOMETIMES THAT...SHAKES THINGS LOOSE, LIKE. SET IT TO LOW, AND IT SCRAMBLES THE EGGS IN JUST THE RIGHT WAY.
SERIOUSLY?
HEY, IT AIN'T YOUR HEAD. I DO IT ALL THE TIME. DON'T WORRY ABOUT IT.
UHH...
DID IT WORK?

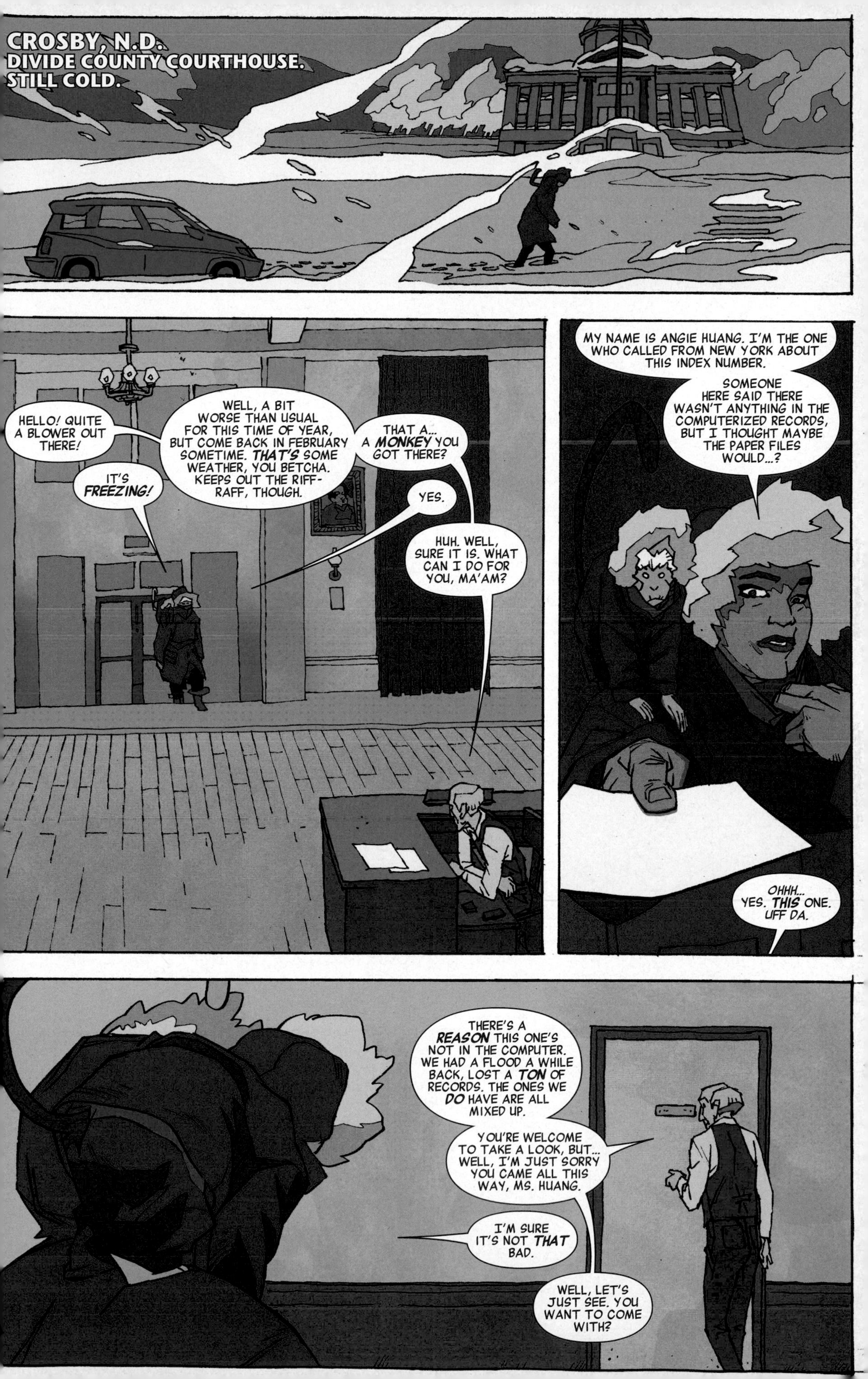
CROSBY, N.D.
DIVIDE COUNTY COURTHOUSE.
STILL COLD.
HELLO! QUITE A BLOWER OUT THERE!
IT'S FREEZING!
WELL, A BIT WORSE THAN USUAL FOR THIS TIME OF YEAR, BUT COME BACK IN FEBRUARY SOMETIME. THAT'S SOME WEATHER, YOU BETCHA. KEEPS OUT THE RIFF-RAFF, THOUGH.
THAT A... A MONKEY YOU GOT THERE?
YES.
HUH. WELL, SURE IT IS. WHAT CAN I DO FOR YOU, MA'AM?
MY NAME IS ANGIE HUANG. I'M THE ONE WHO CALLED FROM NEW YORK ABOUT THIS INDEX NUMBER.
SOMEONE HERE SAID THERE WASN'T ANYTHING IN THE COMPUTERIZED RECORDS, BUT I THOUGHT MAYBE THE PAPER FILES WOULD...?
OHHH... YES. THIS ONE. UFF DA.
THERE'S A REASON THIS ONE'S NOT IN THE COMPUTER. WE HAD A FLOOD A WHILE BACK, LOST A TON OF RECORDS. THE ONES WE DO HAVE ARE ALL MIXED UP.
YOU'RE WELCOME TO TAKE A LOOK, BUT... WELL, I'M JUST SORRY YOU CAME ALL THIS WAY, MS. HUANG.
I'M SURE IT'S NOT THAT BAD.
WELL, LET'S JUST SEE. YOU WANT TO COME WITH?

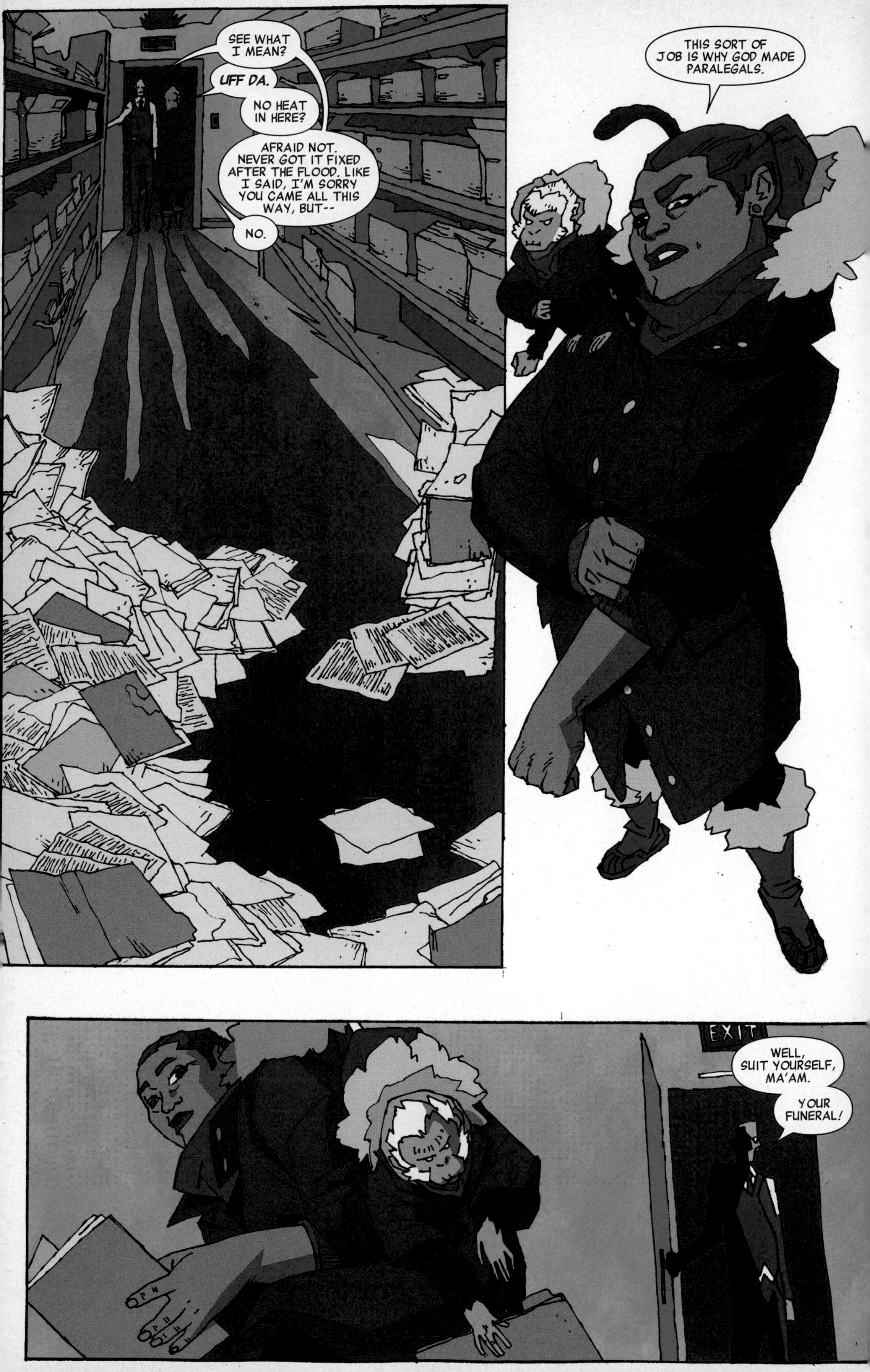

SEE WHAT I MEAN?
UFF DA.
NO HEAT IN HERE?
AFRAID NOT. NEVER GOT IT FIXED AFTER THE FLOOD. LIKE I SAID, I'M SORRY YOU CAME ALL THIS WAY, BUT--
NO.
THIS SORT OF JOB IS WHY GOD MADE PARALEGALS.
EXIT
WELL, SUIT YOURSELF, MA'AM.
YOUR FUNERAL!

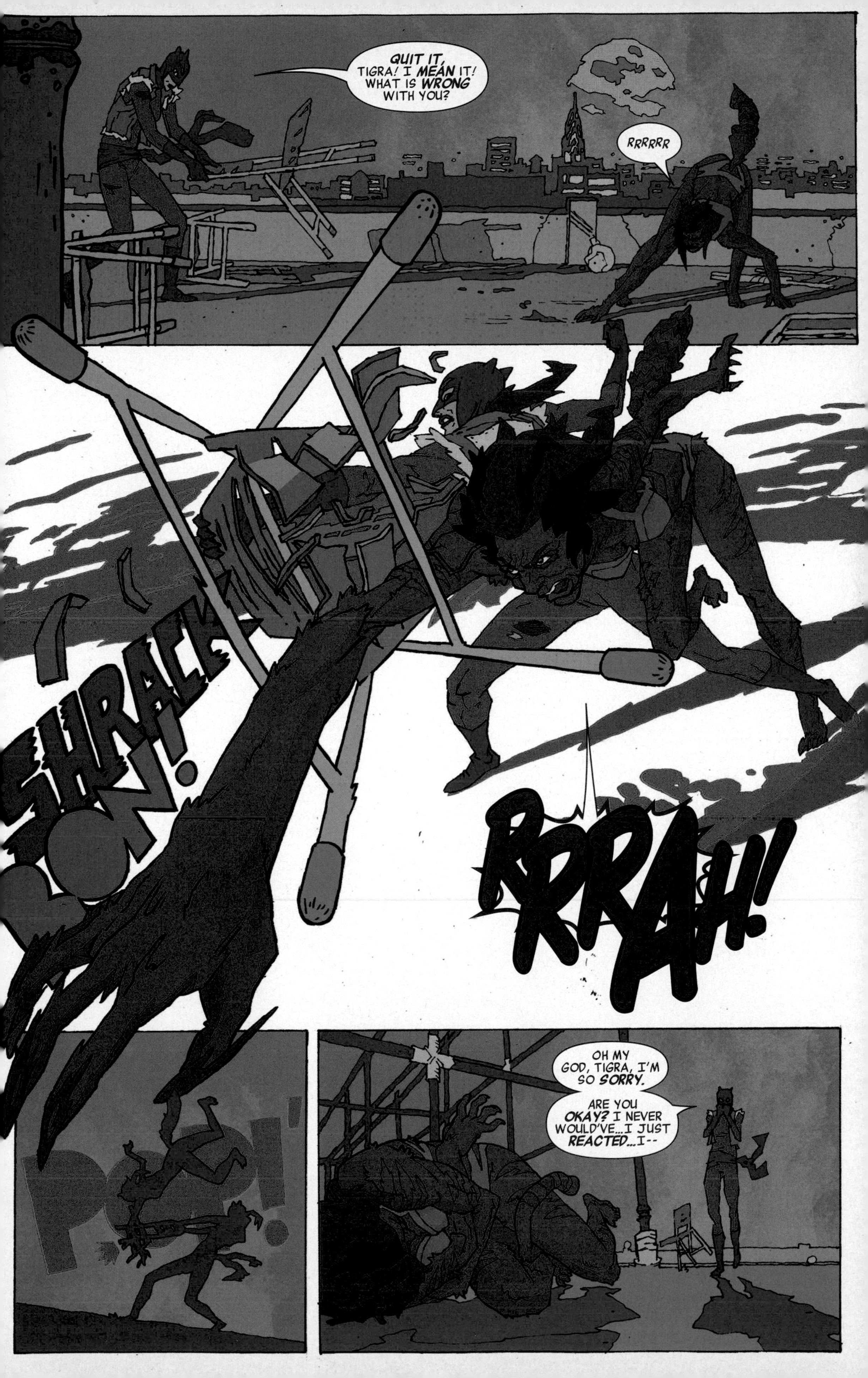
QUIT IT, TIGRA! I MEAN IT! WHAT IS WRONG WITH YOU?
RRRRRR
SHRACK!
RRRAH!
POP!
OH MY GOD, TIGRA, I'M SO SORRY.
ARE YOU OKAY? I NEVER WOULD'VE...I JUST REACTED...I--

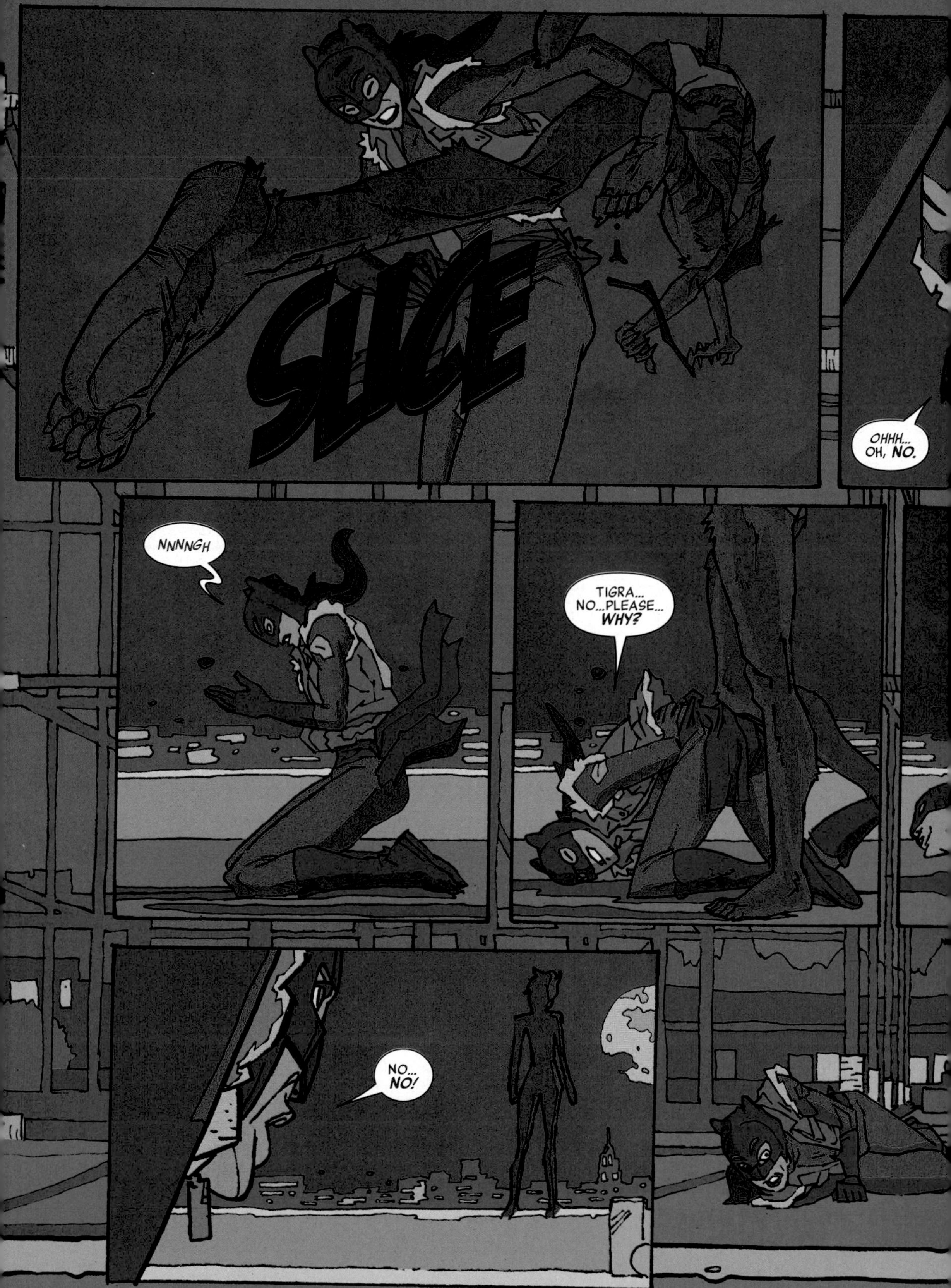
SLICE
OHHH... OH, NO.
NNNNGH
TIGRA... NO...PLEASE... WHY?
NO... NO!

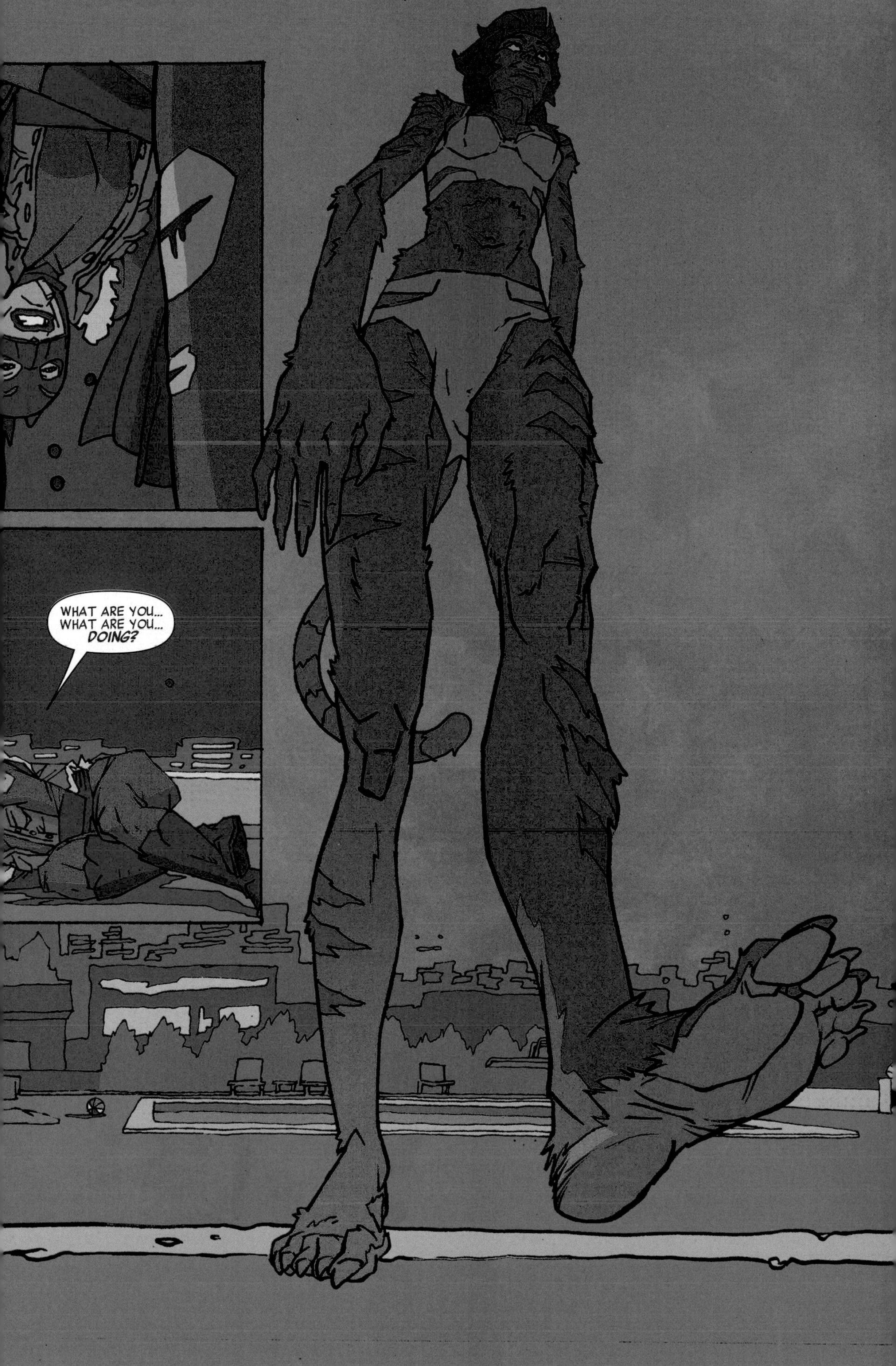
WHAT ARE YOU... WHAT ARE YOU... DOING?

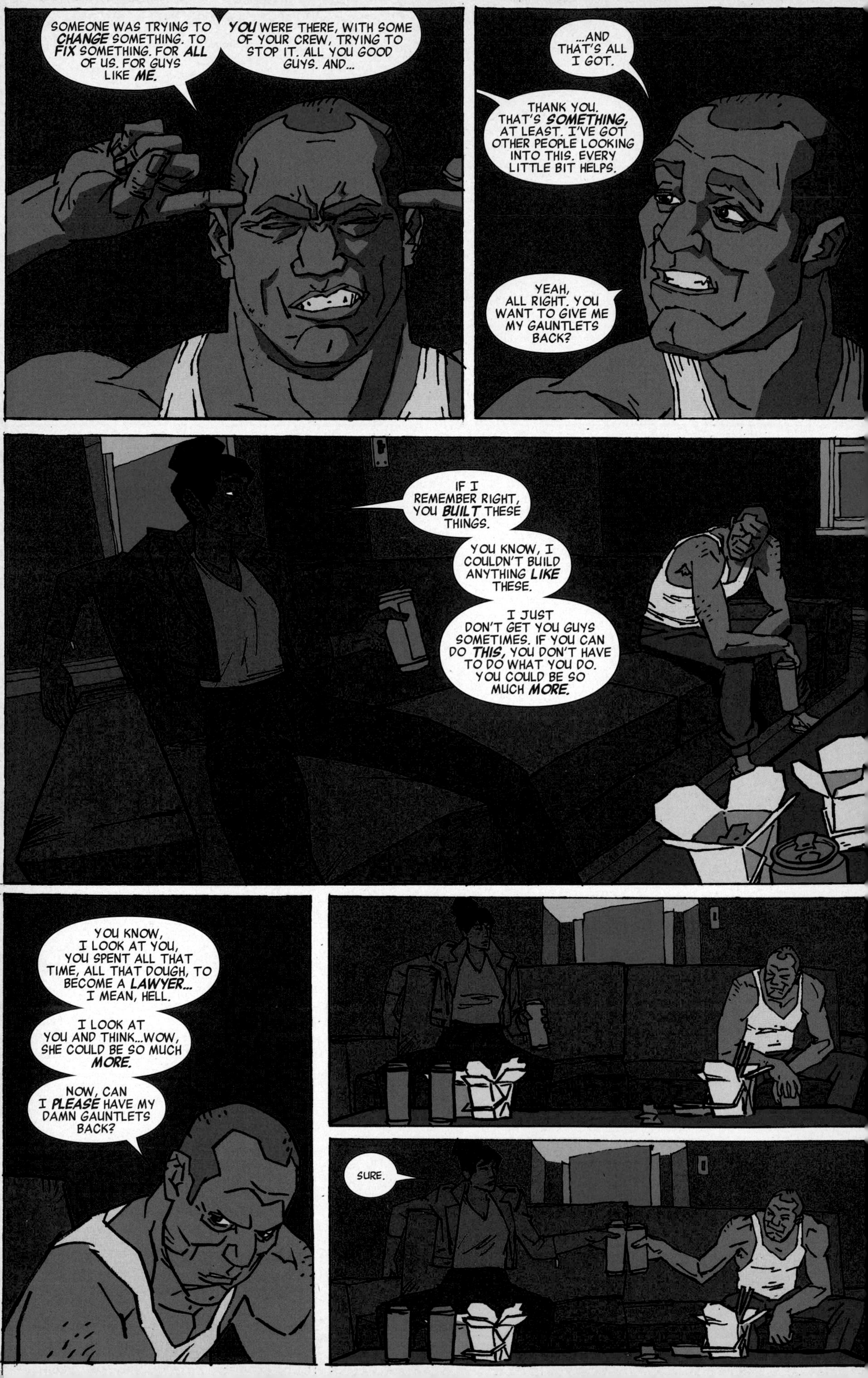
SOMEONE WAS TRYING TO CHANGE SOMETHING. TO FIX SOMETHING. FOR ALL OF US. FOR GUYS LIKE ME.
YOU WERE THERE, WITH SOME OF YOUR CREW, TRYING TO STOP IT. ALL YOU GOOD GUYS. AND...
...AND THAT'S ALL I GOT.
THANK YOU. THAT'S SOMETHING, AT LEAST. I'VE GOT OTHER PEOPLE LOOKING INTO THIS. EVERY LITTLE BIT HELPS.
YEAH, ALL RIGHT. YOU WANT TO GIVE ME MY GAUNTLETS BACK?
IF I REMEMBER RIGHT, YOU BUILT THESE THINGS.
YOU KNOW, I COULDN'T BUILD ANYTHING LIKE THESE.
I JUST DON'T GET YOU GUYS SOMETIMES. IF YOU CAN DO THIS, YOU DON'T HAVE TO DO WHAT YOU DO. YOU COULD BE SO MUCH MORE.
YOU KNOW, I LOOK AT YOU, YOU SPENT ALL THAT TIME, ALL THAT DOUGH, TO BECOME A LAWYER... I MEAN, HELL.
I LOOK AT YOU AND THINK...WOW, SHE COULD BE SO MUCH MORE.
NOW, CAN I PLEASE HAVE MY DAMN GAUNTLETS BACK?
SURE.

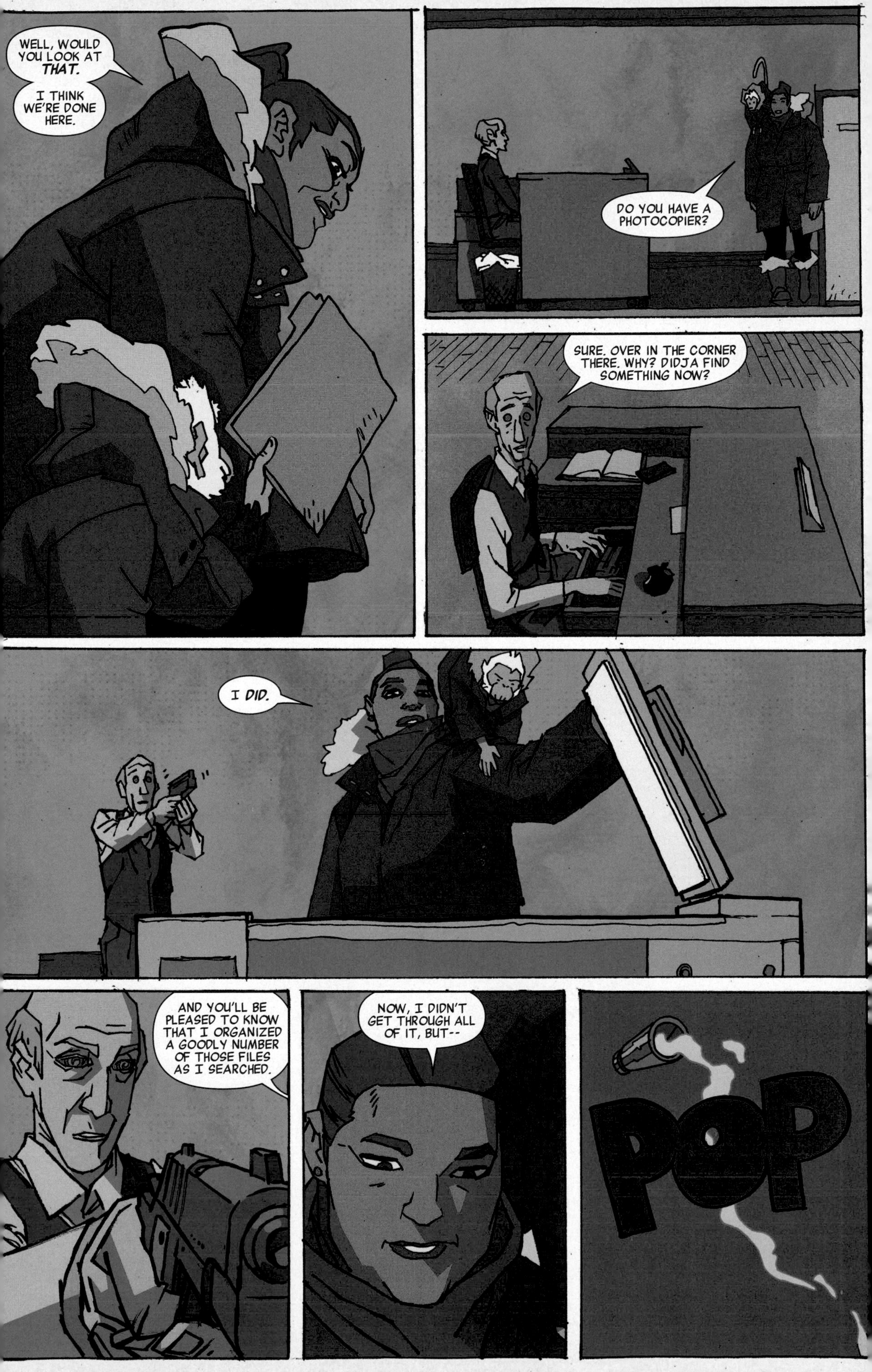

WELL, WOULD YOU LOOK AT *THAT.*
I THINK WE'RE DONE HERE.
DO YOU HAVE A PHOTOCOPIER?
SURE. OVER IN THE CORNER THERE. WHY? DIDJA FIND SOMETHING NOW?
I *DID.*
AND YOU'LL BE PLEASED TO KNOW THAT I ORGANIZED A GOODLY NUMBER OF THOSE FILES AS I SEARCHED.
NOW, I DIDN'T GET THROUGH ALL OF IT, BUT--
POP

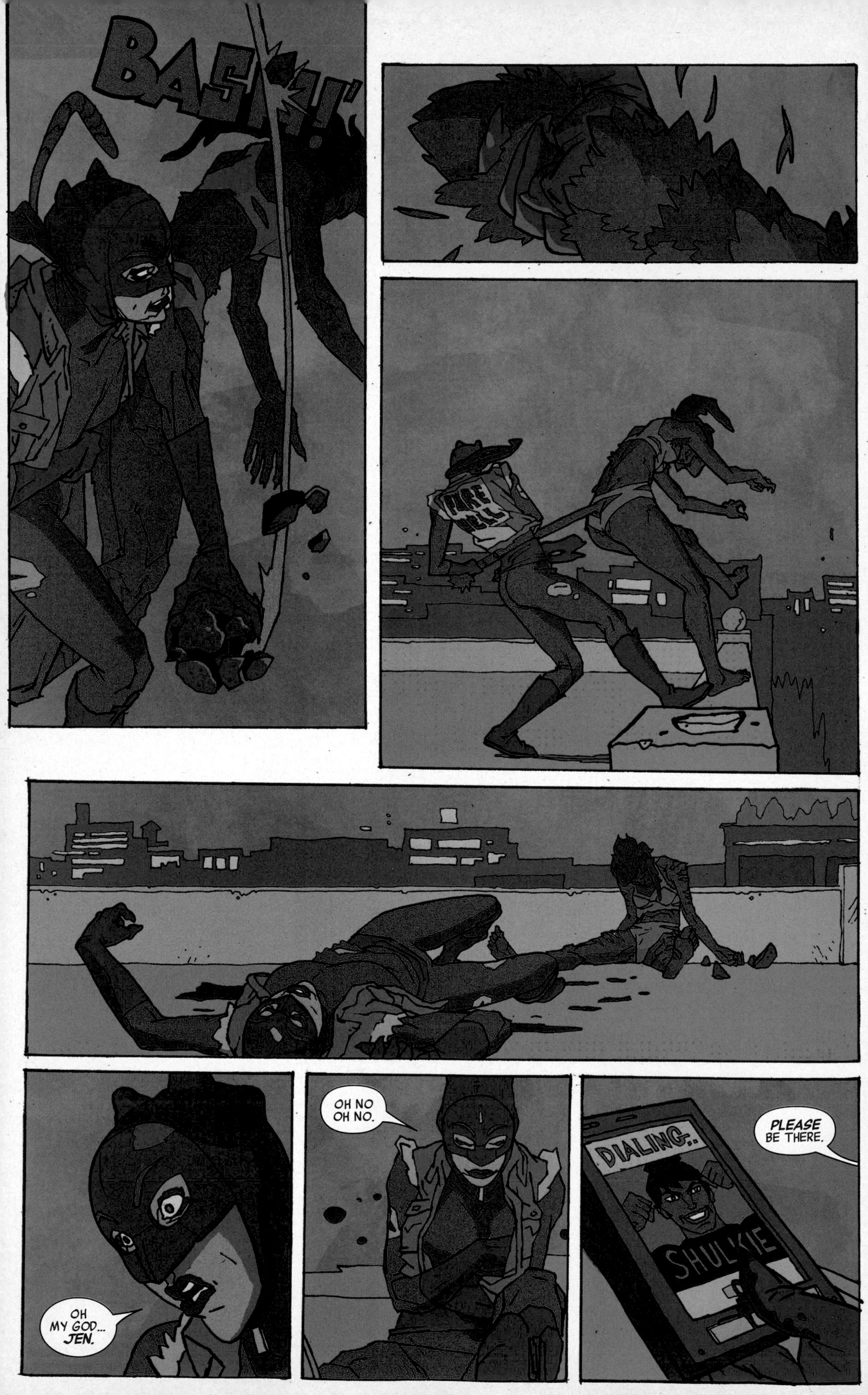
BASH!
FIRE HELL
OH MY GOD... JEN.
OH NO OH NO.
DIALING..
SHULKIE
PLEASE BE THERE.

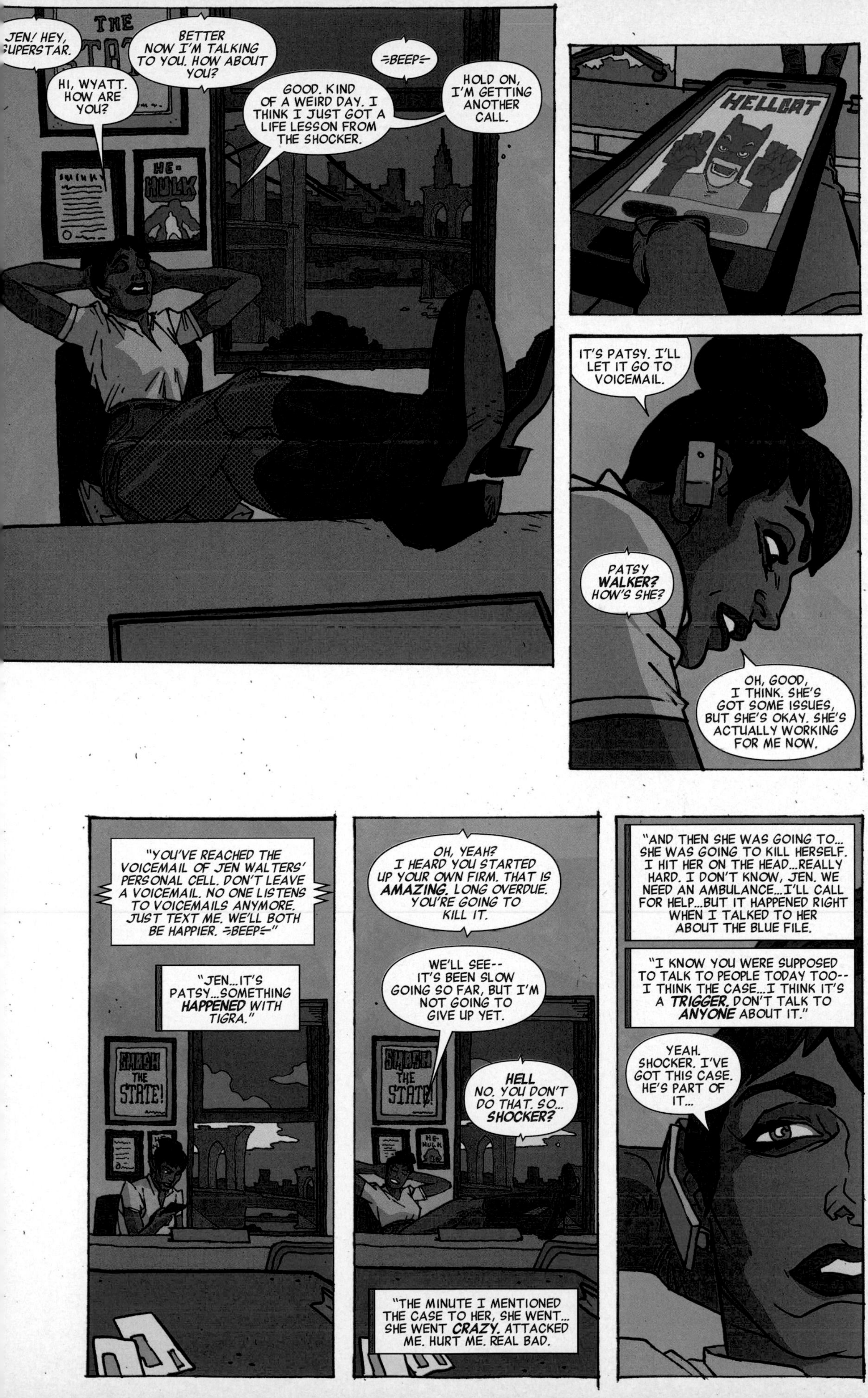

THE STATE
JEN! HEY, SUPERSTAR.
HI, WYATT. HOW ARE YOU?
BETTER NOW I'M TALKING TO YOU. HOW ABOUT YOU?
GOOD. KIND OF A WEIRD DAY. I THINK I JUST GOT A LIFE LESSON FROM THE SHOCKER.
HE-HULK
=BEEP=
HOLD ON, I'M GETTING ANOTHER CALL.
HELLCAT
IT'S PATSY. I'LL LET IT GO TO VOICEMAIL.
PATSY **WALKER?** HOW'S SHE?
OH, GOOD, I THINK. SHE'S GOT SOME ISSUES, BUT SHE'S OKAY. SHE'S ACTUALLY WORKING FOR ME NOW.
"YOU'VE REACHED THE VOICEMAIL OF JEN WALTERS' PERSONAL CELL. DON'T LEAVE A VOICEMAIL. NO ONE LISTENS TO VOICEMAILS ANYMORE. JUST TEXT ME. WE'LL BOTH BE HAPPIER. =BEEP="
"JEN...IT'S PATSY...SOMETHING **HAPPENED** WITH TIGRA."
SMASH THE STATE!
OH, YEAH? I HEARD YOU STARTED UP YOUR OWN FIRM. THAT IS **AMAZING.** LONG OVERDUE. YOU'RE GOING TO KILL IT.
WE'LL SEE-- IT'S BEEN SLOW GOING SO FAR, BUT I'M NOT GOING TO GIVE UP YET.
HELL NO. YOU DON'T DO THAT. SO... **SHOCKER?**
"THE MINUTE I MENTIONED THE CASE TO HER, SHE WENT... SHE WENT **CRAZY.** ATTACKED ME. HURT ME. REAL BAD.
"AND THEN SHE WAS GOING TO... SHE WAS GOING TO KILL HERSELF. I HIT HER ON THE HEAD...REALLY HARD. I DON'T KNOW, JEN. WE NEED AN AMBULANCE...I'LL CALL FOR HELP...BUT IT HAPPENED RIGHT WHEN I TALKED TO HER ABOUT THE BLUE FILE.
"I KNOW YOU WERE SUPPOSED TO TALK TO PEOPLE TODAY TOO-- I THINK THE CASE...I THINK IT'S A **TRIGGER.** DON'T TALK TO **ANYONE** ABOUT IT."
YEAH. SHOCKER. I'VE GOT THIS CASE. HE'S PART OF IT...

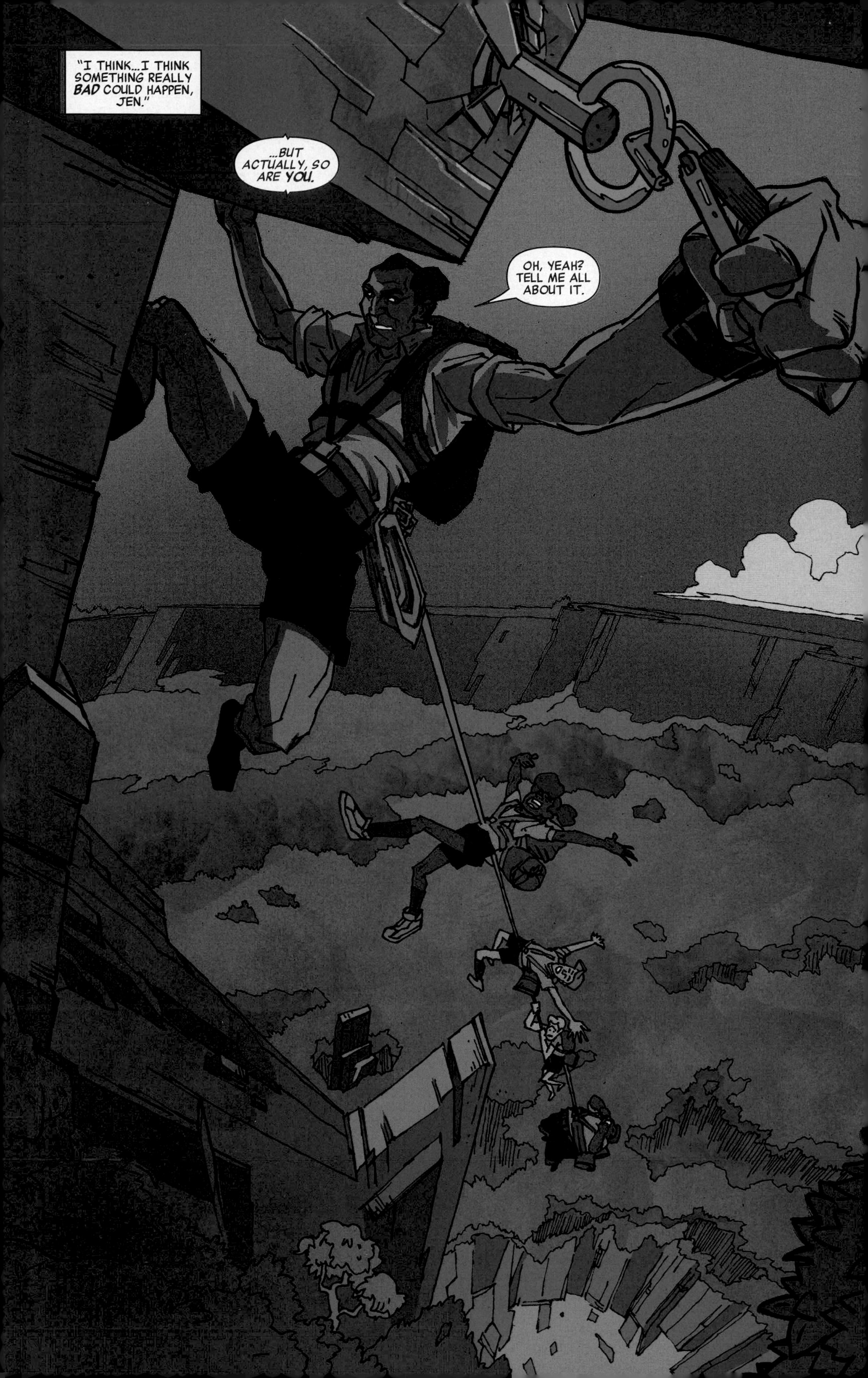
"I THINK...I THINK SOMETHING REALLY BAD COULD HAPPEN, JEN."
...BUT ACTUALLY, SO ARE YOU.
OH, YEAH? TELL ME ALL ABOUT IT.

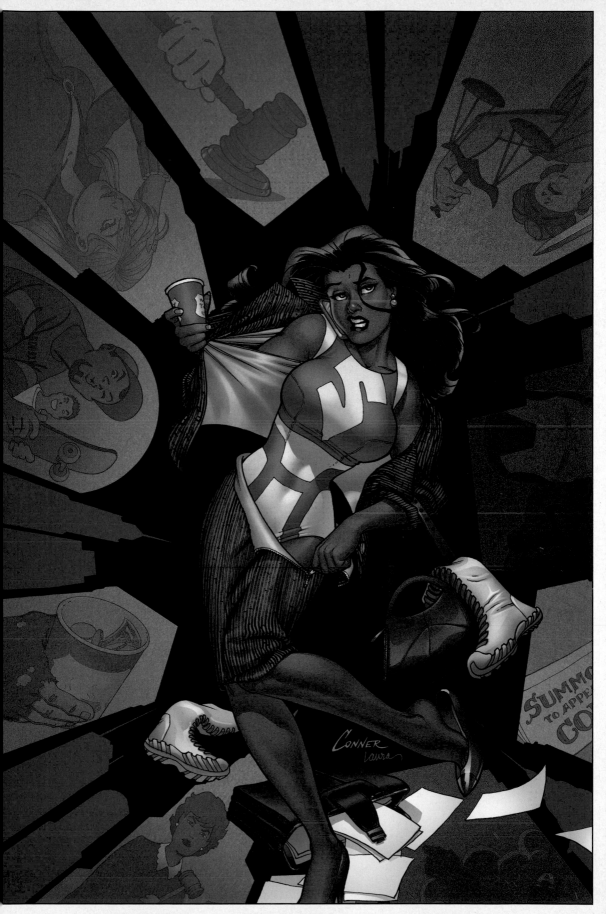

SHE-HULK #2 VARIANT BY AMANDA CONNER & LAURA MARTIN

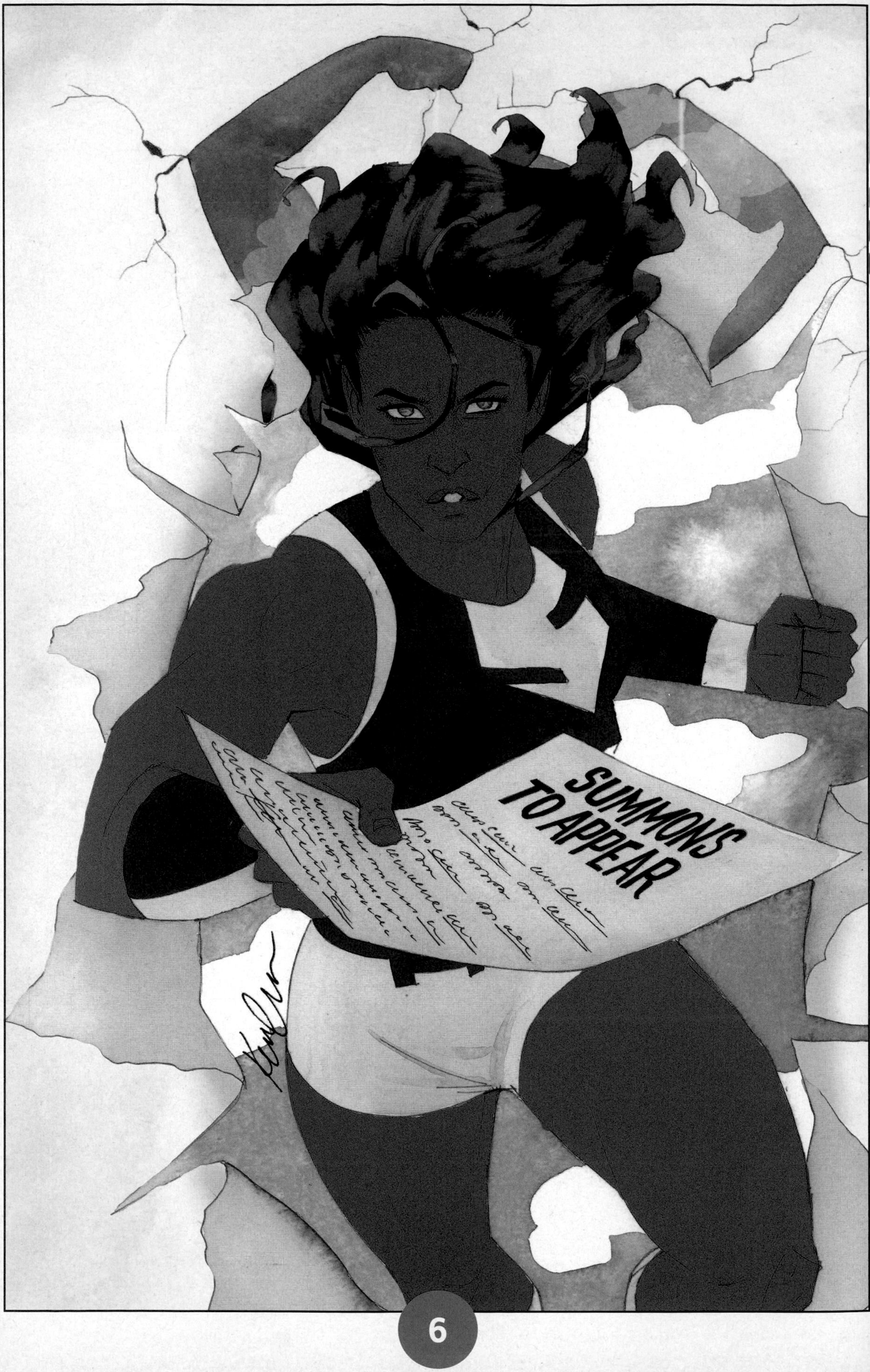
SUMMONS TO APPEAR

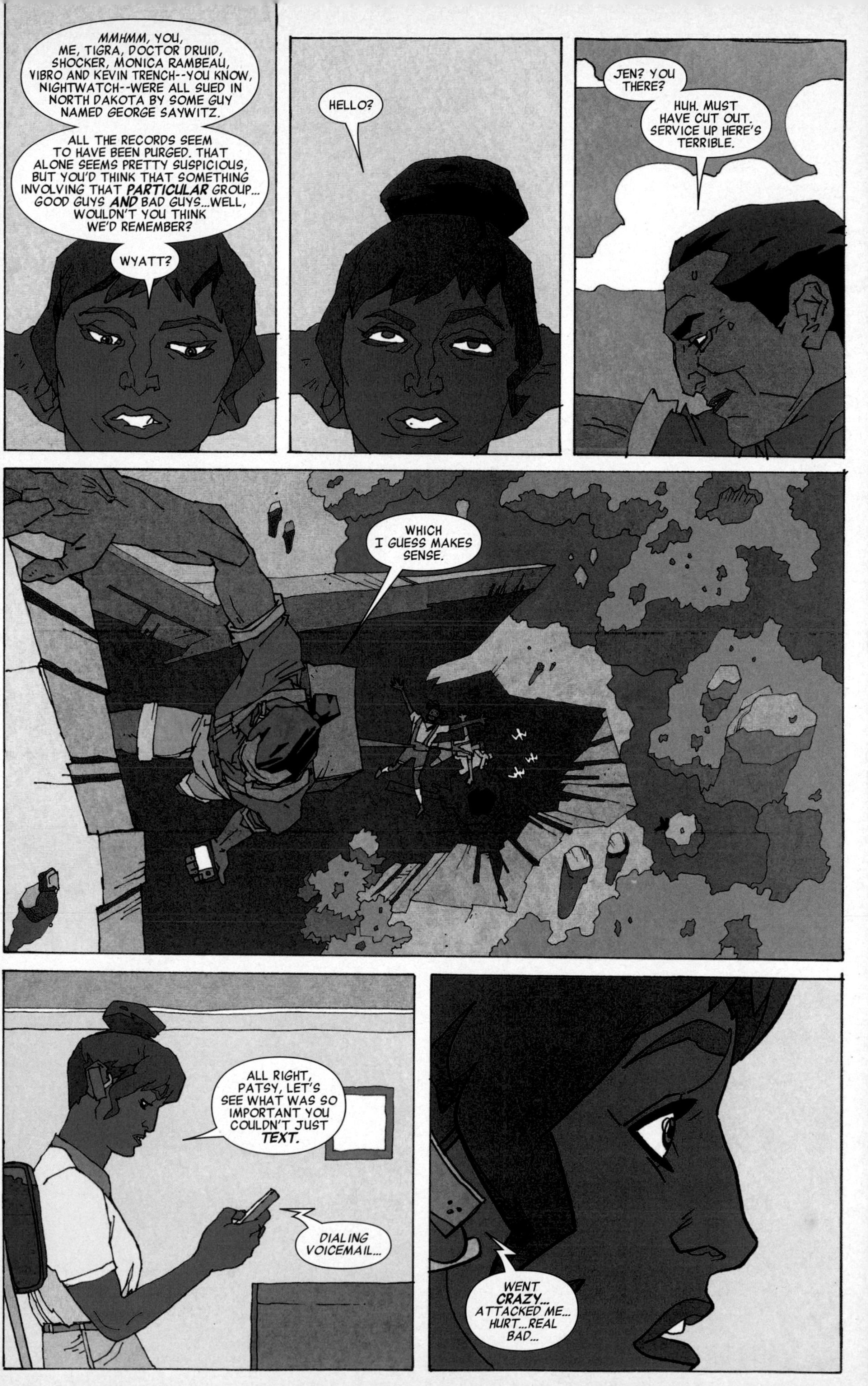
MMHMM, YOU, ME, TIGRA, DOCTOR DRUID, SHOCKER, MONICA RAMBEAU, VIBRO AND KEVIN TRENCH--YOU KNOW, NIGHTWATCH--WERE ALL SUED IN NORTH DAKOTA BY SOME GUY NAMED GEORGE SAYWITZ.
ALL THE RECORDS SEEM TO HAVE BEEN PURGED. THAT ALONE SEEMS PRETTY SUSPICIOUS, BUT YOU'D THINK THAT SOMETHING INVOLVING THAT PARTICULAR GROUP... GOOD GUYS AND BAD GUYS...WELL, WOULDN'T YOU THINK WE'D REMEMBER?
WYATT?
HELLO?
JEN? YOU THERE?
HUH. MUST HAVE CUT OUT. SERVICE UP HERE'S TERRIBLE.
WHICH I GUESS MAKES SENSE.
ALL RIGHT, PATSY, LET'S SEE WHAT WAS SO IMPORTANT YOU COULDN'T JUST TEXT.
DIALING VOICEMAIL...
WENT CRAZY... ATTACKED ME... HURT...REAL BAD...

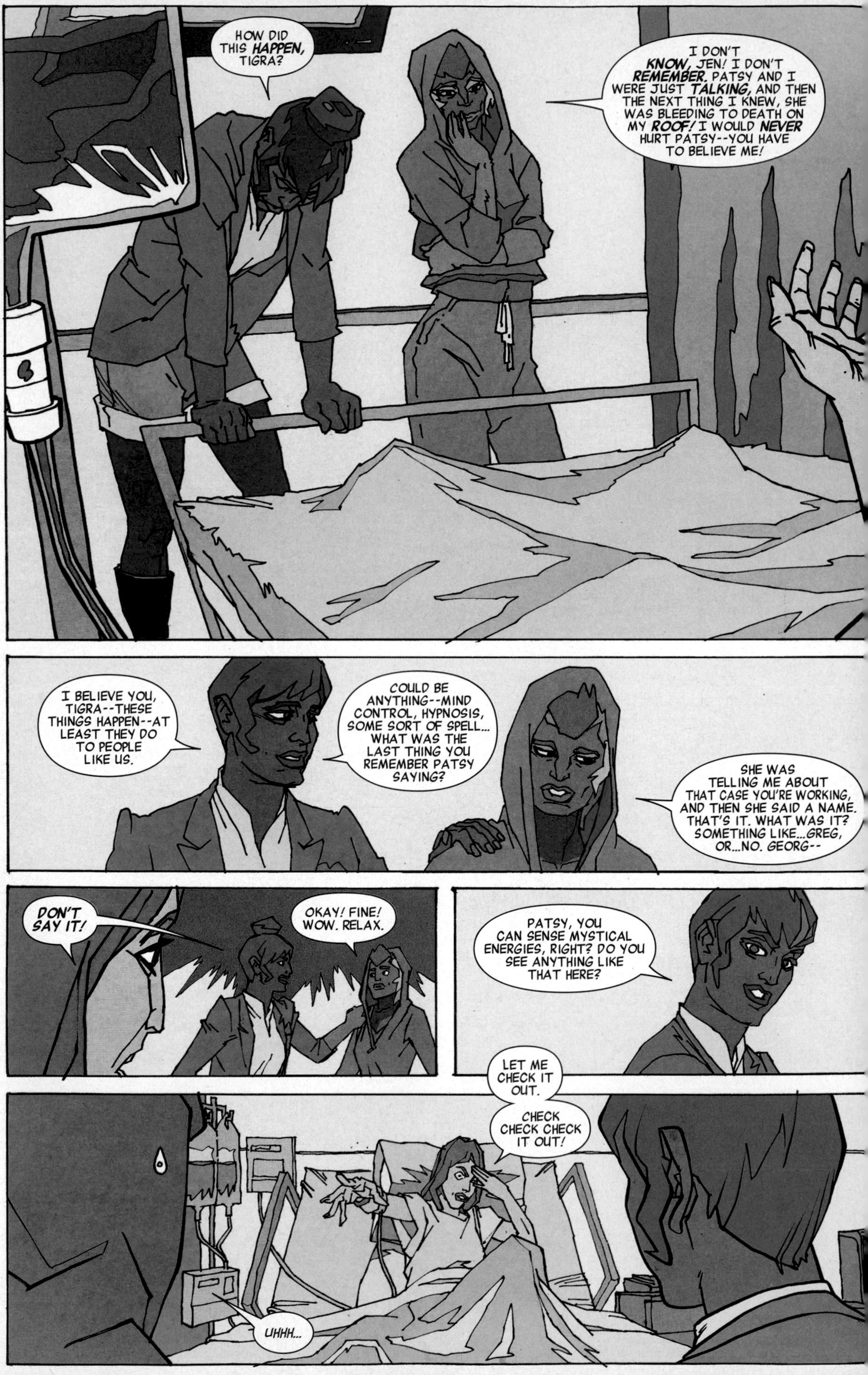
HOW DID THIS HAPPEN, TIGRA?
I DON'T KNOW, JEN! I DON'T REMEMBER. PATSY AND I WERE JUST TALKING, AND THEN THE NEXT THING I KNEW, SHE WAS BLEEDING TO DEATH ON MY ROOF! I WOULD NEVER HURT PATSY--YOU HAVE TO BELIEVE ME!
I BELIEVE YOU, TIGRA--THESE THINGS HAPPEN--AT LEAST THEY DO TO PEOPLE LIKE US.
COULD BE ANYTHING--MIND CONTROL, HYPNOSIS, SOME SORT OF SPELL... WHAT WAS THE LAST THING YOU REMEMBER PATSY SAYING?
SHE WAS TELLING ME ABOUT THAT CASE YOU'RE WORKING, AND THEN SHE SAID A NAME. THAT'S IT. WHAT WAS IT? SOMETHING LIKE...GREG, OR...NO. GEORG--
DON'T SAY IT!
OKAY! FINE! WOW. RELAX.
PATSY, YOU CAN SENSE MYSTICAL ENERGIES, RIGHT? DO YOU SEE ANYTHING LIKE THAT HERE?
LET ME CHECK IT OUT.
CHECK CHECK CHECK IT OUT!
UHHH...

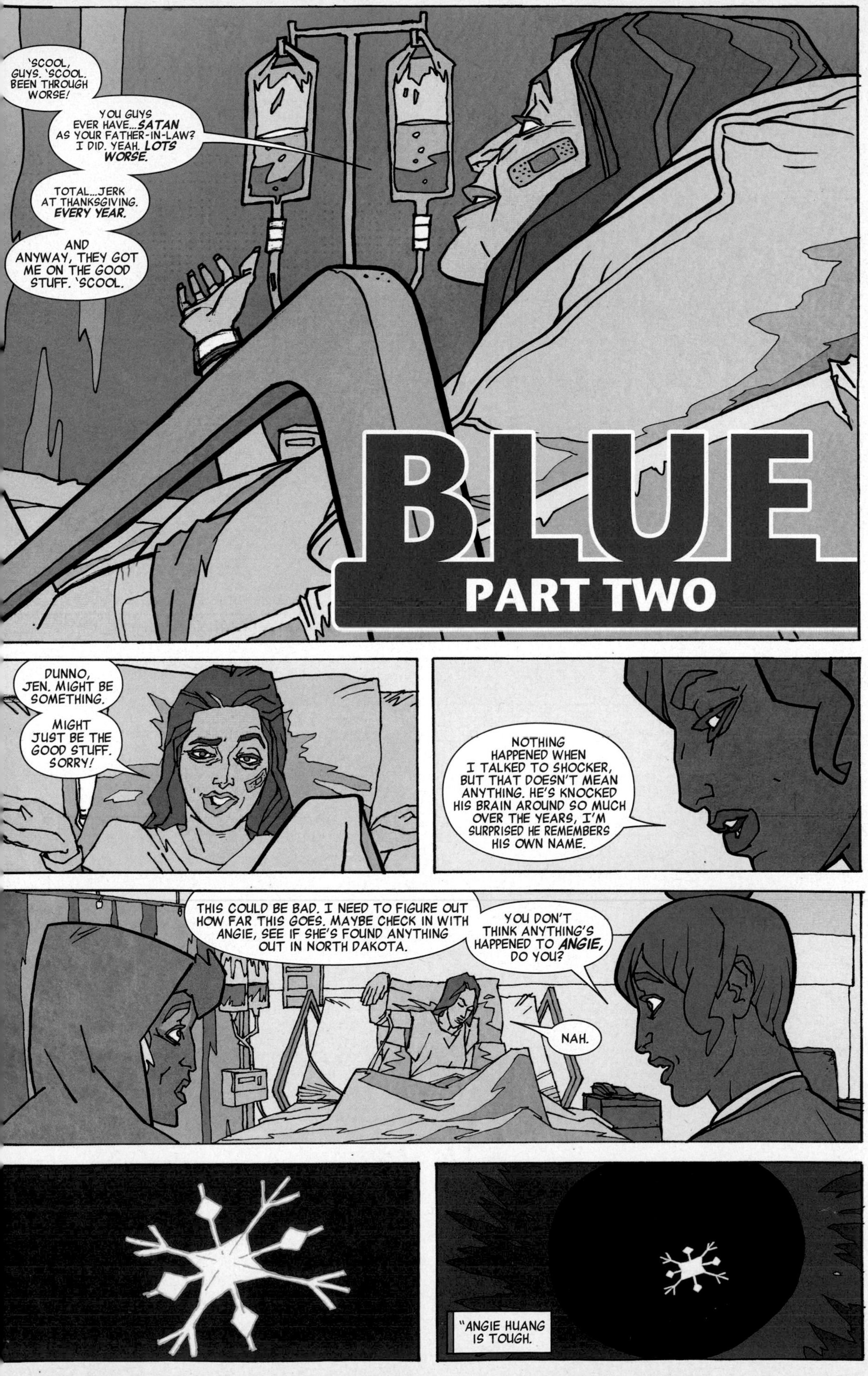
'SCOOL, GUYS. 'SCOOL. BEEN THROUGH WORSE!
YOU GUYS EVER HAVE... SATAN AS YOUR FATHER-IN-LAW? I DID. YEAH. LOTS WORSE.
TOTAL... JERK AT THANKSGIVING. EVERY YEAR.
AND ANYWAY, THEY GOT ME ON THE GOOD STUFF. 'SCOOL.
BLUE
PART TWO
DUNNO, JEN. MIGHT BE SOMETHING.
MIGHT JUST BE THE GOOD STUFF. SORRY!
NOTHING HAPPENED WHEN I TALKED TO SHOCKER, BUT THAT DOESN'T MEAN ANYTHING. HE'S KNOCKED HIS BRAIN AROUND SO MUCH OVER THE YEARS, I'M SURPRISED HE REMEMBERS HIS OWN NAME.
THIS COULD BE BAD. I NEED TO FIGURE OUT HOW FAR THIS GOES. MAYBE CHECK IN WITH ANGIE, SEE IF SHE'S FOUND ANYTHING OUT IN NORTH DAKOTA.
YOU DON'T THINK ANYTHING'S HAPPENED TO ANGIE, DO YOU?
NAH.
"ANGIE HUANG IS TOUGH.

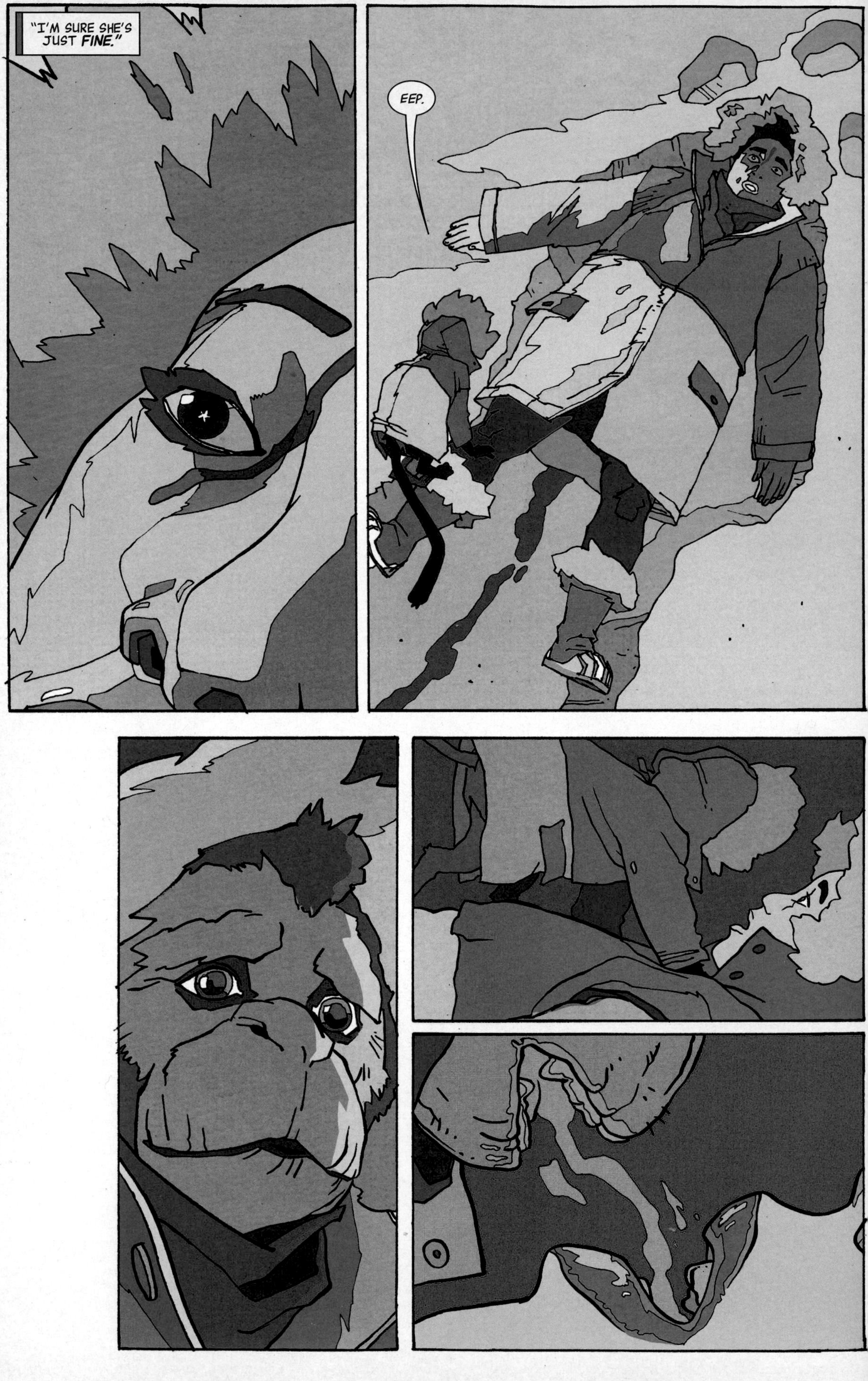
"I'M SURE SHE'S JUST FINE."
EEP.

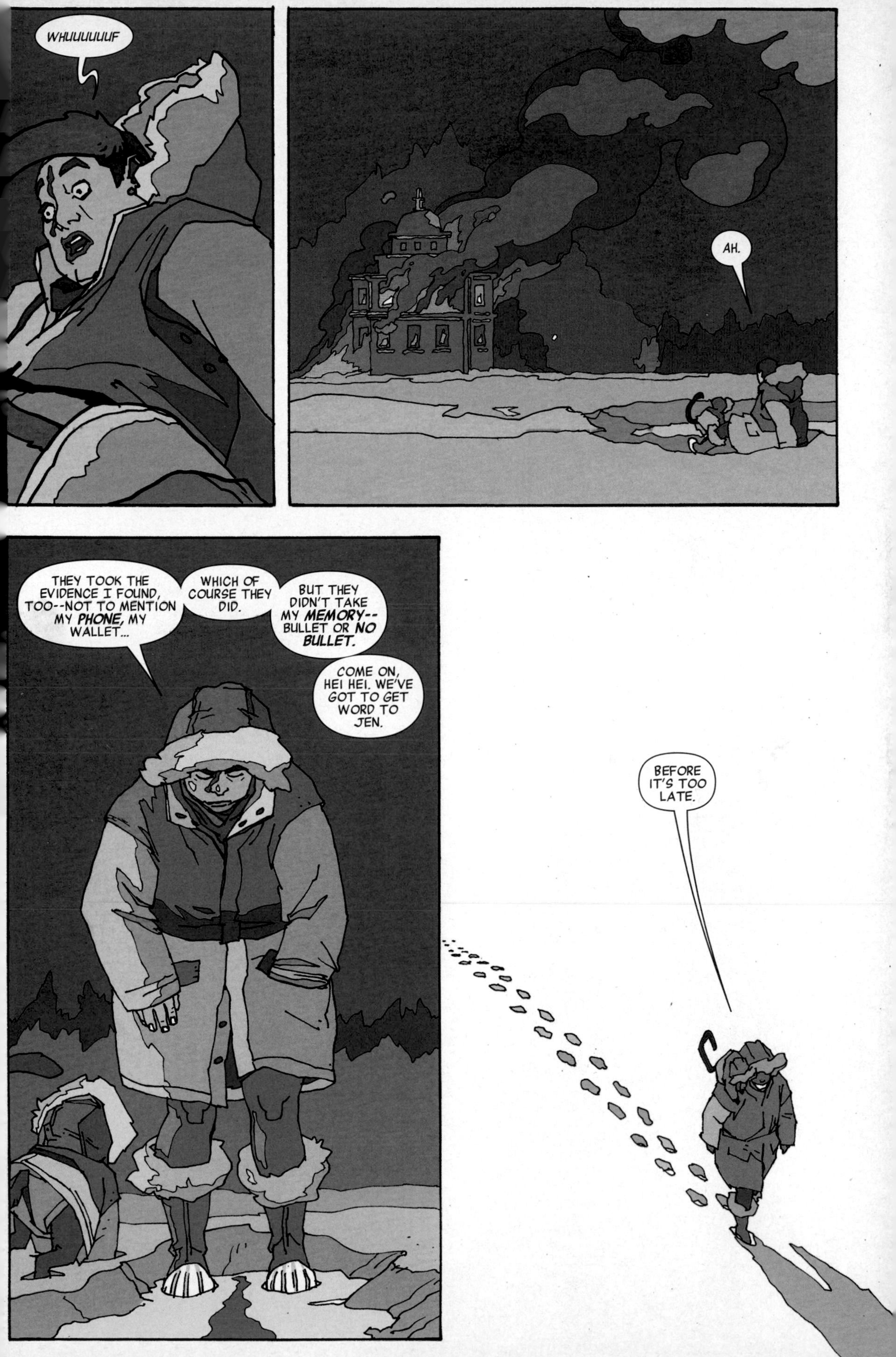
WHUUUUUUF
AH.
THEY TOOK THE EVIDENCE I FOUND, TOO--NOT TO MENTION MY PHONE, MY WALLET...
WHICH OF COURSE THEY DID.
BUT THEY DIDN'T TAKE MY MEMORY-- BULLET OR NO BULLET.
COME ON, HEI HEI. WE'VE GOT TO GET WORD TO JEN.
BEFORE IT'S TOO LATE.

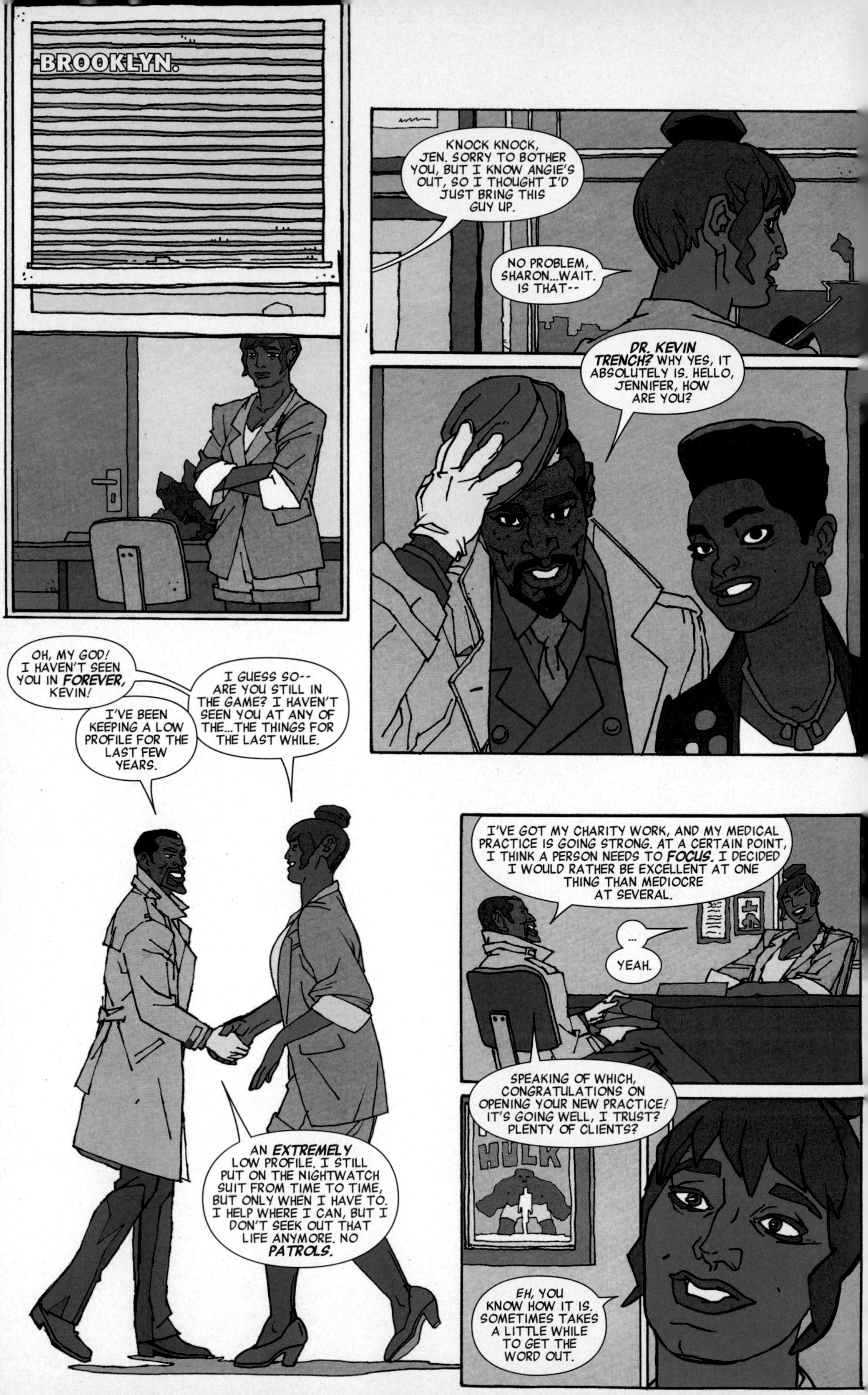
BROOKLYN.
KNOCK KNOCK, JEN. SORRY TO BOTHER YOU, BUT I KNOW ANGIE'S OUT, SO I THOUGHT I'D JUST BRING THIS GUY UP.
NO PROBLEM, SHARON...WAIT. IS THAT--
DR. KEVIN TRENCH? WHY YES, IT ABSOLUTELY IS. HELLO, JENNIFER, HOW ARE YOU?
OH, MY GOD! I HAVEN'T SEEN YOU IN FOREVER, KEVIN!
I GUESS SO-- ARE YOU STILL IN THE GAME? I HAVEN'T SEEN YOU AT ANY OF THE...THE THINGS FOR THE LAST WHILE.
I'VE BEEN KEEPING A LOW PROFILE FOR THE LAST FEW YEARS.
AN EXTREMELY LOW PROFILE. I STILL PUT ON THE NIGHTWATCH SUIT FROM TIME TO TIME, BUT ONLY WHEN I HAVE TO. I HELP WHERE I CAN, BUT I DON'T SEEK OUT THAT LIFE ANYMORE. NO PATROLS.
I'VE GOT MY CHARITY WORK, AND MY MEDICAL PRACTICE IS GOING STRONG. AT A CERTAIN POINT, I THINK A PERSON NEEDS TO FOCUS. I DECIDED I WOULD RATHER BE EXCELLENT AT ONE THING THAN MEDIOCRE AT SEVERAL.
...
YEAH.
SPEAKING OF WHICH, CONGRATULATIONS ON OPENING YOUR NEW PRACTICE! IT'S GOING WELL, I TRUST? PLENTY OF CLIENTS?
HULK
EH, YOU KNOW HOW IT IS. SOMETIMES TAKES A LITTLE WHILE TO GET THE WORD OUT.

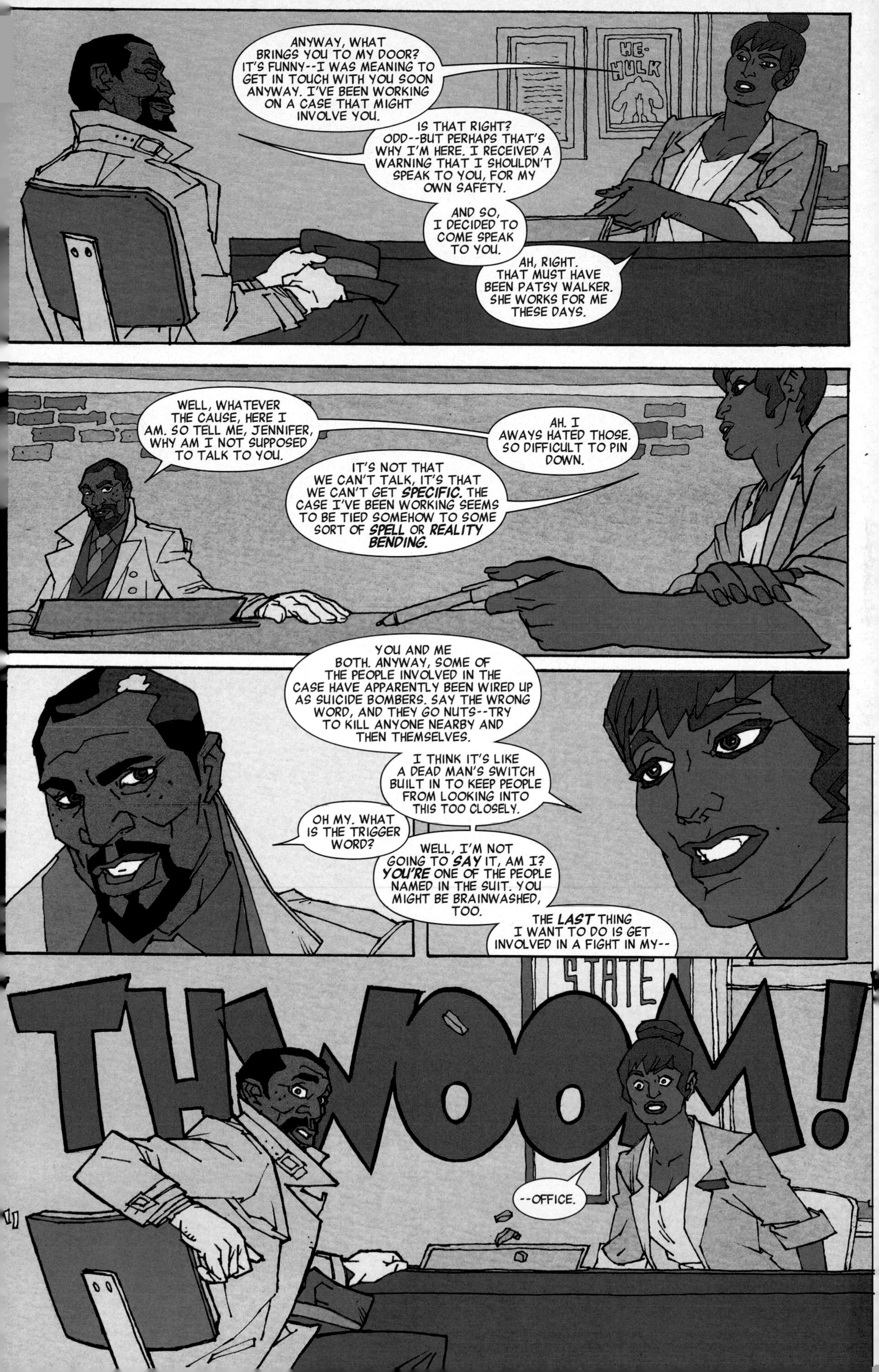
ANYWAY, WHAT BRINGS YOU TO MY DOOR? IT'S FUNNY--I WAS MEANING TO GET IN TOUCH WITH YOU SOON ANYWAY. I'VE BEEN WORKING ON A CASE THAT MIGHT INVOLVE YOU.
IS THAT RIGHT? ODD--BUT PERHAPS THAT'S WHY I'M HERE. I RECEIVED A WARNING THAT I SHOULDN'T SPEAK TO YOU, FOR MY OWN SAFETY.
AND SO, I DECIDED TO COME SPEAK TO YOU.
AH, RIGHT. THAT MUST HAVE BEEN PATSY WALKER. SHE WORKS FOR ME THESE DAYS.
HE-HULK
WELL, WHATEVER THE CAUSE, HERE I AM. SO TELL ME, JENNIFER, WHY AM I NOT SUPPOSED TO TALK TO YOU.
IT'S NOT THAT WE CAN'T TALK, IT'S THAT WE CAN'T GET SPECIFIC. THE CASE I'VE BEEN WORKING SEEMS TO BE TIED SOMEHOW TO SOME SORT OF SPELL OR REALITY BENDING.
AH. I AWAYS HATED THOSE. SO DIFFICULT TO PIN DOWN.
YOU AND ME BOTH. ANYWAY, SOME OF THE PEOPLE INVOLVED IN THE CASE HAVE APPARENTLY BEEN WIRED UP AS SUICIDE BOMBERS. SAY THE WRONG WORD, AND THEY GO NUTS--TRY TO KILL ANYONE NEARBY AND THEN THEMSELVES.
I THINK IT'S LIKE A DEAD MAN'S SWITCH BUILT IN TO KEEP PEOPLE FROM LOOKING INTO THIS TOO CLOSELY.
OH MY. WHAT IS THE TRIGGER WORD?
WELL, I'M NOT GOING TO SAY IT, AM I? YOU'RE ONE OF THE PEOPLE NAMED IN THE SUIT. YOU MIGHT BE BRAINWASHED, TOO.
THE LAST THING I WANT TO DO IS GET INVOLVED IN A FIGHT IN MY--
STATE
THWOOM!
--OFFICE.

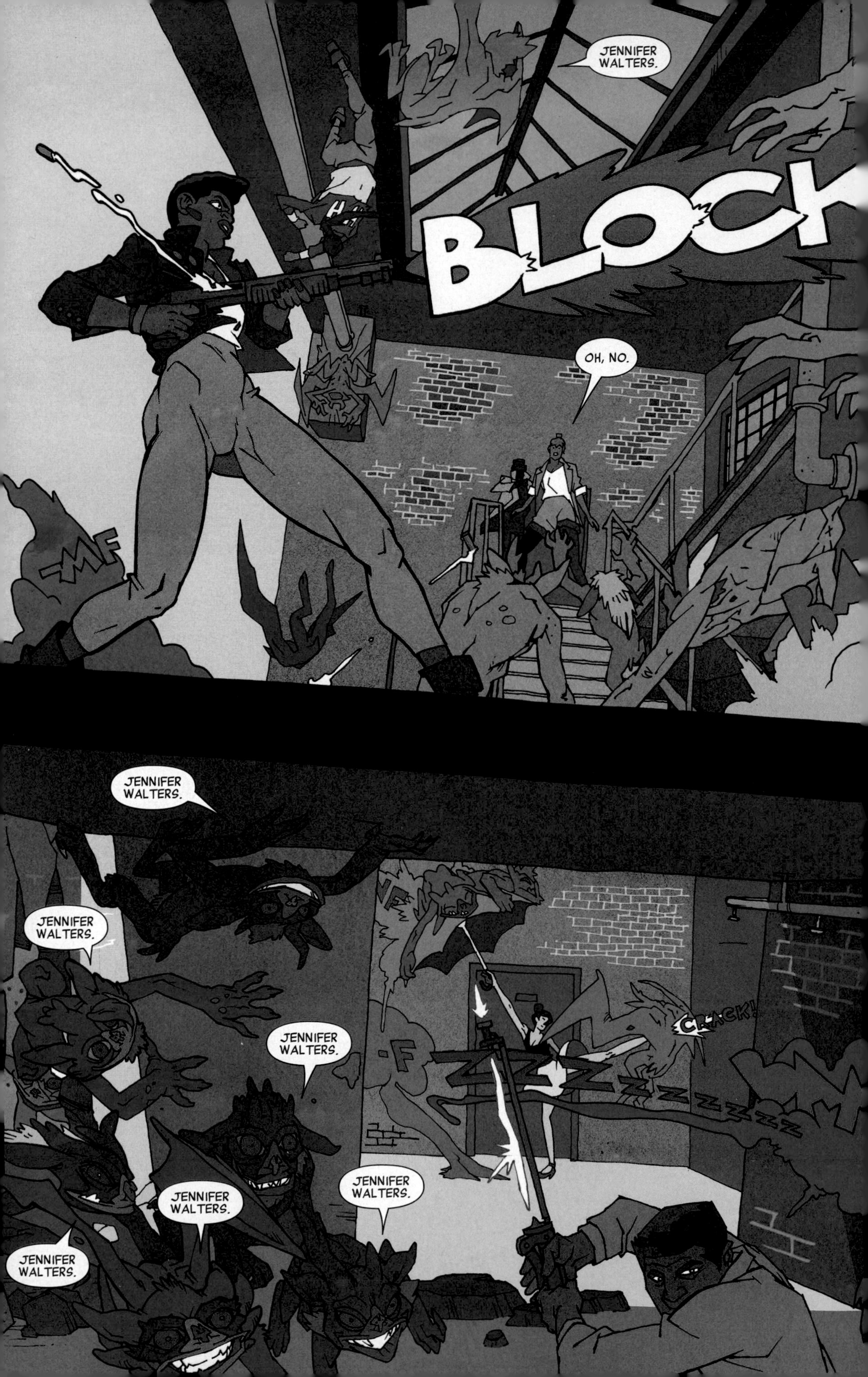
JENNIFER WALTERS.
BLOCK
-MF
OH, NO.
JENNIFER WALTERS.
JENNIFER WALTERS.
JENNIFER WALTERS.
-F
CRACK!
ZZZZZZZZZ
JENNIFER WALTERS.
JENNIFER WALTERS.
JENNIFER WALTERS.

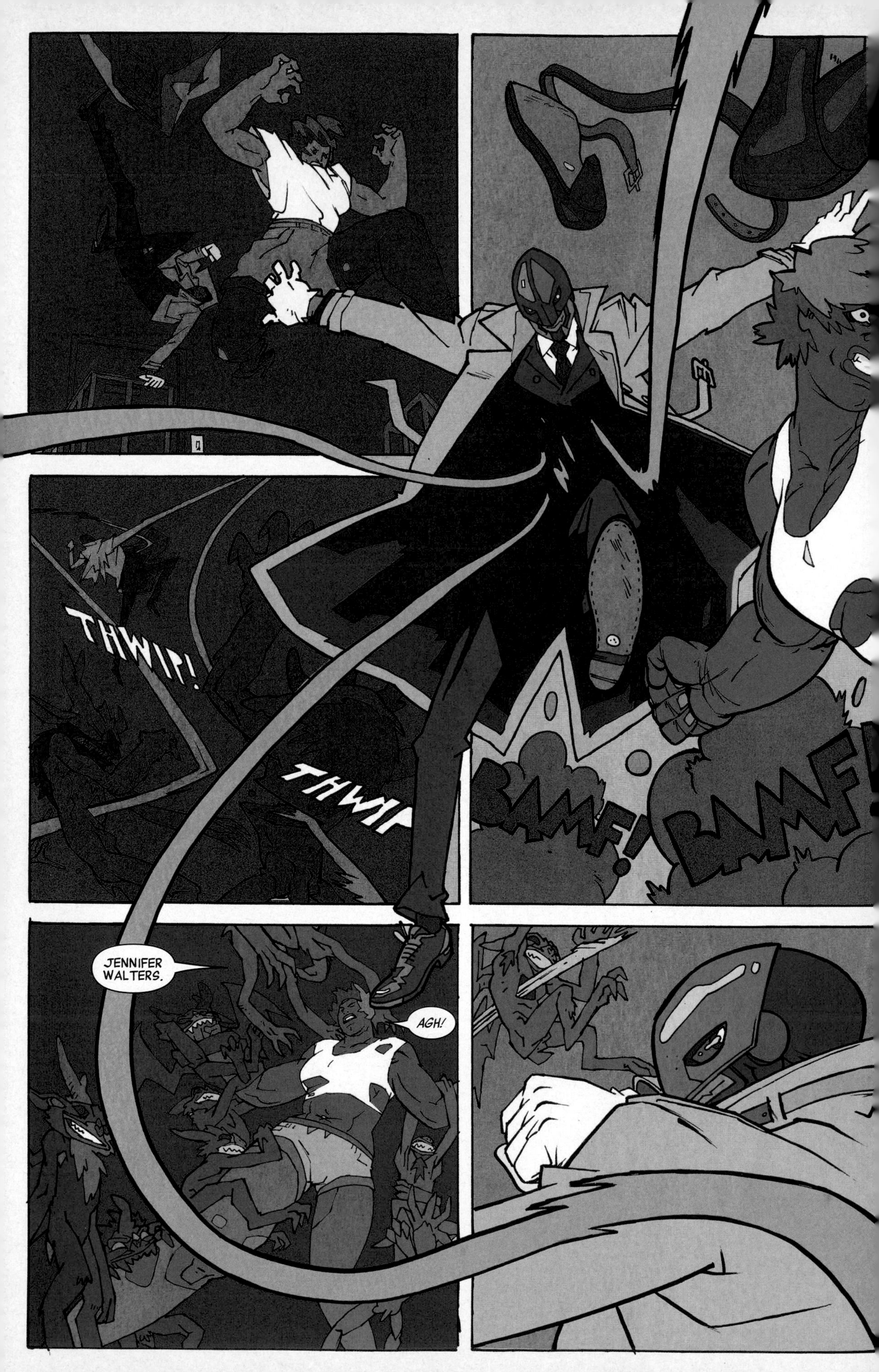
THWIP!
THWIP!
BAMF!
BAMF!
JENNIFER WALTERS.
AGH!

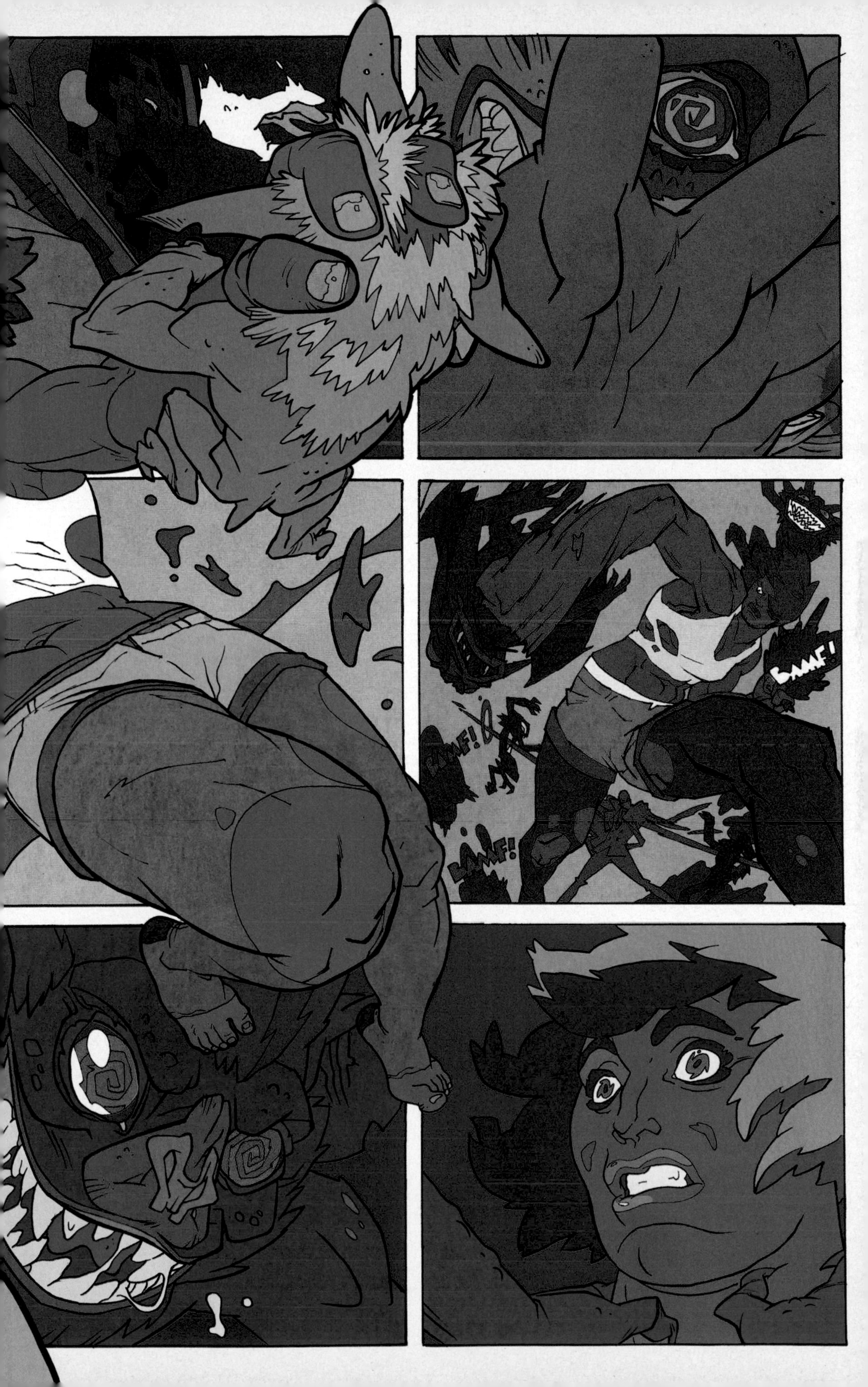
BAMF!
BAMF!
BAMF!

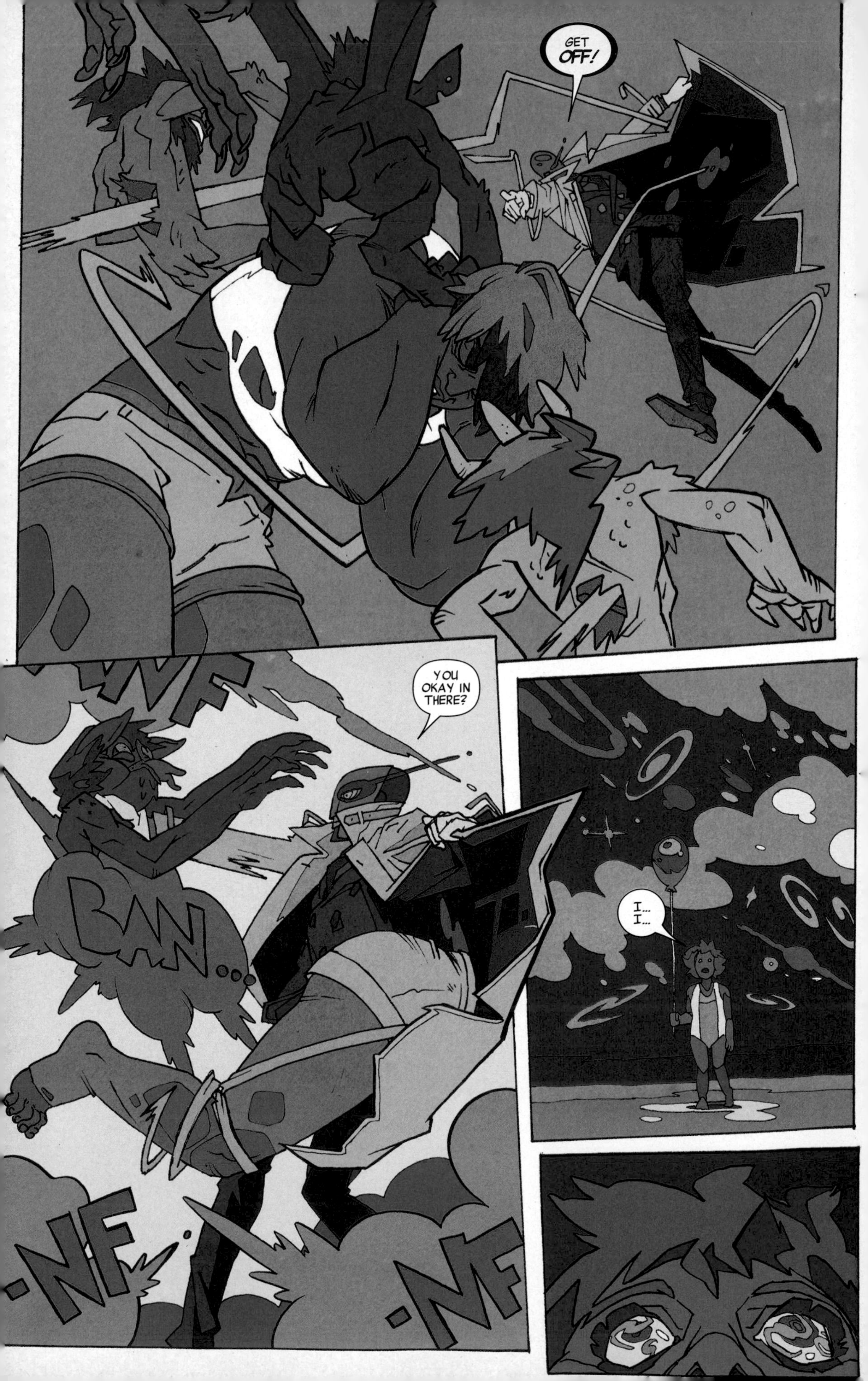
GET OFF!
WNF
YOU OKAY IN THERE?
BAN...
-NF
-NF
I...
I...

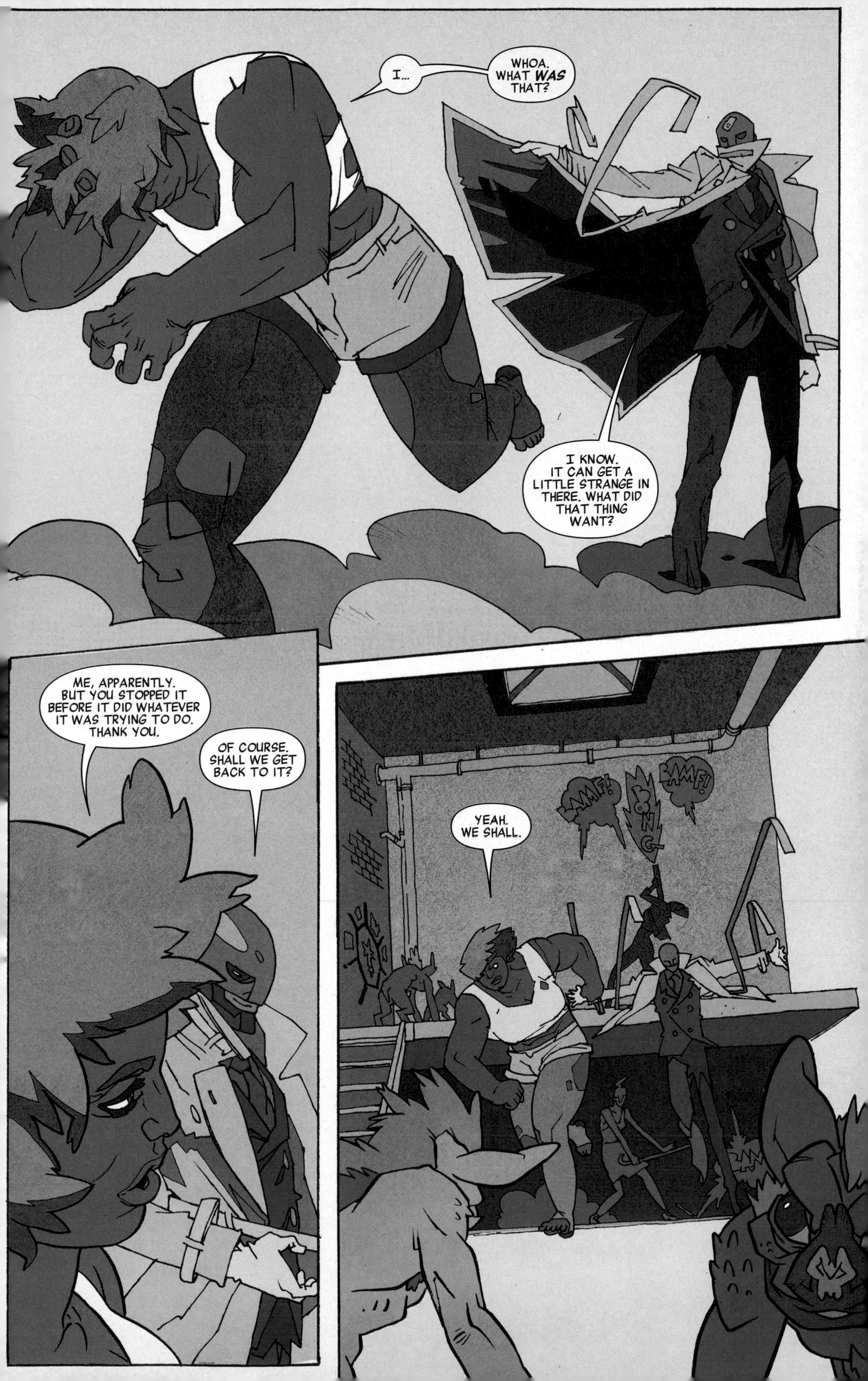
I...
WHOA. WHAT WAS THAT?
I KNOW. IT CAN GET A LITTLE STRANGE IN THERE. WHAT DID THAT THING WANT?
ME, APPARENTLY. BUT YOU STOPPED IT BEFORE IT DID WHATEVER IT WAS TRYING TO DO. THANK YOU.
OF COURSE. SHALL WE GET BACK TO IT?
BAMF!
BONG
BAMF!
YEAH. WE SHALL.

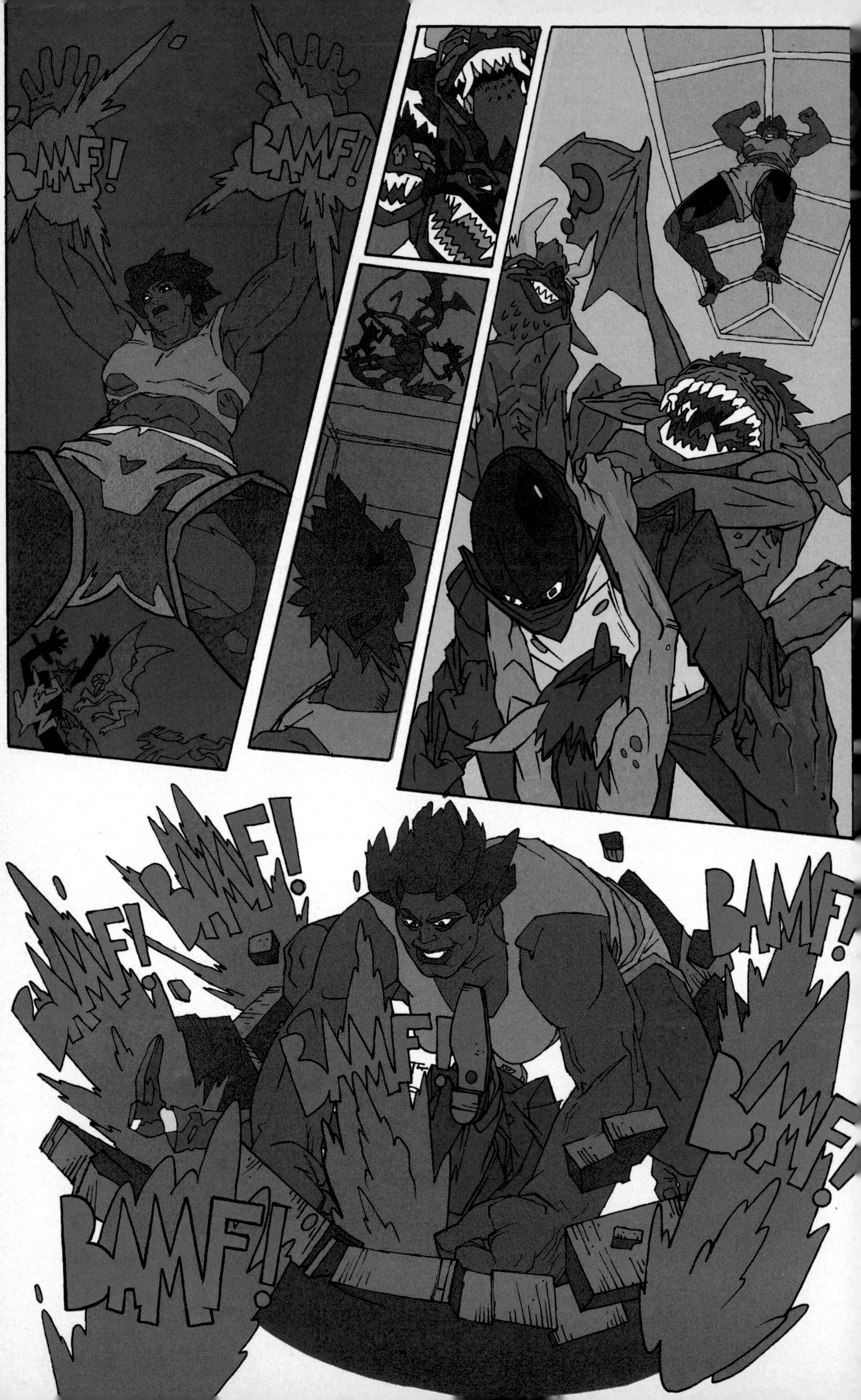
BAMF!
BAMF!
BAMF!
BAMF!
BAMF!
BAMF!
BAMF!
BAMF!

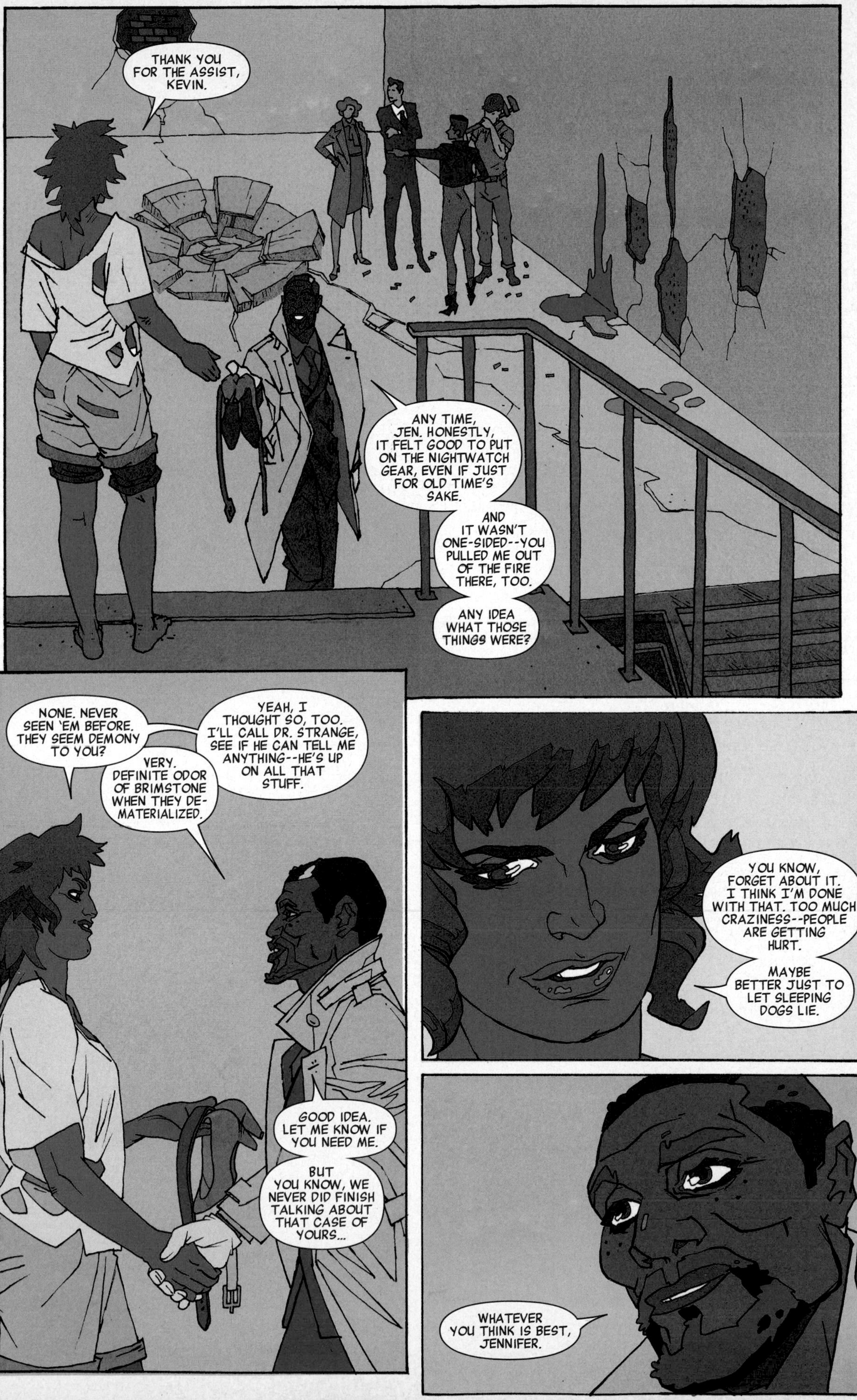
THANK YOU FOR THE ASSIST, KEVIN.
ANY TIME, JEN. HONESTLY, IT FELT GOOD TO PUT ON THE NIGHTWATCH GEAR, EVEN IF JUST FOR OLD TIME'S SAKE.
AND IT WASN'T ONE-SIDED--YOU PULLED ME OUT OF THE FIRE THERE, TOO.
ANY IDEA WHAT THOSE THINGS WERE?
NONE. NEVER SEEN 'EM BEFORE. THEY SEEM DEMONY TO YOU?
VERY. DEFINITE ODOR OF BRIMSTONE WHEN THEY DE-MATERIALIZED.
YEAH, I THOUGHT SO, TOO. I'LL CALL DR. STRANGE, SEE IF HE CAN TELL ME ANYTHING--HE'S UP ON ALL THAT STUFF.
GOOD IDEA. LET ME KNOW IF YOU NEED ME.
BUT YOU KNOW, WE NEVER DID FINISH TALKING ABOUT THAT CASE OF YOURS...
YOU KNOW, FORGET ABOUT IT. I THINK I'M DONE WITH THAT. TOO MUCH CRAZINESS--PEOPLE ARE GETTING HURT.
MAYBE BETTER JUST TO LET SLEEPING DOGS LIE.
WHATEVER YOU THINK IS BEST, JENNIFER.

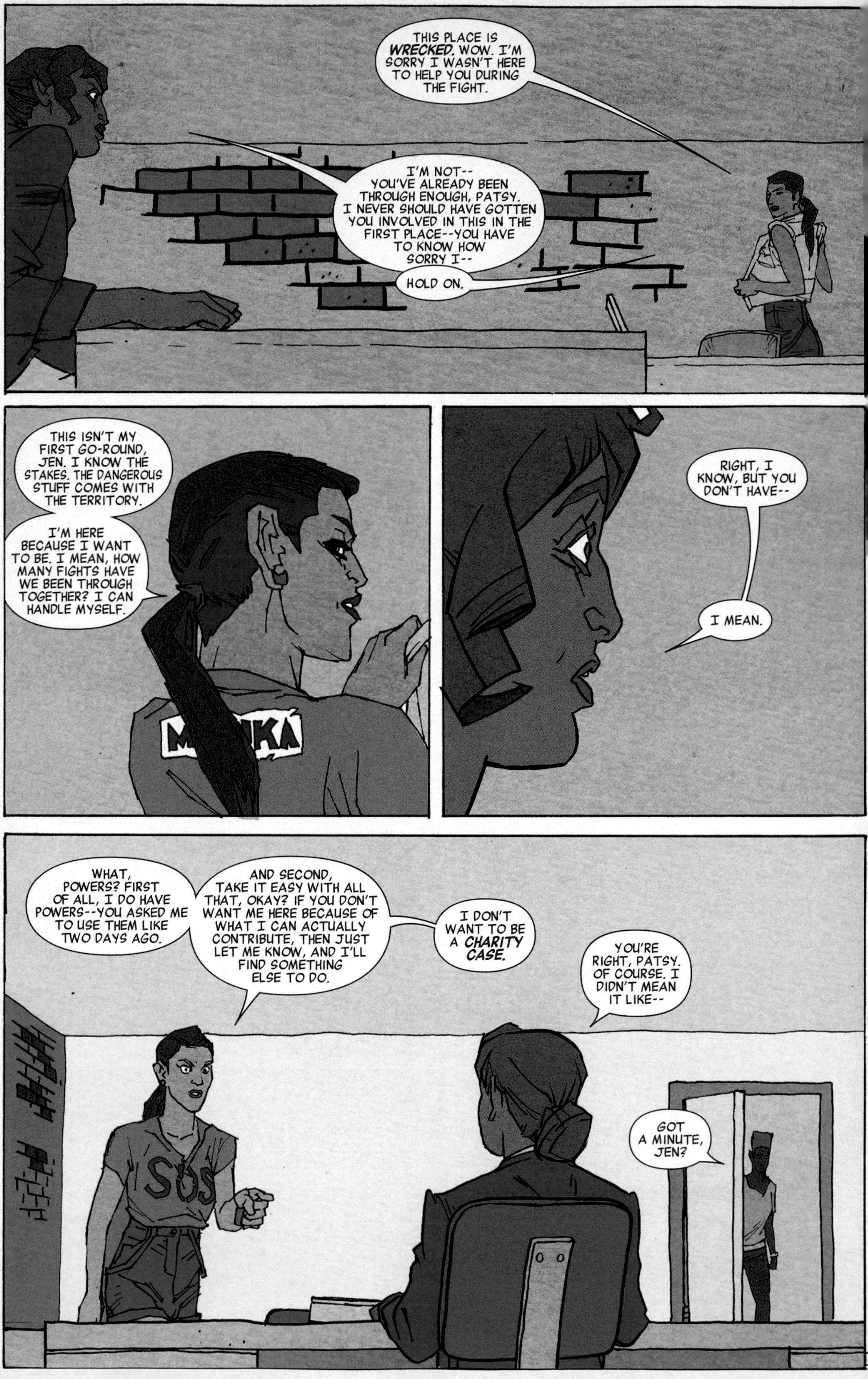

THIS PLACE IS WRECKED. WOW. I'M SORRY I WASN'T HERE TO HELP YOU DURING THE FIGHT.
I'M NOT-- YOU'VE ALREADY BEEN THROUGH ENOUGH, PATSY. I NEVER SHOULD HAVE GOTTEN YOU INVOLVED IN THIS IN THE FIRST PLACE--YOU HAVE TO KNOW HOW SORRY I--
HOLD ON.
THIS ISN'T MY FIRST GO-ROUND, JEN. I KNOW THE STAKES. THE DANGEROUS STUFF COMES WITH THE TERRITORY.
I'M HERE BECAUSE I WANT TO BE. I MEAN, HOW MANY FIGHTS HAVE WE BEEN THROUGH TOGETHER? I CAN HANDLE MYSELF.
RIGHT, I KNOW, BUT YOU DON'T HAVE--
I MEAN.
WHAT, POWERS? FIRST OF ALL, I DO HAVE POWERS--YOU ASKED ME TO USE THEM LIKE TWO DAYS AGO.
AND SECOND, TAKE IT EASY WITH ALL THAT, OKAY? IF YOU DON'T WANT ME HERE BECAUSE OF WHAT I CAN ACTUALLY CONTRIBUTE, THEN JUST LET ME KNOW, AND I'LL FIND SOMETHING ELSE TO DO.
I DON'T WANT TO BE A CHARITY CASE.
YOU'RE RIGHT, PATSY. OF COURSE. I DIDN'T MEAN IT LIKE--
GOT A MINUTE, JEN?

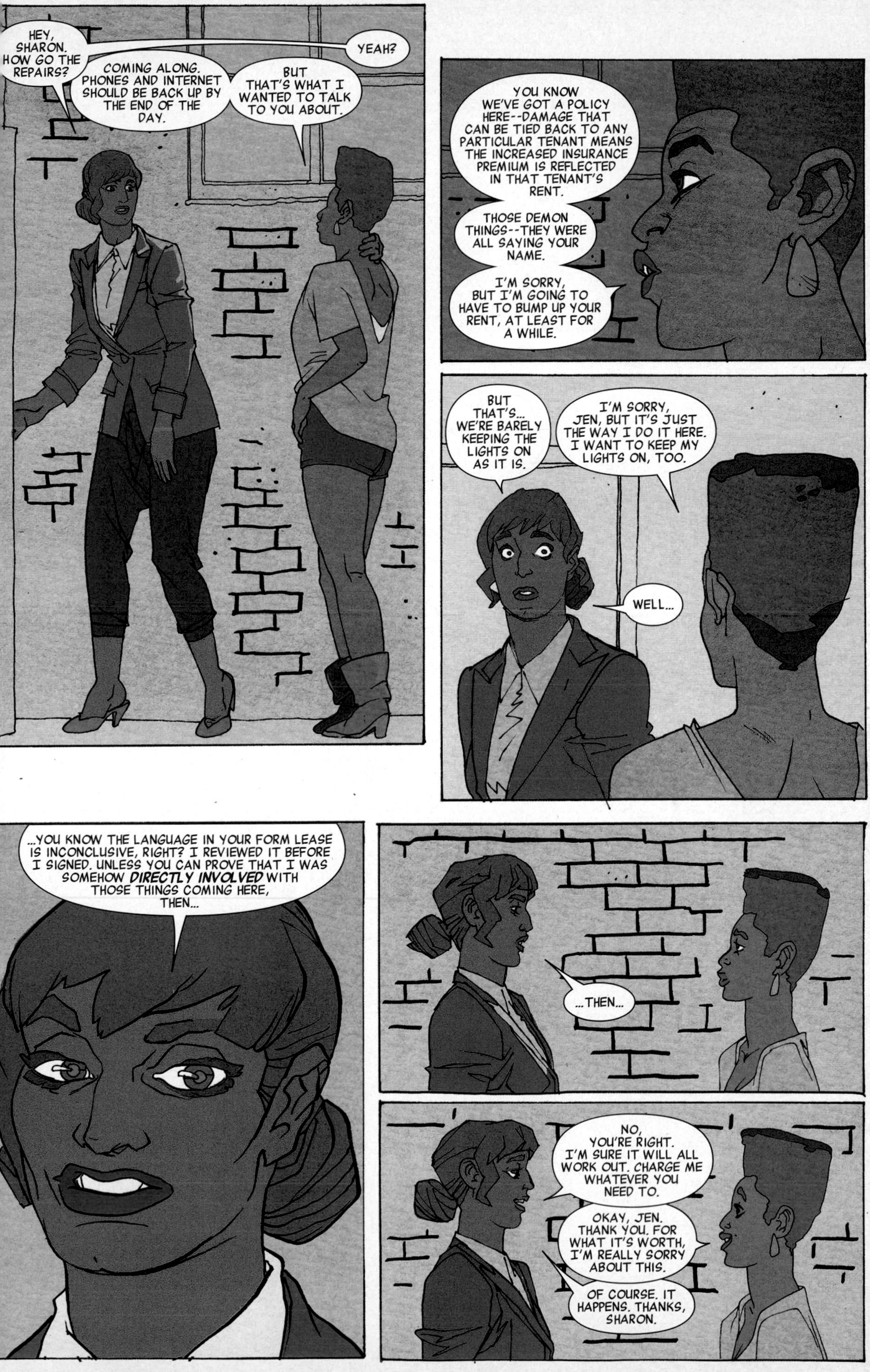
HEY, SHARON. HOW GO THE REPAIRS?
YEAH?
COMING ALONG. PHONES AND INTERNET SHOULD BE BACK UP BY THE END OF THE DAY.
BUT THAT'S WHAT I WANTED TO TALK TO YOU ABOUT.
YOU KNOW WE'VE GOT A POLICY HERE--DAMAGE THAT CAN BE TIED BACK TO ANY PARTICULAR TENANT MEANS THE INCREASED INSURANCE PREMIUM IS REFLECTED IN THAT TENANT'S RENT.
THOSE DEMON THINGS--THEY WERE ALL SAYING YOUR NAME.
I'M SORRY, BUT I'M GOING TO HAVE TO BUMP UP YOUR RENT, AT LEAST FOR A WHILE.
BUT THAT'S... WE'RE BARELY KEEPING THE LIGHTS ON AS IT IS.
I'M SORRY, JEN, BUT IT'S JUST THE WAY I DO IT HERE. I WANT TO KEEP MY LIGHTS ON, TOO.
WELL...
...YOU KNOW THE LANGUAGE IN YOUR FORM LEASE IS INCONCLUSIVE, RIGHT? I REVIEWED IT BEFORE I SIGNED. UNLESS YOU CAN PROVE THAT I WAS SOMEHOW DIRECTLY INVOLVED WITH THOSE THINGS COMING HERE, THEN...
...THEN...
NO, YOU'RE RIGHT. I'M SURE IT WILL ALL WORK OUT. CHARGE ME WHATEVER YOU NEED TO.
OKAY, JEN. THANK YOU. FOR WHAT IT'S WORTH, I'M REALLY SORRY ABOUT THIS.
OF COURSE. IT HAPPENS. THANKS, SHARON.

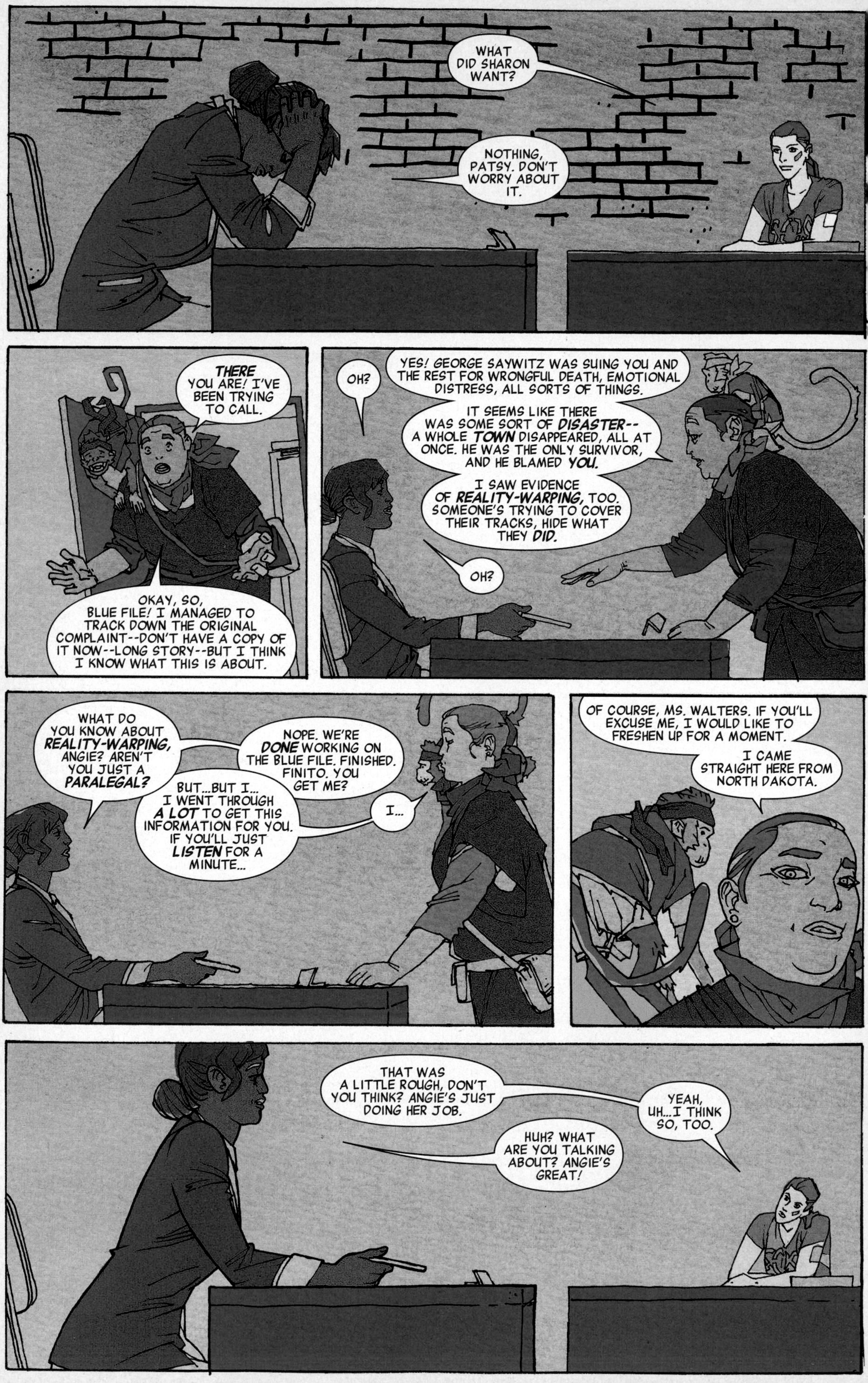
WHAT DID SHARON WANT?
NOTHING, PATSY. DON'T WORRY ABOUT IT.
THERE YOU ARE! I'VE BEEN TRYING TO CALL.
OKAY, SO, BLUE FILE! I MANAGED TO TRACK DOWN THE ORIGINAL COMPLAINT--DON'T HAVE A COPY OF IT NOW--LONG STORY--BUT I THINK I KNOW WHAT THIS IS ABOUT.
OH?
YES! GEORGE SAYWITZ WAS SUING YOU AND THE REST FOR WRONGFUL DEATH, EMOTIONAL DISTRESS, ALL SORTS OF THINGS.
IT SEEMS LIKE THERE WAS SOME SORT OF DISASTER-- A WHOLE TOWN DISAPPEARED, ALL AT ONCE. HE WAS THE ONLY SURVIVOR, AND HE BLAMED YOU.
I SAW EVIDENCE OF REALITY-WARPING, TOO. SOMEONE'S TRYING TO COVER THEIR TRACKS, HIDE WHAT THEY DID.
OH?
WHAT DO YOU KNOW ABOUT REALITY-WARPING, ANGIE? AREN'T YOU JUST A PARALEGAL?
NOPE. WE'RE DONE WORKING ON THE BLUE FILE. FINISHED. FINITO. YOU GET ME?
BUT...BUT I... I WENT THROUGH A LOT TO GET THIS INFORMATION FOR YOU. IF YOU'LL JUST LISTEN FOR A MINUTE...
I...
OF COURSE, MS. WALTERS. IF YOU'LL EXCUSE ME, I WOULD LIKE TO FRESHEN UP FOR A MOMENT.
I CAME STRAIGHT HERE FROM NORTH DAKOTA.
THAT WAS A LITTLE ROUGH, DON'T YOU THINK? ANGIE'S JUST DOING HER JOB.
YEAH, UH...I THINK SO, TOO.
HUH? WHAT ARE YOU TALKING ABOUT? ANGIE'S GREAT!

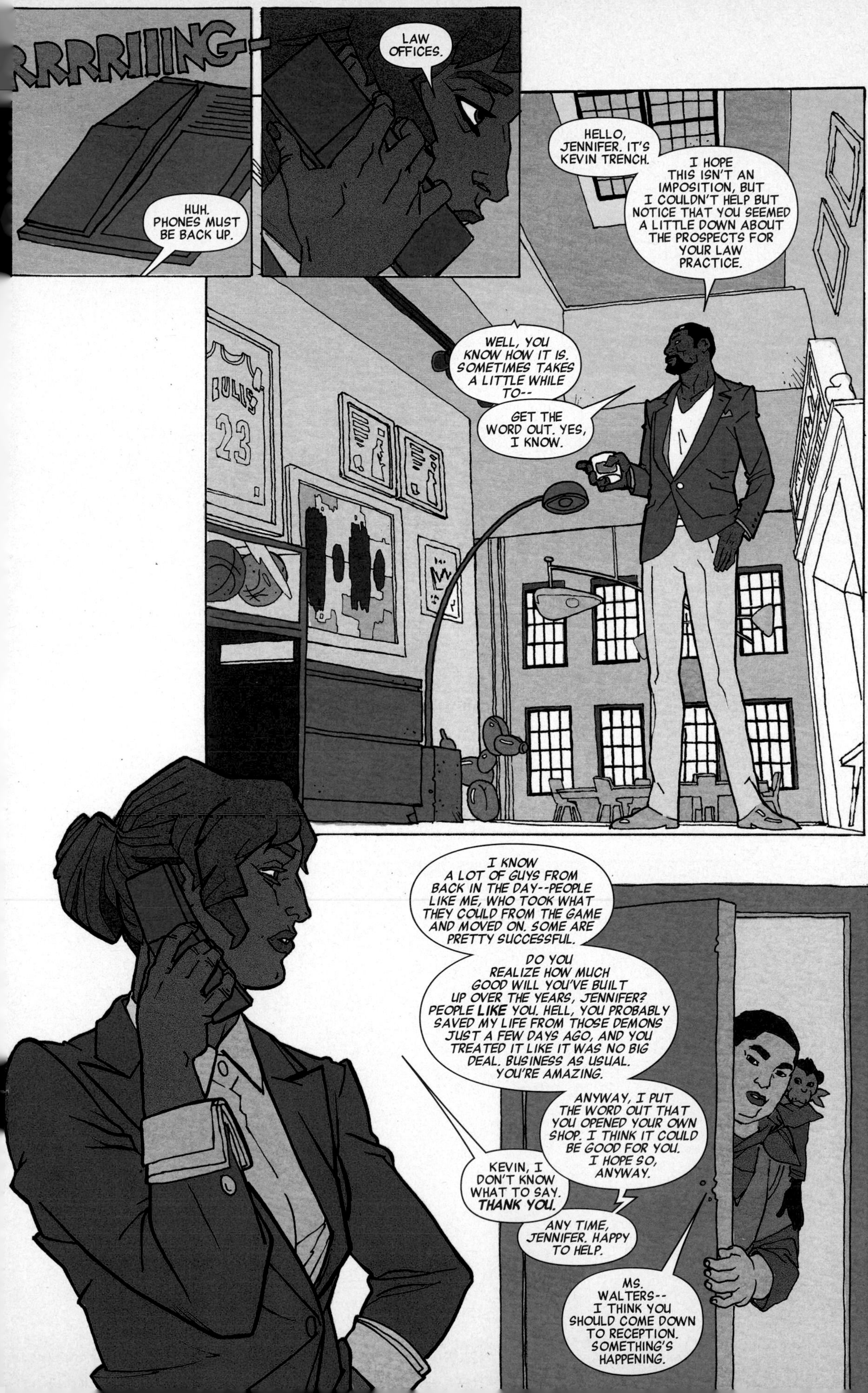
RRRRIIIING-
HUH. PHONES MUST BE BACK UP.
LAW OFFICES.
HELLO, JENNIFER. IT'S KEVIN TRENCH.
I HOPE THIS ISN'T AN IMPOSITION, BUT I COULDN'T HELP BUT NOTICE THAT YOU SEEMED A LITTLE DOWN ABOUT THE PROSPECTS FOR YOUR LAW PRACTICE.
WELL, YOU KNOW HOW IT IS. SOMETIMES TAKES A LITTLE WHILE TO--
GET THE WORD OUT. YES, I KNOW.
BULLS 23
I KNOW A LOT OF GUYS FROM BACK IN THE DAY--PEOPLE LIKE ME, WHO TOOK WHAT THEY COULD FROM THE GAME AND MOVED ON. SOME ARE PRETTY SUCCESSFUL.
DO YOU REALIZE HOW MUCH GOOD WILL YOU'VE BUILT UP OVER THE YEARS, JENNIFER? PEOPLE **LIKE** YOU. HELL, YOU PROBABLY SAVED MY LIFE FROM THOSE DEMONS JUST A FEW DAYS AGO, AND YOU TREATED IT LIKE IT WAS NO BIG DEAL. BUSINESS AS USUAL. YOU'RE AMAZING.
ANYWAY, I PUT THE WORD OUT THAT YOU OPENED YOUR OWN SHOP. I THINK IT COULD BE GOOD FOR YOU. I HOPE SO, ANYWAY.
KEVIN, I DON'T KNOW WHAT TO SAY. **THANK YOU.**
ANY TIME, JENNIFER. HAPPY TO HELP.
MS. WALTERS-- I THINK YOU SHOULD COME DOWN TO RECEPTION. SOMETHING'S HAPPENING.

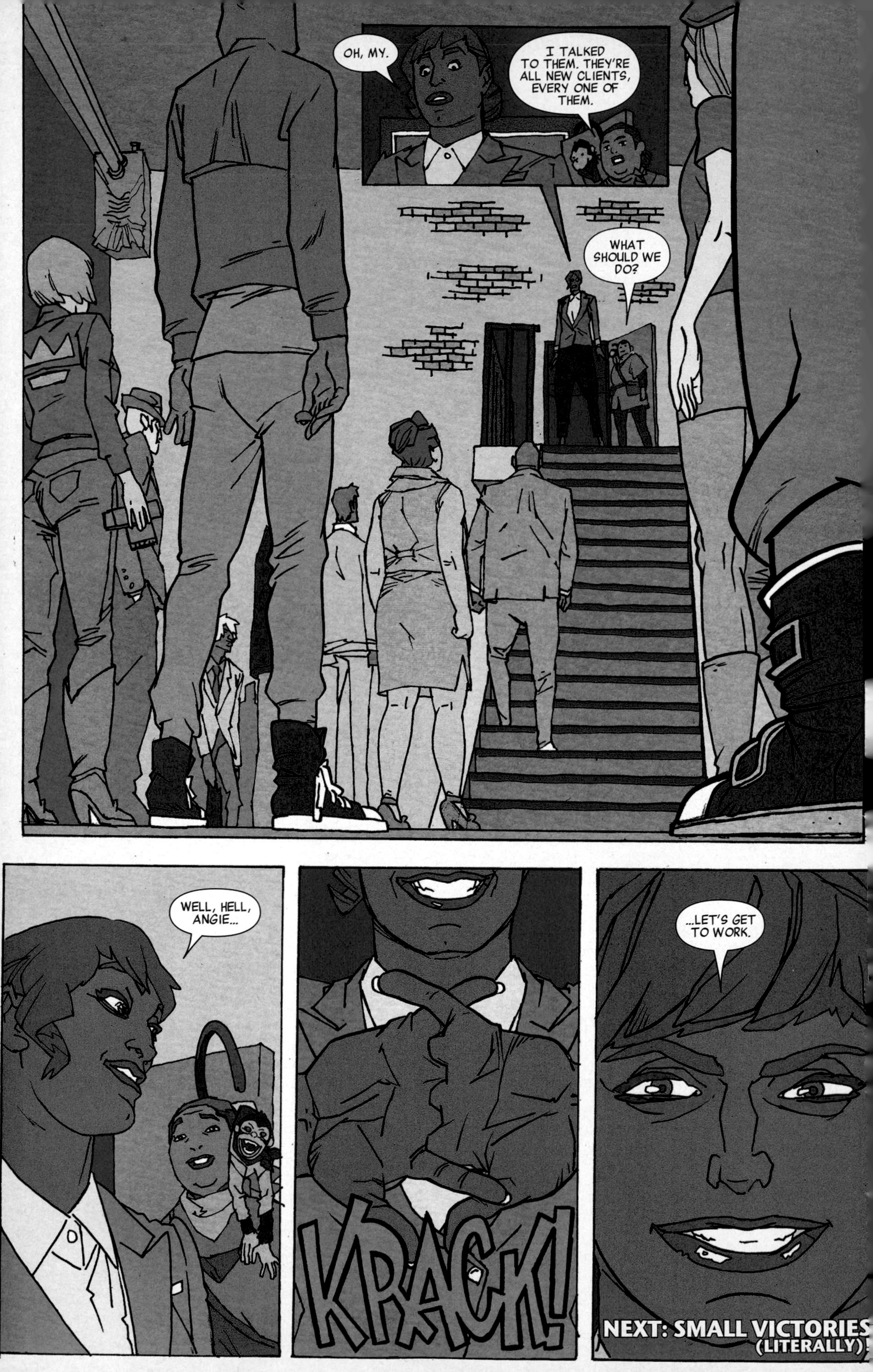

OH, MY.
I TALKED TO THEM. THEY'RE ALL NEW CLIENTS, EVERY ONE OF THEM.
WHAT SHOULD WE DO?
WELL, HELL, ANGIE...
KRACK!
...LET'S GET TO WORK.
NEXT: SMALL VICTORIES (LITERALLY)!

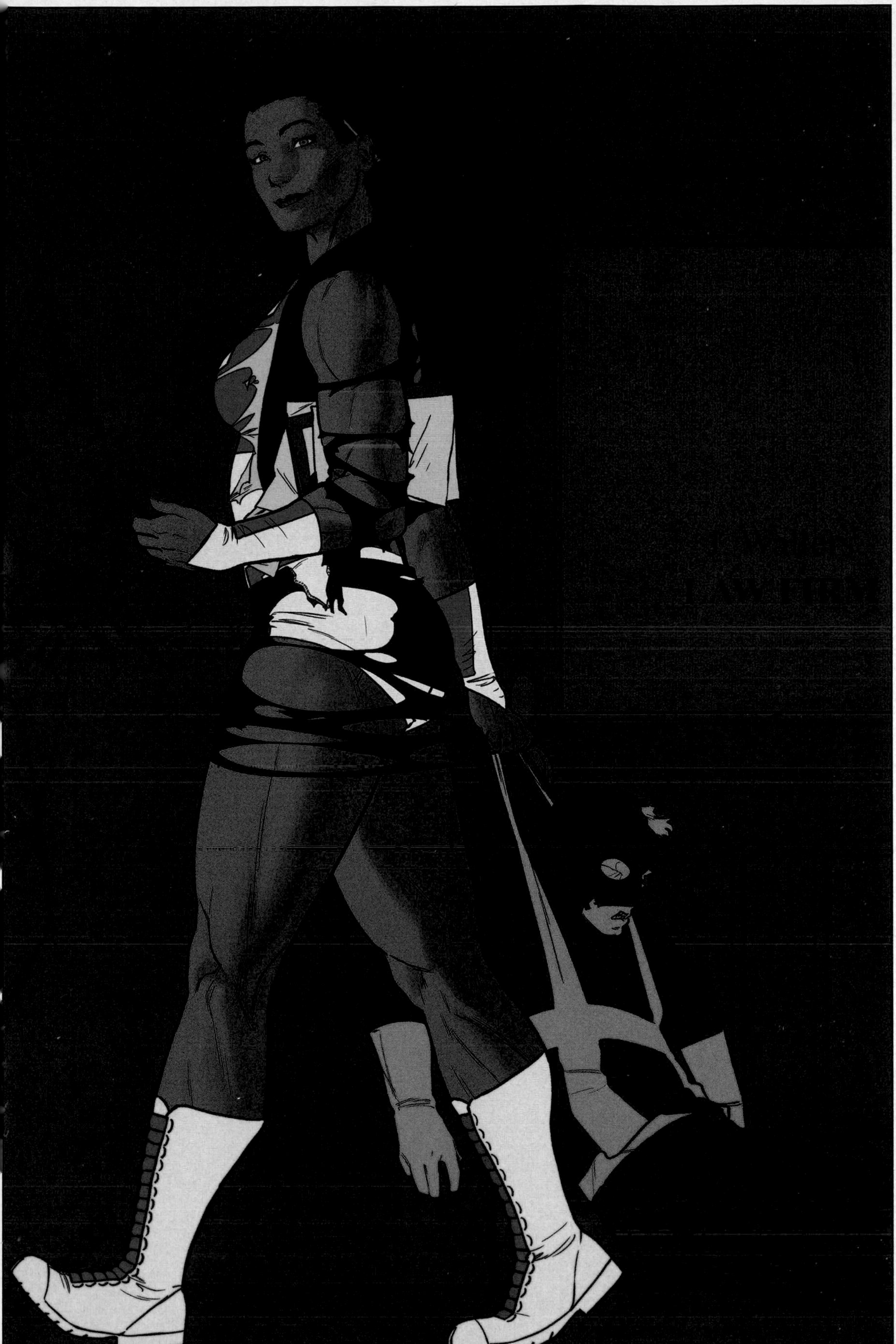

SHE-HULK #1 VARIANT BY KRIS ANKA

ART PROCESS BY JAVIER PULIDO

ISSUE #3, PAGE 1 LAYOUTS

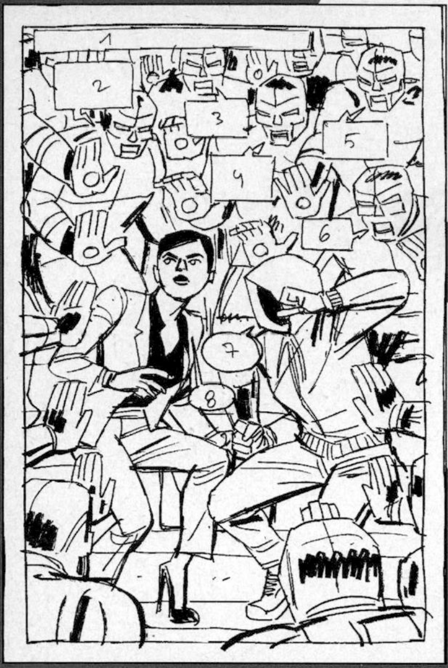

ISSUE #3, PAGES 10-11 LAYOUTS

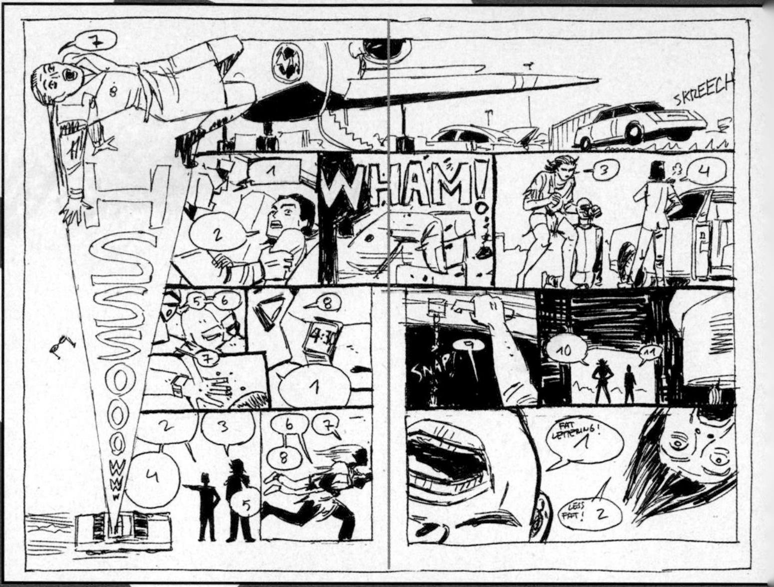
SKREECH
WHAM!
SNAP!
FAT LETTERING! 1
LESS FAT! 2

ISSUE #3, PAGE 1 INKS

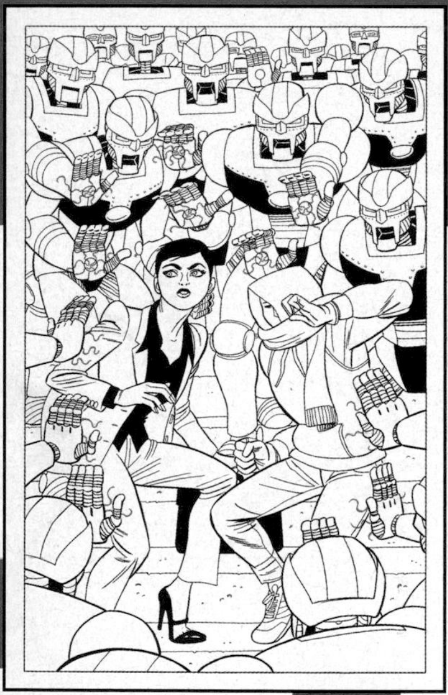

ISSUE #3, PAGES 10-11 INKS

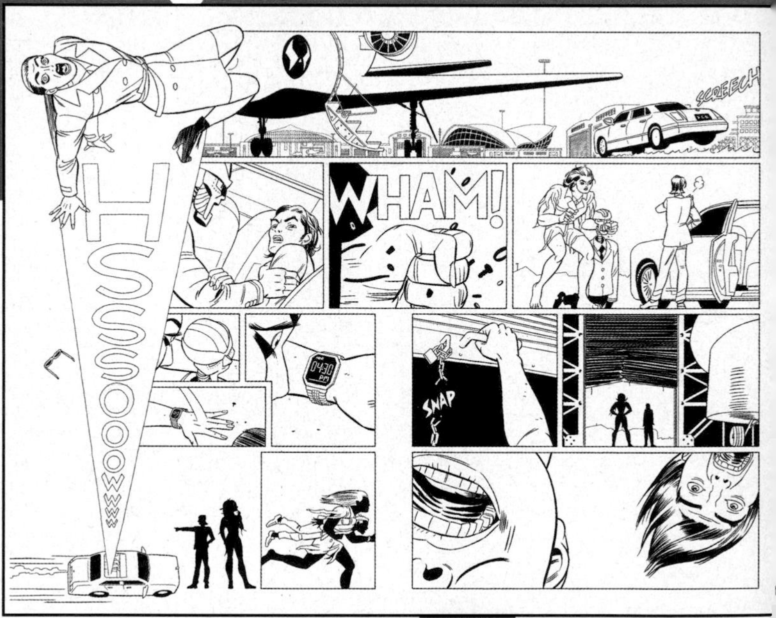
SCREECH
WHAM!
SNAP

ISSUE #3, PAGES 4-5 INKS

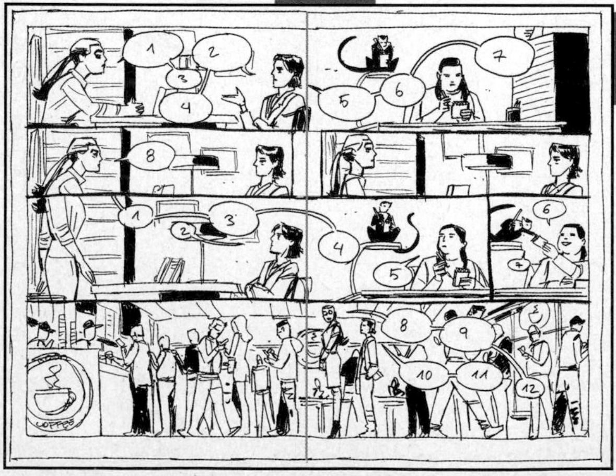

ISSUE #3, PAGES 4-5 INKS

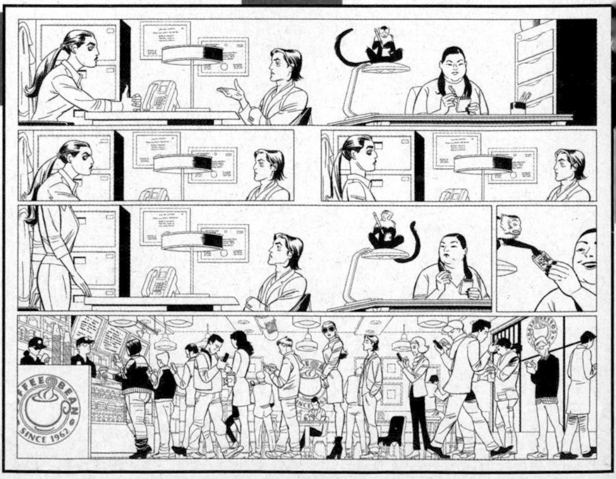
SINCE 1962